Richard Brinsley Sheridan

Plays of Sheridan

Containing the rivals, the school for scandal, the critic

Richard Brinsley Sheridan

Plays of Sheridan
Containing the rivals, the school for scandal, the critic

ISBN/EAN: 9783337281946

Printed in Europe, USA, Canada, Australia, Japan

Cover: Foto ©Andreas Hilbeck / pixelio.de

More available books at **www.hansebooks.com**

PLAYS OF SHERIDAN.

CONTAINING

THE RIVALS.

THE SCHOOL FOR SCANDAL.

THE CRITIC.

LONDON: GEORGE BELL & SONS, YORK STREET,
COVENT GARDEN.
1889.

CONTENTS.

THE RIVALS.

A COMEDY.

PREFACE

A PREFACE to a play seems generally to be considered as a kind of closet-prologue, in which—if his piece has been successful—the author solicits that indulgence from the reader which he had before experienced from the audience : but as the scope and immediate object of a play is to please a mixed assembly in *representation* (whose judgment in the theatre at least is decisive), its degree of reputation is usually as determined as public, before it can be prepared for the cooler tribunal of the study. Thus any farther solicitude on the part of the writer becomes unnecessary at least, if not an intrusion : and if the piece has been condemned in the performance, I fear an address to the closet, like an appeal to posterity, is constantly regarded as the procrastination of a suit, from a consciousness of the weakness of the cause. From these considerations, the following comedy would certainly have been submitted to the reader, without any farther introduction than what it had in the representation, but that its success has probably been founded on a circumstance which the author is informed has not before attended a theatrical trial, and which consequently ought not to pass unnoticed.

I need scarcely add, that the circumstance alluded to was the withdrawing of the piece, to remove those imperfections in the first representation which were too obvious to escape reprehension, and too numerous to admit of a hasty correction. There are few writers, I believe, who, even in the fullest consciousness of error, do not wish to palliate the faults which they acknowledge ; and, however, trifling the performance, to second their confession of its deficiencies, by whatever plea seems least disgraceful to their ability. In the present instance, it cannot be said to amount either to candour or modesty in me, to acknowledge an extreme inexperience and want of judgment on matters, in which, without guidance from practice, or spur from success, a young man should scarcely boast of being an adept. If it be said, that under such disadvantages no one should attempt to write a play, I must beg leave to dissent from the position, while the first point of experience that I have gained on the subject is, a knowledge of the candour and judgment with which an impartial public distinguishes between the errors of inexperience and incapacity, and the indulgence which it shows even to a disposition to remedy the defects of either.

It were unnecessary to enter into any farther extenuation of what was thought exceptionable in this play, but that it has been said, that the managers should have prevented some of the defects before its appearance to the public—and in particular the uncommon length of the piece as represented

B

the first night.   It were an ill return for the most liberal and gentlemanly
conduct on their side, to suffer any censure to rest where none was deserved.
Hurry in writing has long been exploded as an excuse for an author ;—however, in the dramatic line, it may happen, that both an author and a manager
may wish to fill a chasm in the entertainment of the public with a hastiness
not altogether culpable.   The season was advanced when I first put the play
into Mr. Harris's hands : it was at that time at least double the length of
any acting comedy.   I profited by his judgment and experience in the cur-
tailing of it—till, I believe, his feeling for the vanity of a young author got
the better of his desire for correctness, and he left many excrescences remain-
ing, because he had assisted in pruning so many more.   Hence, though I
was not uninformed that the acts were still too long, I flattered myself that,
after the first trial, I might with safer judgment proceed to remove what
should appear to have been most dissatisfactory.   Many other errors there
were, which might in part have arisen from my being by no means conversant with plays in general, either in reading or at the theatre.   Yet I own
that, in one respect, I did not regret my ignorance : for as my first wish in
attempting a play was to avoid every appearance of plagiary, I thought I
should stand a better chance of effecting this from being in a walk which I
had not frequented, and where, consequently, the progress of invention was
less likely to be interrupted by starts of recollection : for on subjects on which
the mind has been much informed, invention is slow of exerting itself.   Faded
ideas float in the fancy like half-forgotten dreams ; and the imagination in its
fullest enjoyments becomes suspicious of its offspring, and doubts whether it
has created or adopted.

   With regard to some particular passages which on the first night's representation seemed generally disliked, I confess, that if I felt any emotion of
surprise at the disapprobation, it was not that they were disapproved of, but
that I had not before perceived that they deserved it.   As some part of the
attack on the piece was begun too early to pass for the sentence of *judgment,*
which is ever tardy in condemning, it has been suggested to me, that much
of the disapprobation must have arisen from virulence of malice, rather than
severity of criticism : but as I was more apprehensive of there being just
grounds to excite the latter than conscious of having deserved the former, I
continue not to believe that probable, which I am sure must have been unprovoked.   However, if it was so, and I could even mark the quarter from
whence it came, it would be ungenerous to retort : for no passion suffers
more than malice from disappointment.   For my own part, I see no reason
why the author of a play should not regard a first night's audience as a can-
did and judicious friend attending, in behalf of the public, at his last rehearsal.   If he can dispense with flattery, he is sure at least of sincerity, and
even though the annotation be rude, he may rely upon the justness of the com-
ment.   Considered in this light, that audience, whose *fiat* is essential to the
poet's claim, whether his object be fame or profit, has surely a right to expect some deference to its opinion, from principles of politeness at least, if not
from gratitude.

   As for the little puny critics, who scatter their peevish strictures in private
circles, and scribble at every author who has the eminence of being unconnected
with them, as they are usually spleen-swoln from a vain idea of increasing
their consequence, there will always be found a petulance and illiberality in

their remarks, which should place them as far beneath the notice of a gentleman, as their original dulness had sunk them from the level of the most unsuccessful author.

It is not without pleasure that I catch at an opportunity of justifying myself from the charge of intending any national reflection in the character of Sir Lucius O'Trigger. If any gentleman opposed the piece from that idea, I thank them sincerely for their opposition; and if the condemnation of this comedy (however misconceived the provocation) could have added one spark to the decaying flame of national attachment to the country supposed to be reflect d on, I should have been happy in its fate; and might with truth have boasted, that it had done more real service in its failure, than the successful morality of a thousand stage-novels will ever effect.

It is usual, I believe, to thank the performers in a new play, for the exertion of their several abilities. But where (as in this instance) their merit has been so striking and uncontroverted, as to call for the warmest and truest applause from a number of judicious audiences, the poet's after-praise comes like the feeble acclamation of a child to close the shouts of a multitude. The conduct, however, of the principals in a theatre cannot be so apparent to the public. I think it therefore but justice to declare, that from this theatre (the only one I can speak of from experience) those writers who wish to try the dramatic line will meet with that candour and liberal attention, which are generally allowed to be better calculated to lead genius into excellence, than either the precepts of judgment, or the guidance of experience.

THE AUTHOR.

DRAMATIS PERSONÆ

AS ORIGINALLY ACTED AT COVENT-GARDEN THEATRE IN 1775.

SIR ANTHONY ABSOLUTE . . } *Mr. Shuter.*	THOMAS . . . . *Mr. Fearon.*
	MRS. MALAPROP . *Mrs. Green.*
CAPTAIN ABSOLUTE *Mr. Woodward.*	LYDIA LANGUISH . *Miss Barsanti*
FAULKLAND . . . *Mr. Lewis.*	JULIA . . . . . *Mrs. Bulkley.*
ACRES . . . . *Mr. Quick.*	LUCY . . . . { *Mrs. Lessingham.*
SIR LUCIUS O'TRIGGER . . } *Mr. Lee.*	
FAG . . . . . *Mr. Lee Lewes.*	Maid, Boy, Servants, &c.
DAVID . . . . *Mr. Dunstal.*	

SCENE—BATH.

Time of Action—Five Hours.

PROLOGUE.

BY THE AUTHOR.

Enter SERJEANT-AT-LAW, *and* ATTORNEY *following, and giving
a paper.*

Serj. WHAT's here!—a vile cramp hand! I cannot see
Without my spectacles.
    Att.   He means his fee.
Nay, Mr. Serjeant, good sir, try again.   *[Gives money*
    Serj. The scrawl improves! *[more]* O come, 'tis pretty plain
Hey! how's this? Dibble!—sure it cannot be!
A poet's brief! a poet and a fee!
    Att. Yes, sir! though you without reward, I know,
Would gladly plead the Muse's cause.
    Serj.   So!—so!
    Att. And if the fee offends, your wrath should fall
On me.
    Serj.   Dear Dibble, no offence at all.
    Att. Some sons of Phœbus in the courts we meet,
    Serj. And fifty sons of Phœbus in the Fleet!
    Att. Nor pleads he worse, who with a decent sprig
Of bays adorns his legal waste of wig.
    Serj. Full-bottom'd heroes thus, on signs, unfurl
A leaf of laurel in a grove of curl!
Yet tell your client, that, in adverse days,
This wig is warmer than a bush of bays.
    Att. Do you, then, sir, my client's place supply,
Profuse of robe, and prodigal of tie——
Do you, with all those blushing powers of face,
And wonted bashful hesitating grace,
Rise in the court, and flourish on the case.   *[Exit.*
    Serj. For practice then suppose—this brief will show it,—
Me, Serjeant Woodward,—counsel for the poet.
Used to the ground, I know 'tis hard to deal
With this dread court, from whence there's no appeal;
No tricking here, to blunt the edge of law,
Or, damn'd in equity, escape by flaw:
But judgment given, your sentence must remain;
No writ of error lies—to Drury-lane:

Yet when so kind you seem, 'tis past dispute
We gain some favour, if not costs of suit.
No spleen is here! I see no hoarded fury;—
I think I never faced a milder jury!
Sad else our plight! where frowns are transportation,
A hiss the gallows, and a groan damnation!
But such the public candour, without fear
My client waves all right of challenge here.
No newsman from our session is dismiss'd,
Nor wit nor critic we scratch off the list;
His faults can never hurt another's ease,
His crime, at worst, a bad attempt to please:
Thus, all respecting, he appeals to all,
And by the general voice will stand or fall.

PROLOGUE.

BY THE AUTHOR.

SPOKEN ON THE TENTH NIGHT, BY MRS. BULKLEY.

GRANTED our cause, our suit and trial o'er,
The worthy serjeant need appear no more:
In pleasing I a different client choose,
He served the Poet—I would serve the Muse·
Like him, I'll try to merit your applause,
A female counsel in a female's cause.
    Look on this form *,—where humour, quaint and sly,
Dimples the cheek, and points the beaming eye;
Where gay invention seems to boast its wiles
In amorous hint, and half-triumphant smiles;
While her light mask or covers satire's strokes,
Or hides the conscious blush her wit provokes.
Look on her well—does she seem form'd to teach?
Should you expect to hear this lady preach?
Is grey experience suited to her youth?
Do solemn sentiments become that mouth?
Bid her be grave, those lips should rebel prove
To every theme that slanders mirth or love.
    Yet, thus adorn'd with every graceful art
To charm the fancy and yet reach the heart——

* Pointing to the figure of Comedy.

Must we displace her? And instead advance
The goddess of the woful countenance—
The sentimental Muse!—Her emblems view,
The Pilgrim's Progress, and a sprig of rue!
View her—too chaste to look like flesh and blood—
Primly portray'd on emblematic wood!
There, fix'd in usurpation, should she stand,
She 'll snatch the dagger from her sister's hand:
And having made her votaries weep a flood,
Good heaven! she 'll end her comedies in blood—
Bid Harry Woodward break poor Dunstal's crown:
Imprison Quick, and knock Ned Shuter down;
While sad Barsanti, weeping o'er the scene,
Shall stab herself—or poison Mrs. Green.

     Such dire encroachments to prevent in time,
Demands the critic's voice—the poet's rhyme.
Can our light scenes add strength to holy laws!
Such puny patronage but hurts the cause:
Fair virtue scorns our feeble aid to ask;
And moral truth disdains the trickster's mask
For here their favourite stands *, whose brow severe
And sad, claims youth's respect, and pity's tear;
Who, when oppress'd by foes her worth creates,
Can point a poniard at the guilt she hates.

ACT I.

Scene I.—*A Street.*

Enter Thomas; *he crosses the Stage;* Fag *follows, looking
after him.*

     Fag. What! Thomas! sure 'tis he?—What! Thomas!
Thomas!

     Thos. Hey!—Odd's life! Mr. Fag!—give us your hand,
my old fellow-servant.

     Fag. Excuse my glove, Thomas:—I'm devilish glad to see
you, my lad. Why, my prince of charioteers, you look as
hearty!—but who the deuce thought of seeing you in Bath?

            * Pointing to Tragedy.

Thos. Sure, master, Madam Julia, Harry, Mrs. Kate, and the postillion, be all come.

Fag. Indeed!

Thos. Ay, master thought another fit of the gout was coming to make him a visit;—so he 'd a mind to gi't the slip, and whip! we were all off at an hour's warning.

Fag. Ay, ay, hasty in every thing, or it would not be Sir Anthony Absolute!

Thos. But tell us, Mr. Fag, how does young master? Odd! Sir Anthony will stare to see the Captain here!

Fag. I do not serve Captain Absolute now.

Thos. Why sure!

Fag. At present I am employed by Ensign Beverley

Thos. I doubt, Mr. Fag, you ha'n't changed for the better.

Fag. I have not changed, Thomas.

Thos. No! Why didn't you say you had left young master?

Fag. No.—Well, honest Thomas, I must puzzle you no farther:—briefly then—Captain Absolute and Ensign Beverley are one and the same person.

Thos. The devil they are!

Fag. So it is indeed, Thomas; and the ensign half of my master being on guard at present—the captain has nothing to do with me.

Thos. So, so!—What, this is some freak, I warrant!—Do tell us, Mr Fag, the meaning o't—you know I ha' trusted you.

Fag. You 'll be secret, Thomas?

Thos. As a coach-horse.

Fag. Why then the cause of all this is—Love,—Love, Thomas, who (as you may get read to you) has been a masquerader ever since the days of Jupiter.

Thos. Ay, ay;—I guessed there was a lady in the case:— but pray, why does your master pass only for ensign?—Now if he had shammed general indeed——

Fag. Ah! Thomas, there lies the mystery o' the matter Hark'ee, Thomas, my master is in love with a lady of a very singular taste: a lady who likes him better as a half pay ensign than if she knew he was son and heir to Sir Anthony Absolute, a baronet of three thousand a year.

Thos. That is an odd taste indeed!—But has she got the stuff, Mr. Fag? Is she rich, hey?

Faj. Rich!—Why, I believe she owns half the stocks! Zounds! Thomas, she could pay the national debt as easily as I could my washerwoman! She has a lapdog that eats out of gold,—she feeds her parrot with small pearls,—and all her thread-papers are made of bank-notes!

Thos. Bravo, faith!—Odd! I warrant she has a set of thousands at least:—but does she draw kindly with the captain?

Fag. As fond as pigeons.

Thos. May one hear her name?

Fag. Miss Lydia Languish.—But there is an old tough aunt in the way; though, by the by, she has never seen my master—for we got acquainted with miss while on a visit in Gloucestershire.

Thos Well—I wish they were once harnessed together in matrimony.—But pray, Mr. Fag, what kind of a place is this Bath?—I ha' heard a deal of it—here 's a mort o' merrymaking, hey?

Fag. Pretty well, Thomas, pretty well—'tis a good lounge; in the morning we go to the pump-room (though neither my master nor I drink the waters); after breakfast we saunter on the parades, or play a game at billiards; at night we dance; but damn the place, I 'm tired of it: their regular hours stupify me--not a fiddle nor a card after eleven!—However, Mr. Faulkland's gentleman and I keep it up a little in private parties;—I 'll introduce you there, Thomas—you 'll like him much.

Thos. Sure I know Mr. Du-Peigne—you know his master is to marry Madam Julia.

Fag. I had forgot.—But, Thomas, you must polish a little —indeed you must.—Here now—this wig!—What the devil do you do with a wig, Thomas?—None of the London whips of any degree of *ton* wear wigs now.

Thos. More 's the pity! more 's the pity! I say.—Odd's life! when I heard how the lawyers and doctors had took to their own hair, I thought how 'twould go next:—odd rabbit it! when the fashion had got foot on the bar, I guessed 'twould mount to the box!—but 'tis all out of character, believe me, Mr. Fag: and look'ee, I 'll never gi' up mine— the lawyers and doctors may do as they will.

Fag. Well, Thomas, we 'll not quarrel about that

Thos Why, bless you, the gentlemen of the professions ben't all of a mind—for in our village now, thoff Jack Gauge, the exciseman, has ta'en to his carrots, there's little Dick the farrier swears he'll never forsake his bob, though all the college should appear with their own heads!

Fag. Indeed! well said, Dick!—But hold—mark! mark! Thomas.

Thos. Zooks! 'tis the captain.—Is that the lady with him?

Fag. No, no, that is Madam Lucy, my master's mistress's maid. They lodge at that house—but I must after him to tell him the news.

Thos. Odd! he's giving her money!—Well, Mr. Fag——

Fag. Good-bye, Thomas. I have an appointment in Gyde's Porch this evening at eight; meet me there, and we'll make a little party.　　　　　　　　　　　　[*Exeunt severally.*

SCENE II.—*A Dressing-room in* MRS. MALAPROP'S *Lodgings.*

LYDIA *sitting on a sofa, with a book in her hand.* LUCY, *as just returned from a message*

Lucy. Indeed, ma'am, I traversed half the town in search of it: I don't believe there's a circulating library in Bath I ha'n't been at.

Lyd. And could not you get *The Reward of Constancy?*

Lucy. No, indeed, ma'am.

Lyd. Nor *The Fatal Connexion?*

Lucy. No, indeed, ma'am

Lyd. Nor *The Mistakes of the Heart?*

Lucy. Ma'am, as ill luck would have it, Mr. Bull said Miss Sukey Saunter had just fetched it away.

Lyd. Heigh-ho!—Did you inquire for *The Delicate Distress?*

Lucy. Or, *The Memoirs of Lady Woodford?* Yes, indeed, ma'am. I asked every where for it; and I might have brought it from Mr. Frederick's, but Lady Slattern Lounger, who had just sent it home, had so soiled and dog's-eared it, it wa'n't fit for a Christian to read.

Lyd. Heigh-ho!—Yes, I always know when Lady Slattern has been before me. She has a most observing thumb; and, I believe, cherishes her nails for the convenience of making marginal notes.—Well, child, what have you brought me?

Lucy. Oh! here, ma'am.—[*Taking books from under her cloak, and from her pockets.*] This is *The Gordian Knot,—*

and this *Peregrine Pickle.* Here are *The Tears of Sensibility*, and *Humphrey Clinker.* This is *The Memoirs of a Lady of Quality, written by herself*, and here the second volume of *The Sentimental Journey.*

Lyd. Heigh-ho!—What are those books by the glass?

Lucy. The great one is only *The Whole Duty of Man*, where I press a few blonds, ma'am.

Lyd. Very well—give me the sal volatile.

Lucy. Is it in a blue cover, ma'am?

Lyd. My smelling-bottle, you simpleton!

Lucy. Oh, the drops!—here, ma'am.

Lyd. Hold!—here's some one coming—quick, see who it is.—[*Exit* Lucy.] Surely I heard my cousin Julia's voice.

Re-enter Lucy.

Lucy. Lud! ma'am, here is Miss Melville.

Lyd. Is it possible!—   [*Exit* Lucy.

Enter Julia.

Lyd. My dearest Julia, how delighted am I!—[*Embrace.*] How unexpected was this happiness!

Jul. True, Lydia—and our pleasure is the greater.—But what has been the matter?—you were denied to me at first!

Lyd. Ah, Julia, I have a thousand things to tell you!—But first inform me what has conjured you to Bath?—Is Sir Anthony here?

Jul. He is—we are arrived within this hour—and I suppose he will be here to wait on Mrs. Malaprop as soon as he is dressed.

Lyd. Then before we are interrupted, let me impart to you some of my distress!—I know your gentle nature will sympathize with me, though your prudence may condemn me! My letters have informed you of my whole connection with Beverley; but I have lost him, Julia! My aunt has discovered our intercourse by a note she intercepted, and has confined me ever since! Yet, would you believe it? she has absolutely fallen in love with a tall Irish baronet she met one night since we have been here, at Lady Macshuffle's rout.

Jul. You jest, Lydia!

Lyd. No, upon my word.—She really carries on a kind of correspondence with him, under a feigned name though, till she chooses to be known to him;—but it is a Delia or a Celia, I assure you.

Jul. Then, surely, she is now more indulgent to her niece.

Lyd. Quite the contrary.   Since she has discovered her own frailty, she is become more suspicious of mine.   Then I must inform you of another plague!—That odius Acres is to be in Bath to-day; so that I protest I shall be teased out of all spirits!

Jul Come, come, Lydia, hope for the best—Sir Anthony shall use his interest with Mrs. Malaprop.

Lyd. But you have not heard the worst.   Unfortunately I had quarrelled with my poor Beverley, just before my aunt made the discovery, and I have not seen him since, to make it up.

Jul. What was his offence?

Lyd. Nothing at all!—But, I don't know how it was, as often as we had been together, we had never had a quarrel, and, somehow, I was afraid he would never give me an opportunity.   So, last Thursday, I wrote a letter to myself, to inform myself that Beverley was at that time paying his addresses to another woman.   I signed it *your friend unknown*, showed it to Beverley, charged him with his falsehood, put myself in a violent passion, and vowed I'd never see him more.

Jul. And you let him depart so, and have not seen him since?

Lyd. 'Twas the next day my aunt found the matter out. I intended only to have teased him three days and a half, and now I've lost him for ever.

Jul. If he is as deserving and sincere as you have represented him to me, he will never give you up so.   Yet consider, Lydia, you tell me he is but an ensign, and you have thirty thousand pounds

Lyd. But you know I lose most of my fortune if I marry without my aunt's consent, till of age; and that is what I have determined to do, ever since I knew the penalty.   Nor could I love the man, who would wish to wait a day for the alternative.

Jul. Nay, this is caprice!

Lyd. What, does Julia tax me with caprice?—I thought her lover Faulkland had inured her to it.

Jul. I do not love even his faults.

Lyd. But apropos--you have sent to him, I suppose?

Jul. Not yet, upon my word—nor has he the least idea of my being in Bath. Sir Anthony's resolution was so sudden, I could not inform him of it.

Lyd. Well, Julia, you are your own mistress, (though under the protection of Sir Anthony,) yet have you, for this long year, been a slave to the caprice, the whim. the jealousy of this ungrateful Faulkland, who will ever delay assuming the right of a husband, while you suffer him to be equally imperious as a lover.

Jul. Nay, you are wrong entirely. We were contracted before my father's death. That, and some consequent embarrassments, have delayed what I know to be my Faulkland's most ardent wish. He is too generous to trifle on such a point:—and for his character, you wrong him there too. No, Lydia, he is too proud, too noble to be jealous; if he is captious, 'tis without dissembling; if fretful, without rudeness. Unused to the fopperies of love, he is negligent of the little duties expected from a lover—but being unhackneyed in the passion, his affection is ardent and sincere; and as it engrosses his whole soul, he expects every thought and emotion of his mistress to move in unison with his. Yet, though his pride calls for this full return, his humility makes him undervalue those qualities in him which would entitle him to it; and not feeling why he should be loved to the degree he wishes, he still suspects that he is not loved enough. This temper, I must own, has cost me many unhappy hours; but I have learned to think myself his debtor, for those imperfections which arise from the ardour of his attachment.

Lyd. Well, I cannot blame you for defending him. But tell me candidly, Julia, had he never saved your life, do you think you should have been attached to him as you are?—Believe me, the rude blast that overset your boat was a prosperous gale of love to him.

Jul. Gratitude may have strengthened my attachment to Mr. Faulkland, but I loved him before he had preserved me; yet surely that alone were an obligation sufficient.

Lyd. Obligation! why a water spaniel would have done as much!—Well, I should never think of giving my heart to a man because he could swim

Jul. Come, Lydia, you are too inconsiderate

Lyd. Nay, I do but jest.—What's here?

Re-enter LUCY *in a hurry.*

Lucy. O ma'am, here is Sir Anthony Absolute just come home with your aunt.

Lyd. They'll not come here.—Lucy, do you watch.

[*Exit* LUCY.

Jul. Yet I must go. Sir Anthony does not know I am here, and if we meet, he'll detain me, to show me the town. I'll take another opportunity of paying my respects to Mrs. Malaprop, when she shall treat me, as long as she chooses, with her select words so ingeniously misapplied, without being mispronounced.

Re-enter LUCY

Lucy. O Lud! ma'am, they are both coming up stairs

Lyd. Well, I'll not detain you, coz.—Adieu, my dear Julia, I'm sure you are in haste to send to Faulkland.—There— through my room you'll find another staircase.

Jul. Adieu!   [*Embraces* LYDIA, *and exit.*

Lyd. Here, my dear Lucy, hide these books. Quick, quick.—*Fling Peregrine Pickle* under the toilet—throw *Roderick Random* into the closet—put *The Innocent Adultery* into *The Whole Duty of Man*—thrust *Lord Aimworth* under the sofa—cram *Ovid* behind the bolster—there—put *The Man of Feeling* into your pocket—so, so—now lay *Mrs. Chapone* in sight, and leave *Fordyce's Sermons* open on the table.

Lucy. O burn it, ma'am! the hair-dresser has torn away as far as *Proper Pride*

Lyd. Never mind—open at *Sobriety.*—Fling me *Lord Chesterfield's Letters.*—Now for 'em.   [*Exit* LUCY.

Enter Mrs. MALAPROP, *and* Sir ANTHONY ABSOLUTE.

Mrs. Mal. There, Sir Anthony, there sits the deliberate simpleton who wants to disgrace her family, and lavish herself on a fellow not worth a shilling.

Lyd. Madam, I thought you once——

Mrs. Mal. You thought, miss! I don't know any business you have to think at all—thought does not become a young .

woman. But the point we would request of you is, that you
will promise to forget this fellow—to illiterate him, I say,
quite from your memory.

Lyd. Ah, madam! our memories are independent of our
wills. It is not so easy to forget.

Mrs. Mal. But I say it is, miss; there is nothing on earth
so easy as to forget, if a person chooses to set about it. I'm
sure I have as much forgot your poor dear uncle as if he had
never existed—and I thought it my duty so to do; and let
me tell you, Lydia, these violent memories don't become a
young woman.

Sir Anth. Why sure she won't pretend to remember what
she's ordered not!—ay, this comes of her reading!

Lyd. What crime, madam, have I committed, to be treated
thus?

Mrs. Mal. Now don't attempt to extirpate yourself from
the matter; you know I have proof controvertible of it.—But
tell me, will you promise to do as you're bid? Will you take
a husband of your friends' choosing?

Lyd. Madam, I must tell you plainly, that had I no preference for any one else, the choice you have made would be my
aversion.

Mrs. Mal. What business have you, miss, with preference
and aversion? They don't become a young woman; and you
ought to know, that as both always wear off, 'tis safest in
matrimony to begin with a little aversion. I am sure I hated
your poor dear uncle before marriage as if he'd been a blacka-
moor—and yet, miss, you are sensible what a wife I made!—
and when it pleased Heaven to release me from him, 'tis
unknown what tears I shed!—But suppose we were going to
give you another choice, will you promise us to give up this
Beverley?

Lyd. Could I belie my thoughts so far as to give that
promise, my actions would certainly as far belie my words.

Mrs. Mal. Take yourself to your room.—You are fit company for nothing but your own ill-humours.

Lyd. Willingly, ma'am—I cannot change for the worse.

[*Exit.*

Mrs. Mal There's a little intricate hussy for you!

Sir Anth. It is not to be wondered at, ma'am,—all this is

the natural consequence of teaching girls to read. Had I a thousand daughters, by Heaven! I'd as soon have them taught the black art as their alphabet!

Mrs. Mal. Nay, nay, Sir Anthony, you are an absolute misanthropy.

Sir Anth. In my way hither, Mrs. Malaprop, I observed your niece's maid coming forth from a circulating library!— She had a book in each hand—they were half-bound volumes, with marble covers!—From that moment I guessed how full of duty I should see her mistress!

Mrs. Mal. Those are vile places, indeed!

Sir Anth. Madam, a circulating library in a town is as an evergreen tree of diabolical knowledge! It blossoms through the year!—And depend on it, Mrs. Malaprop, that they who are so fond of handling the leaves, will long for the fruit at last.

Mrs. Mal. Fy, fy, Sir Anthony! you surely speak laconically.

Sir Anth. Why, Mrs. Malaprop, in moderation now, what would you have a woman know?

Mrs. Mal. Observe me, Sir Anthony. I would by no means wish a daughter of mine to be a progeny of learning; I don't think so much learning becomes a young woman; for instance, I would never let her meddle with Greek, or Hebrew, or algebra, or simony, or fluxions, or paradoxes, or such inflammatory branches of learning—neither would it be necessary for her to handle any of your mathematical, astronomical, diabolical instruments.—But, Sir Anthony, I would send her, at nine years old, to a boarding-school, in order to learn a little ingenuity and artifice. Then, sir, she should have a supercilious knowledge in accounts;—and as she grew up, I would have her instructed in geometry, that she might know something of the contagious countries;—but above all, Sir Anthony, she should be mistress of orthodoxy, that she might not misspell, and mis-pronounce words so shamefully as girls usually do; and likewise that she might reprehend the true meaning of what she is saying. This, Sir Anthony, is what I would have a woman know;—and I don't think there is a superstitious article in it

Sir Anth. Well, well, Mrs. Malaprop, I will dispute the point no further with you; though I must confess, that you are a truly moderate and polite arguer, for almost every third word you say is on my side of the question. But, Mrs. Malaprop, to the more important point in debate—you say you have no objection to my proposal?

Mrs. Mal. None, I assure you. I am under no positive engagement with Mr. Acres, and as Lydia is so obstinate against him, perhaps your son may have better success.

Sir Anth. Well, madam, I will write for the boy directly. He knows not a syllable of this yet, though I have for some time had the proposal in my head. He is at present with his regiment.

Mrs. Mal. We have never seen your son, Sir Anthony; but I hope no objection on his side.

Sir Anth. Objection!—let him object if he dare!—No, no, Mrs. Malaprop, Jack knows that the least demur puts me in a frenzy directly. My process was always very simple—in their younger days, 'twas " Jack, do this; "—if he demurred, I knocked him down—and if he grumbled at that, I always sent him out of the room.

Mrs. Mal. Ay, and the properest way, o' my conscience!— nothing is so conciliating to young people as severity.— Well, Sir Anthony, I shall give Mr. Acres his discharge, and prepare Lydia to receive your son's invocations;—and I hope you will represent her to the captain as an object not alto gether illegible.

Sir Anth. Madam, I will handle the subject prudently.— Well, I must leave you; and let me beg you, Mrs. Malaprop, to enforce this matter roundly to the girl.—Take my advice— keep a tight hand: if she rejects this proposal, clap her under lock and key; and if you were just to let the servants forget to bring her dinner for three or four days, you c n't conceive how she 'd come about.   [*Exit*

Mrs. Mal. Well, at any rate I shall be glad to get her from under my intuition. She has somehow discovered my par- tiality for Sir Lucius O'Trigger—sure, Lucy can't have be- trayed me!—No, the girl is such a simpleton, I should have made her confess it.—Lucy!—Lucy!—[*Calls.*] Had she been one of your artificial ones, I should never have trusted her.

Re-enter LUCY

Lucy. Did you call, ma'am?

Mrs. Mal. Yes, girl.—Did you see Sir Lucius while you was out?

Lucy. No, indeed, ma'am, not a glimpse of him.

Mrs. Mal. You are sure, Lucy, that you never mentioned——

Lucy Oh gemini! I'd sooner cut my tongue out.

Mrs. Mal. Well, don't let your simplicity be imposed on.

Lucy. No, ma'am.

Mrs. Mal. So, come to me presently, and I'll give you another letter to Sir Lucius; but mind, Lucy—if ever you betray what you are entrusted with (unless it be other people's secrets to me), you forfeit my malevolence for ever; and your being a simpleton shall be no excuse for your locality. [*Exit.*

Lucy. Ha! ha! ha!—So, my dear Simplicity, let me give you a little respite.—[*Altering her manner.*] Let girls in my station be as fond as they please of appearing expert, and knowing in their trusts; commend me to a mask of silliness, and a pair of sharp eyes for my own interest under it!—Let me see to what account have I turned my simplicity lately.—[*Looks at a paper.*] For *abetting Miss Lydia Languish in a design of running away with an ensign!—in money, sundry times, twelve pound twelve; gowns, five; hats, ruffles, caps, &c. &c., numberless!—From the said ensign, within this last month, six guineas and a half.*—About a quarter's pay!—Item, *from Mrs Malaprop, for betraying the young people to her*—when I found matters were likely to be discovered—*two guineas, and a black paduasoy.*—Item, *from Mr. Acres, for carrying divers letters*—which I never delivered—*two guineas, and a pair of buckles.*—Item, *from Sir Lucius O'Trigger, three crowns, two gold pocket-pieces, and a silver snuff-box!* —Well done, Simplicity!—Yet I was forced to make my Hibernian believe, that he was corresponding, not with the aunt, but with the niece: for though not over rich, I found he had too much pride and delicacy to sacrifice the feelings of a gentleman to the necessities of his fortune.   [*Exit.*

ACT II.

SCENE I.—CAPTAIN ABSOLUTE'S *Lodgings*.

CAPTAIN ABSOLUTE *and* FAG.

Fag. Sir, while I was there Sir Anthony came in: I told

him, you had sent me to inquire after his health, and to know if he was at leisure to see you.

Abs. And what did he say, on hearing I was at Bath?

Fag. Sir, in my life I never saw an elderly gentleman more astonished! He started back two or three paces, rapped out a dozen interjectural oaths, and asked, what the devil had brought you here.

Abs. Well, sir, and what did you say?

Fag. Oh, I lied, sir—I forget the precise lie; but you may depend on't, he got no truth from me. Yet, with submission, for fear of blunders in future, I should be glad to fix what has brought us to Bath; in order that we may lie a little consistently. Sir Anthony's servants were curious, sir, very curious indeed.

Abs. You have said nothing to them?

Fag. Oh, not a word, sir,—not a word! Mr. Thomas, indeed, the coachman (whom I take to be the discreetest of whips)——

Abs. 'Sdeath!—you rascal! you have not trusted him!

Fag. Oh, no, sir—no—no—not a syllable, upon my veracity!—He was, indeed, a little inquisitive; but I was sly, sir—devilish sly! My master (said I), honest Thomas, (you know, sir, one says honest to one's inferiors,) is come to Bath to recruit—Yes, sir, I said to recruit—and whether for men, money, or constitution, you know, sir, is nothing to him, nor any one else.

Abs. Well, recruit will do—let it be so.

Fag. Oh, sir, recruit will do surprisingly—indeed, to give the thing an air, I told Thomas, that your honour had already enlisted five disbanded chairmen, seven minority waiters, and thirteen billiard-markers.

Abs. You blockhead, never say more than is necessary.

Fag. I beg pardon, sir—I beg pardon—but, with submission, a lie is nothing unless one supports it. Sir, whenever I draw on my invention for a good current lie, I always forge indorsements as well as the bill.

Abs. Well, take care you don't hurt your credit, by offering too much security.—Is Mr. Faulkland returned?

Fag. He is above, sir, changing his dress.

Abs. Can you tell whether he has been informed of Sir Anthony and Miss Melville's arrival?

Fag. I fancy not, sir; he has seen no one since he came in but his gentleman, who was with him at Bristol.—I think, sir, I hear Mr. Faulkland coming down——

Abs. Go, tell him I am here.

Fag. Yes, sir.—[*Going.*] I beg pardon, sir, but should Sir Anthony call, you will do me the favour to remember that we are recruiting, if you please.

Abs. Well, well.

Fag. And, in tenderness to my character, if your honour could bring in the chairmen and waiters, I should esteem it as an obligation; for though I never scruple a lie to serve my master, yet it hurts one's conscience to be found out.

[*Exit.*

Abs. Now for my whimsical friend—if he does not know that his mistress is here, I'll tease him a little before I tell him—

Enter FAULKLAND.

Faulkland, you're welcome to Bath again; you are punctual in your return.

Faulk. Yes; I had nothing to detain me, when I had finished the business I went on. Well, what news since I left you? how stand matters between you and Lydia?

Abs. Faith, much as they were; I have not seen her since our quarrel; however, I expect to be recalled every hour.

Faulk. Why don't you persuade her to go off with you at once?

Abs. What, and lose two-thirds of her fortune? you forget that, my friend.—No, no, I could have brought her to that long ago.

Faulk. Nay then, you trifle too long—if you are sure of her, propose to the aunt in your own character, and write to Sir Anthony for his consent.

Abs. Softly, softly; for though I am convinced my little Lydia would elope with me as Ensign Beverley, yet am I by no means certain that she would take me with the impediment of our friends' consent, a regular humdrum wedding, and the reversion of a good fortune on my side. no, no; I must prepare her gradually for the discovery, and make myself necessary to her, before I risk it.—Well, but Faulkland, you'll dine with us to-day at the hotel?

Faulk. Indeed I cannot; I am not in spirits to be of such a party.

Abs. By heavens! I shall forswear your company. You are the most teasing, captious, incorrigible lover!—Do love like a man

Faulk. I own I am unfit for company.

Abs. Am not I a lover; ay, and a romantic one too? Yet do I carry every where with me such a confounded farrago of doubts, fears, hopes, wishes, and all the flimsy furniture of a country miss's brain!

Faulk. Ah! Jack, your heart and soul are not, like mine, fixed immutably on one only object. You throw for a large stake, but losing, you could stake and throw again:—but I have set my sum of happiness on this cast, and not to succeed, were to be stripped of all.

Abs. But, for Heaven's sake! what grounds for apprehension can your whimsical brain conjure up at present?

Faulk. What grounds for apprehension, did you say? Heavens! are there not a thousand! I fear for her spirits— her health—her life.—My absence may fret her; her anxiety for my return, her fears for me may oppress her gentle temper: and for her health, does not every hour bring me cause to be alarmed? If it rains, some shower may even then have chilled her delicate frame! If the wind be keen, some rude blast may have affected her! The heat of noon, the dews of the evening, may endanger the life of her, for whom only I value mine. O Jack! when delicate and feeling souls are separated, there is not a feature in the sky, not a movement of the elements, not an aspiration of the breeze, but hints some cause for a lover's apprehension!

Abs. Ay, but we may choose whether we will take the hint or not.—So, then, Faulkland, if you were convinced that Julia were well and in spirits, you would be entirely content?

Faulk. I should be happy beyond measure—I am anxious only for that.

Abs. Then to cure your anxiety at once—Miss Melville is in perfect health, and is at this moment in Bath.

Faulk. Nay, Jack—don't trifle with me.

Abs. She is arrived here with my father within this hour.

Faulk. Can you be serious?

Abs. I thought you knew Sir Anthony better than to be

surprised at a sudden whim of this kind.—Seriously, then, it is as I tell you—upon my honour.

Faulk. My dear friend!—Hollo, Du Peigne! my hat.—My dear Jack—now nothing on earth can give me a moment's un-easiness

Re-enter FAG.

Fag. Sir, Mr. Acres, just arrived, is below.

Abs. Stay, Faulkland, this Acres lives within a mile of Sir Anthony, and he shall tell you how your mistress has been ever since you left her.—Fag, show the gentleman up.

[*Exit* FAG.

Faulk. What, is he much acquainted in the family?

Abs. Oh, very intimate: I insist on your not going: besides, his character will divert you.

Faulk. Well, I should like to ask him a few questions.

Abs. He is likewise a rival of mine—that is, of my other self's, for he does not think his friend Captain Absolute ever saw the lady in question; and it is ridiculous enough to hear him complain to me of one Beverley, a concealed skulking rival, who——

Faulk. Hush!—he's here.

Enter ACRES.

Acres. Ha! my dear friend, noble captain, and honest Jack, how do'st thou? just arrived, faith, as you see.—Sir, your humble servant.—Warm work on the roads, Jack!—Odds whips and wheels! I've travelled like a comet, with a tail of dust all the way as long as the Mall.

Abs. Ah! Bob, you are indeed an eccentric planet, but we know your attraction hither.—Give me leave to introduce Mr. Faulkland to you; Mr. Faulkland, Mr. Acres.

Acres. Sir, I am most heartily glad to see you: sir, I solicit your connections.—Hey, Jack—what, this is Mr. Faulkland, who——

Abs. Ay, Bob, Miss Melville's Mr. Faulkland.

Acres. Odso! she and your father can be but just arrived before me:—I suppose you have seen them. Ah! Mr Faulk land, you are indeed a happy man.

Faulk. I have not seen Miss Melville, yet, sir;—I hope she enjoyed full health and spirits in Devonshire?

Acres. Never knew her better in my life, sir,—never better Odds blushes and blooms! she has been as healthy as the German Spa.

Faulk. Indeed!—I did hear that she had been a little indisposed.

Acres. False, false, sir—only said to vex you: quite the reverse, I assure you.

Faulk There, Jack, you see she has the advantage of me; I had almost fretted myself ill.

Abs. Now are you angry with your mistress for not having been sick?

Faulk. No, no, you misunderstand me: yet surely a little trifling indisposition is not an unnatural consequence of absence from those we love.—Now confess—isn't there something unkind in this violent, robust, unfeeling health?

Abs. Oh, it was very unkind of her to be well in your absence, to be sure!

Acres. Good apartments, Jack.

Faulk. Well, sir, but you was saying that Miss Melville has been so exceedingly well—what then she has been merry and gay, I suppose?—Always in spirits—hey?

Acres. Merry, odds crickets! she has been the belle and spirit of the company wherever she has been—so lively and entertaining! so full of wit and humour!

Faulk. There, Jack, there.—Oh, by my soul! there is an innate levity in woman, that nothing can overcome.—What! happy, and I away!

Abs. Have done.—How foolish this is! just now you were only apprehensive for your mistress' spirits.

Faulk. Why, Jack, have I been the joy and spirit of the company?

Abs. No indeed, you have not.

Faulk. Have I been lively and entertaining?

Abs. Oh, upon my word, I acquit you.

Faulk. Have I been full of wit and humour?

Abs. No, faith, to do you justice, you have been confoundedly stupid indeed.

Acres. What's the matter with the gentleman?

Abs. He is only expressing his great satisfaction at hearing that Julia has been so well and happy—that's all—hey, Faulkland?

Faulk. Oh! I am rejoiced to hear it—yes, yes, she has a happy disposition!

Acres. That she has indeed—then she is so accomplished —so sweet a voice—so expert at her harpsichord—such a mistress of flat and sharp, squallante, rumblante, and quiverante!—There was this time month—odds minims and crotchets! how she did chirrup at Mrs. Piano's concert!

Faulk. There again, what say you to this? you see she has been all mirth and song—not a thought of me!

Abs. Pho! man, is not music the food of love?

Faulk. Well, well, it may be so.—Pray, Mr. ——, what 's his damned name?—Do you remember what songs Miss Melville sung?

Acres. Not I indeed.

Abs. Stay, now, they were some pretty melancholy purling-stream airs, I warrant; perhaps you may recollect;—did she sing, *When absent from my soul's delight?*

Acres. No, that wa'n't it.

Abs. Or, *Go, gentle gales!*   [*Sings*

Acres. Oh, no! nothing like it.   Odds! now I recollect one of them—*My heart's my own, my will is free.*   [*Sings.*

Faulk. Fool! fool that I am! to fix all my happiness on such a trifler! 'Sdeath! to make herself the pipe and balladmonger of a circle! to soothe her light heart with catches and glees!—What can you say to this, sir?

Abs. Why, that I should be glad to hear my mistress had been so merry, sir.

Faulk. Nay, nay, nay—I'm not sorry that she has been happy—no, no, I am glad of that—I would not have had her sad or sick—yet surely a sympathetic heart would have shown itself even in the choice of a song—she might have been temperately healthy, and somehow. plaintively gay;—but she has been dancing too, I doubt not!

Acres. What does the gentleman say about dancing?

Abs. He says the lady we speak of dances as well as she sings.

Acres. Ay, truly, does she—there was at our last race ball——

Faulk. Hell and the devil! There!—there—I told you so! I told you so! Oh! she thrives in my absence!—Dancing! but her whole feelings have been in opposition with mine;—I have been anxious, silent, pensive, sedentary—my

days have been hours of care, my nights of watchfulness.—Sho
has been all health! spirit! laugh! song! dance!—Oh!
damned, damned levity!

Abs. For Heaven's sake, Faulkland, don't expose yourself
so!—Suppose she has dance`, what then?—does not the
ceremony of society often oblige——

Faulk. Well, well, I 'll contain myself—perhaps as you say
—for form sake.—What, Mr. Acres, you were praising Miss
Melville's manner of dancing a minuet—hey?

Acres. Oh, I dare insure her for that—but what I was going
to speak of was her country-dancing. Odds swimmings! she
has such an air with her!

Faulk. Now disappointment on her!—Defend this, Abso-
soluto; why don't you defend this?—Country-dances! jigs and
reels! am I to blame now? A minuet I could have forgiven
—I should not have minded that—I say I should not have
regarded a minuet—but country-dances!—Zounds! had she
made one in a cotillion—I believe I could have forgiven even
that—but to be monkey-led for a night!—to run the gauntlet
through a string of amorous palming puppies!—to show paces
like a managed filly!—Oh. Jack, there never can be but one
man in the world whom a truly modest and delicate woman
ought to pair with in a country-dance; and, even then, the
rest of the couples should be her great-uncles and aunts!

Abs. Ay, to be sure!—grandfathers and grandmothers!

Faulk. If there be but one vicious mind in the set, 'twill
spread like a contagion—the action of their pulse beats to
the lascivious movement of the jig—their quivering, warm-
breathed sighs impregnate the very air—the atmosphere becomes electrical to love, and each amorous spark darts through
every link of the chain!—I must leave you—I own I am
somewhat flurried—and that confounded looby has perceived
it   *[Going.*

Abs. Nay, but stay, Faulkland, and thank Mr. Acres for his
good news.

Faulk. Damn his news!   *[Exit.*

Abs. Ha! ha! ha! poor Faulkland five minutes since—
" nothing on earth could give him a moment's uneasiness!"

Acres. The gentleman wa'n't angry at my praising his mistress, was he?

Abs. A little jealous, I believe, Bob

Acres. You don't say so? Ha! ha! jealous of me—that's a good joke.

Abs. There's nothing strange in that, Bob; let me tell you, that sprightly grace and insinuating manner of yours will do some mischief among the girls here.

Acres. Ah! you joke—ha! ha! mischief—ha! ha! but you know I am not my own property, my dear Lydia has forestalled me. She could never abide me in the country, because I used to dress so badly—but odds frogs and tambours! I shan't take matters so here, now ancient madam has no voice in it: I'll make my old clothes know who's master. I shall straight-way cashier the hunting-frock, and render my leather breeches incapable. My hair has been in training some time.

Abs. Indeed!

Acres. Ay—and tho'ff the side curls are a little restive, my hind-part takes it very kindly.

Abs. Oh, you'll polish, I doubt not

Acres. Absolutely I propose so—then if I can find out this Ensign Beverley, odds triggers and flints! I'll make him know the difference o't.

Abs. Spoke like a man! But pray, Bob, I observe you have got an odd kind of a new method of swearing——

Acres. Ha! ha! you've taken notice of it—'tis genteel, isn't it!—I didn't invent it myself though; but a commander in our militia, a great scholar, I assure you, says that there is no meaning in the common oaths, and that nothing but their antiquity makes them respectable;—because, he says, the an cients would never stick to an oath or two, but would say, by Jove! or by Bacchus! or by Mars! or by Venus! or by Pallas, according to the sentiment: so that to swear with propriety, says my little major, the oath should be an echo to the sense; and this we call the *oath referential* or *sentimental swearing*— ha! ha! 'tis genteel, isn't it?

Abs. Very genteel, and very new, indeed!—and I dare say will supplant all other figures of imprecation.

Acres. Ay, ay, the best terms will grow obsolete.—Damns have had their day.

Re-enter FAG.

Fag Sir, there is a gentleman below desires to see you.— Shall I show him into the parlour?

Abs. Ay—you may.

Acres. Well, I must be gone——

Abs. Stay; who is it, Fag?

Fag. Your father, sir.

Abs. You puppy, why didn't you show him up directly?

[*Exit* FAG

Acres. You have business with Sir Anthony.—I expect a message from Mrs. Malaprop at my lodgings. I have sent also to my dear friend Sir Lucius O'Trigger. Adieu, Jack! we must meet at night, when you shall give me a dozen bumpers to little Lydia.

Abs. That I will with all my heart.—[*Exit* ACRES.] Now for a parental lecture—I hope he has heard nothing of the business that has brought me here—I wish the gout had held him fast in Devonshire, with all my soul!

Enter Sir ANTHONY ABSOLUTE.

Sir, I am delighted to see you here; looking so well! your sudden arrival at Bath made me apprehensive for your health.

Sir Anth. Very apprehensive, I dare say, Jack.—What, you are recruiting here, hey?

Abs. Yes, sir, I am on duty.

Sir Anth. Well, Jack, I am glad to see you, though I did not expect it, for I was going to write to you on a little matter of business.—Jack, I have been considering that I grow old and infirm, and shall probably not trouble you long.

Abs. Pardon me, sir, I never saw you look more strong and hearty; and I pray frequently that you may continue so.

Sir Anth. I hope your prayers may be heard, with all my heart. Well then, Jack, I have been considering that I am so strong and hearty I may continue to plague you a long time. Now, Jack, I am sensible that the income of your commission, and what I have hitherto allowed you, is but a small pittance for a lad of your spirit.

Abs. Sir, you are very good

Sir Anth. And it is my wish, while yet I live, to have my boy make some figure in the world. I have resolved, therefore, to fix you at once in a noble independence.

Abs. Sir, your kindness overpowers me—such generosity makes the gratitude of reason more lively than the sensations even of filial affection.

Sir Anth. I am glad you are so sensible of my attention—and you shall be master of a large estate in a few weeks.

Abs. Let my future life, sir, speak my gratitude; I cannot express the sense I have of your munificence.—Yet, sir, I presume you would not wish me to quit the army?

Sir Anth. Oh, that shall be as your wife chooses.

Abs. My wife, sir!

Sir Anth. Ay, ay, settle that between you—settle that between you.

Abs. A wife, sir, did you say?

Sir Anth. Ay, a wife—why, did not I mention her before?

Abs. Not a word of her, sir.

Sir Anth. Odd so!—I mustn't forget her though.—Yes, Jack, the independence I was talking of is by a marriage—the fortune is saddled with a wife—but I suppose that makes no difference.

Abs. Sir! sir!—you amaze me!

Sir Anth. Why, what the devil's the matter with the fool? Just now you were all gratitude and duty.

Abs. I was, sir,—you talked to me of independence and a fortune, but not a word of a wife.

Sir Anth. Why—what difference does that make? Odds life, sir! if you have the estate, you must take it with the live stock on it, as it stands.

Abs. If my happiness is to be the price, I must beg leave to decline the purchase.—Pray, sir, who is the lady?

Sir Anth. What's that to you, sir?—Come, give me your promise to love, and to marry her directly.

Abs. Sure, sir, this is not very reasonable, to summon my affections for a lady I know nothing of!

Sir Anth. I am sure, sir, 'tis more unreasonable in you to object to a lady you know nothing of.

Abs. Then, sir, I must tell you plainly that my inclinations are fixed on another—my heart is engaged to an angel.

Sir Anth. Then pray let it send an excuse. It is very sorry—but business prevents its waiting on her.

Abs. But my vows are pledged to her.

Sir Anth. Let her foreclose, Jack; let her foreclose; they are not worth redeeming; besides, you have the angel's vows in exchange, I suppose; so there can be no loss there

Abs. You must excuse me, sir, if I tell you, once for all, that in this point I cannot obey you

Sir Anth. Hark'ee, Jack;—I have heard you for some timo with patience—I have been cool—quite cool; but take care— you know I am compliance itself—when I am not thwarted; —no one moro easily led—when I have my own way;—but don't put me in a frenzy.

Abs. Sir, I must repeat it—in this I cannot obey you.

Sir Anth. Now damn mo! if ever I call you Jack again while I live!

Abs. Nay, sir, but hear me.

Sir Anth. Sir, I won't hear a word—not a word! not one word! so give me your promise by a nod—and I 'll tell you what, Jack—I mean, you dog—if you don't, by——

Abs. What, sir, promise to link myself to some mass of ugliness! to——

Sir Anth. Zounds! sirrah! the lady shall bo as ugly as I choose: she shall have a hump on each shoulder; she shall be as crooked as the crescent; her one eye shall roll like tho bull's in Cox's Museum; she shall have a skin like a mummy, and the beard of a Jew—sho shall be all this, sirrah!—yet I will make you oglo her all day, and sit up all night to write sonnets on her beauty.

Abs. This is reason and moderation indeed!

Sir Anth. None of your sneering, puppy! no grinning, jackanapes!

Abs. Indeed, sir, I never was in a worse humour for mirth in my life.

Sir Anth. 'Tis false, sir, I know you are laughing in your sleeve; I know you 'll grin when I am gone, sirrah!

Abs. Sir, I hope I know my duty better.

Sir Anth. None of your passion, sir! none of your violencè, if you please!—It won't do with me, I promise you.

Abs. Indeed, sir, I never was cooler in my life.

Sir Anth. 'Tis a confounded lie!—I know you are in a passion in your heart; I know you are, you hypocritical young dog! but it won't do.

Abs. Nay, sir, upon my word——

Sir Anth. So you will fly out! can't you be cool like me? What the devil good can passion do?—Passion is of no ser-

vice, ycu impudent, insolent, overbearing reprobate!—There,
you sneer again! don't provoke me!—but you rely upon the
mildness of my temper—you do, you dog! you play upon the
meekness of my disposition!—Yet take care—the patience of
a saint may be overcome at last!—but mark! I give you six
hours and a half to consider of this: if you then agree, without
any condition, to do every thing on earth that I choose, why—
confound you! I may in time forgive you.—If not, zounds!
don't enter the same hemisphere with me! don't dare to
breathe the same air, or use the same light with me; but get
an atmosphere and a sun of your own! I 'll strip you of your
commission; I 'll lodge a five-and-threepence in the hands of
trustees, and you shall live on the interest.—I 'll disown you,
I 'll disinherit you, I 'll unget you! and damn me! if ever I
call you Jack again!   [*Exit.*

Abs. Mild, gentle, considerate father—I kiss your hands!
—What a tender method of giving his opinion in these matters Sir Anthony has! I dare not trust him with the truth.
—I wonder what old wealthy hag it is that he wants to bestow
on me!—Yet he married himself for love! and was in his
youth a bold intriguer, and a gay companion!

Re-enter FAG.

Fag. Assuredly, sir, your father is wrath to a degree; he
comes down stairs eight or ten steps at a time—muttering,
growling, and thumping the banisters all the way: I and the
cook's dog stand bowing at the door—rap! he gives me a
stroke on the head with his cane; bids me carry that to my
master; then kicking the poor turnspit into the area, damns
us all, for a puppy triumvirate!—Upon my credit, sir, were I
in your place, and found my father such very bad company, I
should certainly drop his acquaintance.

Abs. Cease your impertinence, sir, at present.—Did you
come in for nothing more?—Stand out of the way!
                        [*Pushes him aside, and exit.*

Fag. So! Sir Anthony trims my master: he is afraid to
reply to his father—then vents his spleen on poor Fag!—
When one is vexed by one person, to revenge one's self on
another, who happens to come in the way, is the vilest in-
justice! Ah! it shows the worst temper—the basest——

Enter BOY.

Boy. Mr. Fag! Mr. Fag! your master calls you.

Fag. Well, you little dirty puppy, you need not bawl so!—
The meanest disposition! the——

Boy. Quick, quick, Mr. Fag!

Fag. Quick! quick! you impudent jackanapes! am I to
be commanded by you too? you little impertinent, insolent,
kitchen-bred——   [*Exit kicking and beating him.*

SCENE II.—*The North Parade.*

Enter LUCY.

Lucy. So—I shall have another rival to add to my mistress's
list—Captain Absolute. However, I shall not enter his name
till my purse has received notice in form. Poor Acres is dis-
missed!—Well, I have done him a last friendly office, in
letting him know that Beverley was here before him.—Sir
Lucius is generally more punctual, when he expects to hear
from his *dear Dalia*, as he calls her: I wonder he's not here!
—I have a little scruple of conscience from this deceit;
though I should not be paid so well, if my hero knew that Delia
was near fifty, and her own mistress.

Enter SIR LUCIUS O'TRIGGER.

Sir Luc. Ha! my little ambassadress—upon my conscience,
I have been looking for you; I have been on the South Parade
this half hour.

Lucy. [*Speaking simply.*] O gemini! and I have been
waiting for your worship here on the North.

Sir Luc. Faith!—may be that was the reason we did not
meet; and it is very comical too, how you could go out and I
not see you—for I was only taking a nap at the Parade Coffee-
house, and I chose the window on purpose that I might not
miss you.

Lucy. My stars! Now I'd wager a sixpence I went by
while you were asleep.

Sir Luc. Sure enough it must have been so—and I never
dreamt it was so late, till I waked. Well, but my little girl,
have you got nothing for me?

Lucy. Yes, but I have—I've got a letter for you in my
pocket

Sir Luc. O faith! I guessed you weren't come empty-handed —Well—let me see what the dear creature says.

Lucy. There, Sir Lucius.　　　　　　　[*Gives him a letter.*

Sir Luc. [Reads.] *Sir—there is often a sudden incentive impulse in love, that has a greater induction than years of domestic combination: such was the commotion I felt at the first superfluous view of Sir Lucius O'Trigger.*—Very pretty, upon my word.—*Female punctuation forbids me to say more, yet let me add, that it will give me joy infallible to find Sir Lucius worthy the last criterion of my affections.*　　DELIA. Upon my conscience! Lucy, your lady is a great mistress of language.　Faith, she's quite the queen of the dictionary!— for the devil a word dare refuse coming at her call—though one would think it was quite out of hearing.

Lucy. Ay, sir, a lady of her experience——

Sir Luc. Experience! what, at seventeen?

Lucy. O true, sir—but then she reads so—my stars! how she will read off hand!

Sir Luc. Faith, she must be very deep read to write this way—though she is rather an arbitrary writer too—for here are a great many poor words pressed into the service of this note, that would get their *habeas corpus* from any court in Christendom.

Lucy. Ah! Sir Lucius, if you were to hear how she talks of you!

Sir Luc. Oh, tell her I'll make her the best husband in the world, and Lady O'Trigger into the bargain!—But we must get the old gentlewoman's consent—and do every thing fairly.

Lucy. Nay, Sir Lucius, I thought you wa'n't rich enough to be so nice!

Sir Luc. Upon my word, young woman, you have hit it:— I am so poor, that I can't afford to do a dirty action.—If I did not want money, I'd steal your mistress and her fortune with a great deal of pleasure.—However, my pretty girl, [*Gives her money,*] here's a little something to buy you a ribbon; and meet me in the evening, and I'll give you an answer to this.　So, hussy, take a kiss beforehand to put you in mind.　　　　　　　　　　　　　　[*Kisses her.*

Lucy. O Lud! Sir Lucius—I never seed such a gemman' My lady won't like you if you're so impudent.

Sir Luc. Faith she will, Lucy!--That same--pho! what's the name of it?--modesty--is a quality in a lover more praised by the women than liked; so, if your mistress asks you whether Sir Lucius ever gave you a kiss, tell her fifty--my dear.

Lucy. What, would you have me tell her a lie?

Sir Luc. Ah, then, you baggage! I'll make it a truth presently.

Lucy. For shame now! here is some one coming.

Sir Luc. Oh, faith, I'll quiet your conscience!

[*Exit, humming a tune*

Enter FAG.

Fag. So, so, ma'am! I humbly beg pardon.

Lucy. O Lud! now, Mr. Fag--you flurry one so.

Fag. Come, come, Lucy, here's no one by--so a little less simplicity, with a grain or two more sincerity, if you please.--You play false with us, madam.--I saw you give the baronet a letter.--My master shall know this--and if he don't call him out, I will.

Lucy. Ha! ha! ha! you gentlemen's gentlemen are so hasty.--That letter was from Mrs. Malaprop, simpleton.--She is taken with Sir Lucius's address.

Fag. How! what tastes some people have!--Why, I suppose I have walked by her window a hundred times.--But what says our young lady? any message to my master?

Lucy. Sad news, Mr. Fag.--A worse rival than Acres! Sir Anthony Absolute has proposed his son.

Fag. What, Captain Absolute?

Lucy. Even so--I overheard it all.

Fag. Ha! ha! ha! very good, faith. Good bye, ·Lucy, I must away with this news.

Lucy. Well, you may laugh--but it is true, I assure you.--[*Going.*] But, Mr. Fag, tell your master not to be cast down by this.

Fag. Oh, he'll be so disconsolate!

Lucy. And charge him not to think of quarrelling with young Absolute.

Fag. Never fear! never fear!

Lucy. Be sure--bid him keep up his spirits.

Fag. We will--we will.   [*Exeunt severally.*

ACT III.

SCENE I.—*The North Parade*

Enter CAPTAIN ABSOLUTE.

Abs. 'Tis just as Fag told me, indeed. Whimsical enough, faith! My father wants to force me to marry the very girl I am plotting to run away with! He must not know of my connection with her yet awhile. He has too summary a method of proceeding in these matters. However, I'll read my recantation instantly. My conversion is something sudden, indeed—but I can assure him it is very sincere. So, so—here he comes. He looks plaguy gruff.   [*Steps aside.*

Enter SIR ANTHONY ABSOLUTE.

Sir Anth. No—I'll die sooner than forgive him. Die, did I say? I'll live these fifty years to plague him. At our last meeting, his impudence had almost put me out of temper. An obstinate, passionate, self-willed boy! Who can he take after? This is my return for getting him before all his brothers and sisters!—for putting him, at twelve years old, into a marching regiment, and allowing him fifty pounds a year, besides his pay, ever since! But I have done with him; he's anybody's son for me. I never will see him more, never—never—never.

Abs. [*Aside, coming forward.*] Now for a penitential face.

Sir Anth. Fellow, get out of my way!

Abs. Sir, you see a penitent before you.

Sir Anth. I see an impudent scoundrel before me.

Abs. A sincere penitent. I am come, sir, to acknowledge my error, and to submit entirely to your will.

Sir Anth. What's that?

Abs. I have been revolving, and reflecting, and considering on your past goodness, and kindness, and condescension to me.

Sir Anth. Well, sir?

Abs. I have been likewise weighing and balancing what you were pleased to mention concerning duty, and obedience, and authority.

Sir Anth. Well, puppy?

Abs. Why then, sir, the result of my reflections is—a resolution to sacrifice every inclination of my own to your satisfaction

D

Sir Anth. Why now you talk sense—absolute sense--I never heard any thing more sensible in my life. Confound you! you shall be Jack again

Abs. I am happy in the appellation.

Sir Anth. Why then, Jack, my dear Jack, I will now inform you who the lady really is. Nothing but your passion and violence, you silly fellow, prevented my telling you at first. Prepare, Jack, for wonder and rapture—prepare. What think you of Miss Lydia Languish?

Abs. Languish! What, the Languishes of Worcestershire?

Sir Anth. Worcestershire! no. Did you never meet Mrs. Malaprop and her niece, Miss Languish, who came into our country just before you were last ordered to your regiment?

Abs. Malaprop! Languish! I don't remember ever to have heard the names before. Yet, stay—I think I do recollect something. Languish! Languish! She squints, don't she? A little red-haired girl?

Sir Anth. Squints! A red-haired girl! Zounds! no

Abs. Then I must have forgot; it can't be the same person.

Sir Anth. Jack! Jack! what think you of blooming, love-breathing seventeen?

Abs. As to that, sir, I am quite indifferent. If I can please you in the matter, 'tis all I desire.

Sir Anth. Nay, but Jack, such eyes! such eyes! so innocently wild! so bashfully irresolute! not a glance but speaks and kindles some thought of love! Then, Jack, her cheeks! her cheeks, Jack! so deeply blushing at the insinuations of her tell-tale eyes! Then, Jack, her lips! O Jack, lips smiling at their own discretion; and if not smiling, more sweetly pouting; more lovely in sullenness!

Abs. That's she indeed. Well done, old gentleman. [*Aside.*

Sir Anth. Then, Jack, her neck! O Jack! Jack!

Abs. And which is to be mine, sir, the niece, or the aunt?

Sir Anth. Why, you unfeeling, insensible puppy, I despise you! When I was of your age, such a description would have made me fly like a rocket! The aunt indeed! Odds life! when I ran away with your mother, I would not have touched any thing old or ugly to gain an empire.

Abs. Not to please your father, sir?

Sir Anth. To please my father! zounds! not to please—Oh, my father—odd so!—yes—yes; if my father indeed had desired—that 's quite another matter. Though he wa'n't the indulgent father that I am, Jack.

Abs. I dare say not, sir.

Sir Anth. But, Jack, you are not sorry to find your mistress is so beautiful ?

Abs. Sir, I repeat it—if I please you in this affair, 'tis all I desire. Not that I think a woman the worse for being handsome; but, sir, if you please to recollect, you before hinted something about a hump or two, one eye, and a few more graces of that kind—now, without being very nice, I own I should rather choose a wife of mine to have the usual number of limbs, and a limited quantity of back : and though one eye may be very agreeable, yet as the prejudice has always run in favour of two, I would not wish to affect a singularity in that article.

Sir Anth. What a phlegmatic sot it is ! Why, sirrah, you 're an anchorite !—a vile, insensible stock. You a soldier !— you 're a walking block, fit only to dust the company's regimentals on! Odds life ! I have a great mind to marry the girl myself.

Abs. I am entirely at your disposal, sir : if you should think of addressing Miss Languish yourself, I suppose you would have me marry the aunt; or if you should change your mind, and take the old lady—'tis the same to me—I 'll marry the niece.

Sir Anth. Upon my word, Jack, thou 'rt either a very great hypocrite, or—but, come, I know your indifference on such a subject must be all a lie—I 'm sure it must—come, now—damn your demure face !—come, confess Jack—you have been lying —ha'n't you? You have been playing the hypocrite, hey !— I 'll never forgive you, if you ha'n't been lying and playing the hypocrite.

Abs. I 'm sorry, sir, that the respect and duty which I bear to you should be so mistaken.

Sir Anth. Hang your respect and duty! But come along with me, I 'll write a note to Mrs. Malaprop, and you shall visit the lady directly. Her eyes shall be the Promethean torch to you—come along, I 'll never forgive you, if you don't come back stark mad with rapture and impatience—if you don't, egad, I will marry the girl myself!　　　　　*[Exeunt*

D 2

SCENE II.—JULIA's *Dressing-room.*

FAULKLAND *discovered alone.*

Faulk. They told me Julia would return directly; I wonder she is not yet come! How mean does this captious, unsatisfied temper of mine appear to my cooler judgment! Yet I know not that I indulge it in any other point : but on this one subject, and to this one subject, whom I think I love beyond my life, I am ever ungenerously fretful and madly capricious! I am conscious of it—yet I cannot correct myself! What tender honest joy sparkled in her eyes when we met! how delicate was the warmth of her expressions! I was ashamed to appear less happy—though I had come resolved to wear a face of coolness and upbraiding. Sir Anthony's presence prevented my proposed expostulations: yet I must be satisfied that she has not been so very happy in my absence. She is coming! Yes!—I know the nimbleness of her tread, when she thinks her impatient Faulkland counts the moments of her stay.

Enter JULIA.

Jul. I had not hoped to see you again so soon

Faulk. Could I, Julia, be contented with my first welcome—restrained as we were by the presence of a third person?

Jul. O Faulkland, when your kindness can make me thus happy, let me not think that I discovered something of coldness in your first salutation.

Faulk. 'Twas but your fancy, Julia. I was rejoiced to see you—to see you in such health. Sure I had no cause for coldness?

Jul. Nay then, I see you have taken something ill. You must not conceal from me what it is.

Faulk. Well, then—shall I own to you that my joy at hearing of your health and arrival here, by your neighbour Acres, was somewhat damped by his dwelling much on the high spirits you had enjoyed in Devonshire—on your mirth—your singing—dancing, and I know not what! For such is my temper, Julia, that I should regard every mirthful moment in your absence as a treason to constancy. The mutual tear that steals down the cheek of parting lovers is a compact, that no smile shall live there till they meet again

Jul. Must I never cease to tax my Faulkland with this teasing minute caprice? ‚ Can the idle reports of a silly boor weigh in your breast against my tried affection?

Faulk. They have no weight with me, Julia: No, no—I am happy if you have been so—yet only say, that you did not sing with mirth—say that you thought of Faulkland in the dance.

Jul. I never can be happy in your absence. If I wear a countenance of content, it is to show that my mind holds no doubt of my Faulkland's truth. If I seemed sad, it were to make malice triumph; and say, that I had fixed my heart on one, who left me to lament his roving, and my own credulity. Believe me, Faulkland, I mean not to upbraid you, when I say, that I have often dressed sorrow in smiles, lest my friends should guess whose unkindness had caused my tears.

Faulk. You were ever all goodness to me. Oh, I am a brute, when I but admit a doubt of your true constancy!

Jul. If ever without such cause from you, as I will not suppose possible, you find my affections veering but a point, may I become a proverbial scoff for levity and base ingratitude.

Faulk. Ah! Julia, that last word is grating to me. I would I had no title to your gratitude! Search your heart, Julia; perhaps what you have mistaken for love, is but the warm effusion of a too thankful heart.

Jul. For what quality must I love you?

Faulk. For no quality! To regard me for any quality of mind or understanding, were only to esteem me. And for person—I have often wished myself deformed, to be convinced that I owed no obligation there for any part of your affection.

Jul. Where nature has bestowed a show of nice attention in the features of a man, he should laugh at it as misplaced. I have seen men, who in this vain article, perhaps, might rank above you; but my heart has never asked my eyes if it were so or not.

Faulk. Now this is not well from you, Julia—I despise person in a man—yet if you loved me as I wish, though I were an Æthiop, you 'd think none so fair.

Jul. I see you are determined to be unkind! The contract which my poor father bound us in gives you more than a lover's privilege.

Faulk Again, Julia, you raise ideas that feed and justify

my doubts. I would not have been more free—no—I am proud of my restraint. Yet—yet—perhaps your high respect alone for this solemn compact has fettered your inclinations, which else had made a worthier choice. How shall I be sure, had you remained unbound in thought and promise, that I should still have been the object of your persevering love?

Jul. Then try me now. Let us be free as strangers as to what is past: my heart will not feel more liberty!

Faulk. There now! so hasty, Julia! so anxious to be free! If your love for me were fixed and ardent, you would not lose your hold, even though I wished it!

Jul. Oh! you torture me to the heart! I cannot bear it.

Faulk. I do not mean to distress you. If I loved you less I should never give you an uneasy moment. But hear me. All my fretful doubts arise from this. Women are not used to weigh and separate the motives of their affections: the cold dictates of prudence, gratitude, or filial duty, may sometimes be mistaken for the pleadings of the heart. I would not boast —yet let me say, that I have neither age, person, nor character, to found dislike on; my fortune such as few ladies could be charged with indiscretion in the match. O Julia! when love receives such countenance from prudence, nice minds will be suspicious of its birth.

Jul. I know not whither your insinuations would tend :— but as they seem pressing to insult me, I will spare you the regret of having done so.—I have given you no cause for this!

[Exit in tears.

Faulk. In tears! Stay, Julia: stay but for a moment.— The door is fastened!—Julia!—my soul—but for one moment! —I hear her sobbing!—'Sdeath! what a brute am I to use her thus! Yet stay.—Ay—she is coming now :—how little resolution there is in woman!—how a few soft words can turn them!—No, faith!—she is not coming either.—Why, Julia— my love—say but that you forgive me—come but to tell me that—now this is being too resentful. Stay! she is coming too—I thought she would—no steadiness in any thing: her going away must have been a mere trick then—she sha'nt see that I was hurt by it.—I 'll affect indifference—[*Hums a tune: then listens.*] No—zounds! she 's not coming!—nor don't intend it, I suppose.—This is not steadiness, but obstinacy! Yet I deserve it.—What, after so long an absence to quarrel

with her tenderness!—'twas barbarous and unmanly!—I
should be ashamed to see her now.—I'll wait till her just ro
sentment is abated—and when I distress her so again, may I
lose her for ever! and be linked instead to some antiquo
virago, whose gnawing passions, and long hoarded spleen, shall
make me curse my folly half the day and all the night.

[*Exit.*

SCENE III.—MRS. MALAPROP'S *Lodgings.*

MRS. MALAPROP, *with a letter in her hand, and* CAPTAIN
ABSOLUTE.

Mrs. Mal. Your being Sir Anthony's son, captain, would
itself be a sufficient accommodation; but from the ingenuity
of your appearance, I am convinced you deserve the character
here given of you.

Abs. Permit me to say, madam, that as I never yet have
had the pleasure of seeing Miss Languish, my principal inducement in this affair at present is the honour of being allied
to Mrs. Malaprop; of whose intellectual accomplishments,
elegant manners, and unaffected learning, no tongue is silent.

Mrs. Mal. Sir, you do me infinite honour! I beg, captain,
you'll be seated.—[*They sit.*] Ah! few gentlemen, now-a-
days, know how to value the ineffectual qualities in a woman!
few think how a little knowledge becomes a gentlewoman!—
Men have no sense now but for the worthless flower of
beauty!

Abs. It is but too true, indeed, ma'am;—yet I fear our
ladies should share the blame—they think our admiration of
beauty so great, that knowledge in them would be superfluous.
Thus, like garden-trees, they seldom show fruit, till time has
robbed them of the more specious blossom.—Few, like Mrs.
Malaprop and the orange-tree, are rich in both at once!

Mrs. Mal. Sir, you overpower me with good-breeding.—
He is the very pine-apple of politeness!—You are not ignorant, captain, that this giddy girl has somehow contrived to
fix her affections on a beggarly, strolling, eaves-dropping
ensign, whom none of us have seen, and nobody knows any-
thing of.

Abs. Oh, I have heard the silly affair before.—I'm not at
all prejudiced against her on that account.

Mrs. Mal. You are very good and very considerate, captain.

I am sure I have done every thing in my power since I exploded the affair; long ago I laid my positive conjunctions on her, never to think on the fellow again;—I have since laid Sir Anthony's preposition before her; but, I am sorry to say, she seems resolved to decline every particle that I enjoin her

Abs. It must be very distressing, indeed, ma'am.

Mrs. Mal. Oh! it gives me the hydrostatics to such a degree.—I thought she had persisted from corresponding with him; but, behold, this very day, I have interceded another letter from the fellow; I believe I have it in my pocket.

Abs. Oh, the devil! my last note.   [*Aside.*

Mrs. Mal. Ay, here it is.

Abs Ay, my note indeed! O the little traitress Lucy.
                                                  [*Aside.*

Mrs. Mal. There, perhaps you may know the writing.
                                        [*Gives him the letter.*

Abs. I think I have seen the hand before—yes, I certainly must have seen this hand before—

Mrs. Mal. Nay, but read it, captain.

Abs. [Reads.] *My soul's idol, my adored Lydia!*—Very tender indeed!

Mrs. Mal. Tender! ay, and profane too, o' my conscience

Abs. [Reads.] *I am excessively alarmed at the intelligence you send me, the more so as my new rival*——

Mrs. Mal. That's you, sir.

Abs. [Reads.] *Has universally the character of being an accomplished gentleman and a man of honour.*—Well, that's handsome enough.

Mrs. Mal. Oh, the fellow has some design in writing so.

Abs. That he had, I'll answer for him, ma'am.

Mrs. Mal. But go on, sir—you'll see presently.

Abs. [Reads.] *As for the old weather-beaten she-dragon who guards you*—Who can he mean by that?

Mrs. Mal. Me, sir!—me!—he means me!—There—what do you think now?—but go on a little further.

Abs. Impudent scoundrel!—[Reads.] *it shall go hard but I will elude her vigilance, as I am told that the same ridiculous vanity, which makes her dress up her coarse features, and deck her dull chat with hard words which she don't understand*——

Mrs. Mal. There, sir, an attack upon my language! what do you think of that?—an aspersion upon my parts of speech! was ever such a brute! Sure, if I reprehend any thing in this world, it is the use of my oracular tongue, and a nice derangement of epitaphs!

Abs. He deserves to be hanged and quartered! let me see —[Reads.] *same ridiculous vanity——*

Mrs. Mal. You need not read it again, sir.

Abs. I beg pardon, ma'am.—[Reads.] *does also lay her open to the grossest deceptions from flattery and pretended ad miration—*an impudent coxcomb!—*so that I have a scheme to see you shortly with the old harridan's consent, and even to make her a go-between in our interview.*—Was ever such assurance!

Mrs. Mal. Did you ever hear any thing like it?—he'll elude my vigilance, will he—yes, yes! ha! ha! he's very likely to enter these doors;—we'll try who can plot best!

Abs. So we will, ma'am—so we will! Ha! ha! ha! a conceited puppy, ha! ha! ha!—Well, but Mrs. Malaprop, as the girl seems so infatuated by this fellow, suppose you were to wink at her corresponding with him for a little time—let her even plot an elopement with him—then do you connive at her escape—while I, just in the nick, will have the fellow laid by the heels, and fairly contrive to carry her off in his stead.

Mrs. Mal. I am delighted with the scheme; never was any-thing better perpetrated!

Abs. But, pray, could not I see the lady for a few minutes now?—I should like to try her temper a little.

Mrs. Mal. Why, I don't know—I doubt she is not prepared for a visit of this kind. There is a decorum in these matters.

Abs. O Lord! she won't mind me—only tell her Bever-ley——

Mrs. Mal. Sir!

Abs. Gently, good tongue.   [*Aside*

Mrs. Mal. What did you say of Beverley?

Abs. Oh, I was going to propose that you should tell her, by way of jest, that it was Beverley who was below; she'd come down fast enough then—ha! ha! ha!

Mrs. Mal 'Twould be a trick she well deserves; besides,

you know the fellow tells her he'll get my consent to see
her—ha! ha! Let him if he can, I say again. Lydia, come
down here!—[*Calling.*] He'll make me a go-between in
their interviews!—ha! ha! ha! Come down, I say, Lydia!
I don't wonder at your laughing, ha! ha! ha! his impudence
is truly ridiculous.

Abs. 'Tis very ridiculous, upon my soul, ma'am, ha!
ha! ha!

Mrs. Mal. The little hussy won't hear. Well, I'll go and
tell her at once who it is—she shall know that Captain Absolute is come to wait on her. And I'll make her behave as
becomes a young woman.

Abs. As you please, ma'am.

Mrs. Mal. For the present, captain, your servant. Ah!
you've not done laughing yet, I see—elude my vigilance;
yes, yes; ha! ha! ha!   [*Exit*

Abs. Ha! ha! ha! one would think now that I might
throw off all disguise at once, and seize my prize with security;
but such is Lydia's caprice, that to undeceive were probably
to lose her. I'll see whether she knows me.

[*Walks aside, and seems engaged in looking at the pictures*

Enter LYDIA.

Lyd. What a scene am I now to go through! surely no
thing can be more dreadful than to be obliged to listen to
the loathsome addresses of a stranger to one's heart. I have
heard of girls persecuted as I am, who have appealed in behalf
of their favoured lover to the generosity of his rival suppose I were to try it—there stands the hated rival—an officer
too!—but oh, how unlike my Beverley! I wonder he don't
begin—truly he seems a very negligent wooer!—quite at his
ease, upon my word!—I'll speak first—Mr. Absolute

Abs. Ma'am.   [*Turns round*

Lyd. O heavens! Beverley!

Abs. Hush!—hush, my life! softly! be not surprised!

Lyd. I am so astonished! and so terrified! and so over
joyed!—for Heaven's sake! how came you here?

Abs. Briefly, I have deceived your aunt—I was informed
that my new rival was to visit here this evening, and con-
triving to have him kept away, have passed myself on her
for Captain Absolute

Lyd. O charming! And she really takes you for young Absolute?

Abs. Oh, she's convinced of it.

Lyd Ha! ha! ha! I can't forbear laughing to think how her sagacity is overreached!

Abs. But we trifle with our precious moments—such another opportunity may not occur; then let me now conjure my kind, my condescending angel, to fix the time when I may rescue her from undeserving persecution, and with a licensed warmth plead for my reward.

Lyd. Will you then, Beverley, consent to forfeit that portion of my paltry wealth?— that burden on the wings of love?

Abs. Oh, come to me—rich only thus—in loveliness! Bring no portion to me but thy love—'twill be generous in you, Lydia—for well you know, it is the only dower your poor Beverley can repay.

Lyd. How persuasive are his words!—how charming will poverty be with him! [*Aside.*

Abs. Ah! my soul, what a life will we then live! Love shall be our idol and support! we will worship him with a monastic strictness; abjuring all worldly toys, to centre every thought and action there. Proud of calamity, we will enjoy the wreck of wealth; while the surrounding gloom of adversity shall make the flame of our pure love show doubly bright. By Heavens! I would fling all goods of fortune from me with a prodigal hand, to enjoy the scene where I might clasp my Lydia to my bosom, and say, the world affords no smile to me but here—[*Embracing her.*] If she holds out now, the devil is in it! [*Aside.*

Lyd. Now could I fly with him to the antipodes! but my persecution is not yet come to a crisis [*Aside.*

Re-enter MRS. MALAPROP, *listening*

Mrs. Mal. I am impatient to know how the little hussy deports herself. [*Aside*

Abs So pensive, Lydia!—is then your warmth abated?

Mrs. Mal. Warmth abated!—so!—she has been in a passion, I suppose. [*Aside.*

Lyd. No—nor ever can while I have life.

Mrs. Mal. An ill tempered little devil! She'll be in a passion all her life—will she?   [*Aside.*

Lyd. Think not the idle threats of my ridiculous aunt can ever have any weight with me.

Mrs. Mal. Very dutiful, upon my word!   [*Aside.*

Lyd. Let her choice be Captain Absolute, but Beverley is mine.

Mrs. Mal. I am astonished at her assurance!—to his face—this is to his face!   [*Aside*

Abs. Thus then let me enforce my suit.   [*Kneeling.*

Mrs. Mal. [*Aside.*] Ay, poor young man!—down on his knees entreating for pity!—I can contain no longer.—[*Coming forward.*] Why, thou vixen!—I have overheard you.

Abs. Oh, confound her vigilance!   [*Aside*

Mrs. Mal. Captain Absolute, I know not how to apologize for her shocking rudeness.

Abs. [*Aside.*] So all's safe, I find.—[*Aloud.*] I have hopes, madam, that time will bring the young lady——

Mrs. Mal. Oh, there's nothing to be hoped for from her! she's as headstrong as an allegory on the banks of Nile.

Lyd. Nay, madam, what do you charge me with now?

Mrs. Mal. Why, thou unblushing rebel—didn't you tell this gentleman to his face that you loved another better?—didn't you say you never would be his?

Lyd. No, madam—I did not.

Mrs. Mal. Good Heavens! what assurance!—Lydia, Lydia, you ought to know that lying don't become a young woman!—Didn't you boast that Beverley, that stroller Beverley, possessed your heart?—Tell me that, I say.

Lyd. 'Tis true, ma'am, and none but Beverley——

Mrs. Mal. Hold!—hold, Assurance!—you shall not be so rude.

Abs. Nay, pray, Mrs. Malaprop, don't stop the young lady's speech: she's very welcome to talk thus—it does not hurt me in the least, I assure you.

Mrs. Mal. You are too good, captain—too amiably patient—but come with me, miss.—Let us see you again soon, captain—remember what we have fixed.

Abs. I shall ma'am.

Mrs. Mal. Come, take a graceful leave of the gentleman

Lyd. May every blessing wait on my Beverley, my loved Bev——

Mrs. Mal. Hussy! I'll choke the word in your throat!—come along—come along.

[*Exeunt severally;* CAPTAIN ABSOLUTE *kissing his hand to* LYDIA—Mrs. MALAPROP *stopping her from speaking*

SCENE IV.—ACRES' *Lodgings.*

ACRES, *as just dressed, and* DAVID

Acres. Indeed, David—do you think I become it so?

Dav. You are quite another creature, believe me, master, by the mass! an' we've any luck we shall see the Devon mon kerony in all the print-shops in Bath!

Acres. Dress does make a difference, David.

Dav. 'Tis all in all, I think.—Difference! why, an' you were to go now to Clod-hall, I am certain the old lady wouldn't know you: master Butler wouldn't believe his own eyes, and Mrs. Pickle would cry, Lard presarve me! our dairy-maid would come giggling to the door, and I warrant Dolly Tester, your honour's favourite, would blush like my waistcoat.— Oons! I'll hold a gallon, there an't a dog in the house but would bark, and I question whether Phillis would wag a hair of her tail!

Acres. Ay, David, there's nothing like polishing.

Dav. So I says of your honour's boots; but the boy never heeds me!

Acres. But, David, has Mr. De-la-grace been here? I must rub up my balancing, and chasing, and boring.

Dav. I'll call again, sir

Acres. Do—and see if there are any letters for me at the post-office

Dav. I will.—By the mass, I can't help looking at your head!—if I hadn't been by at the cooking, I wish I may die if I should have known the dish again myself! [*Exit*

Acres. [*Practising a dancing-step.*] Sink, slide—coupee.— Confound the first inventors of cotillons! say I—they are as bad as algebra to us country gentlemen—I can walk a minuet easy enough when I am forced!—and I have been accounted a good stick in a country-dance.—Odds jigs and tabors! I never valued your cross-over to couple—figure in—right and left—and I'd foot it with e'er a captain in the county!--but

these outlandish heathen allemandes and cotillons are quite
beyond me!—I shall never prosper at 'em, that's sure—mine
are true-born English legs—they don't understand their curst
French lingo!—their *pas* this, and *pas* that, and *pas* t'other!
—damn me! my feet don't like to be called paws! no, 'tis
certain I have most Antigallican toes!

Enter SERVANT.

Serv. Here is Sir Lucius O'Trigger to wait on you, sir.
Acres. Show him in.   [*Exit* SERVANT.

Enter SIR LUCIUS O'TRIGGER.

Sir Luc. Mr. Acres, I am delighted to embrace you.
Acres. My dear Sir Lucius, I kiss your hands.
Sir Luc. Pray, my friend, what has brought you so sud
denly to Bath?
Acres. Faith! I have followed Cupid's Jack-a-lantern, and
find myself in a quagmire at last.—In short, I have been very
ill used, Sir Lucius.—I don't choose to mention names, but
look on me as on a very ill-used gentleman.
Sir Luc. Pray what is the case?—I ask no names.
Acres. Mark me, Sir Lucius, I fall as deep as need be in
love with a young lady—her friends take my part—I follow
her to Bath—send word of my arrival; and receive answer,
that the lady is to be otherwise disposed of.—This, Sir Lucius, I call being ill used.
Sir Luc. Very ill, upon my conscience.—Pray, can you divine the cause of it?
Acres. Why, there's the matter; she has another lover,
one Beverley, who, I am told, is now in Bath.—Odds slanders
and lies! he must be at the bottom of it.
Sir Luc. A rival in the case, is there?—and you think he
has supplanted you unfairly?
Acres. Unfairly! to be sure he has. He never could have
done it fairly.
Sir Luc. Then sure you know what is to be done!
Acres. Not I, upon my soul!
Sir Luc. We wear no swords here, but you understand me.
Acres. What! fight him!
Sir Luc. Ay, to be sure: what can I mean else?
Acres. But he has given me no provocation.
Sir Luc. Now, I think he has given you the greatest pro

vocation in the world. Can a man commit a more heinous offence against another than to fall in love with the same woman? Oh, by my soul! it is the most unpardonable breach of friendship.

Acres. Breach of friendship! ay, ay; but I have no acquaintance with this man. I never saw him in my life.

Sir Luc. That's no argument at all—he has the less right then to take such a liberty.

Acres. Gad, that's true—I grow full of anger, Sir Lucius! —I fire apace! Odds hilts and blades! I find a man may have a deal of valour in him, and not know it! But couldn't I contrive to have a little right of my side?

Sir Luc. What the devil signifies right, when your honour is concerned? Do you think Achilles, or my little Alexander the Great, ever inquired where the right lay? No, by my soul, they drew their broad-swords, and left the lazy sons of peace to settle the justice of it.

Acres. Your words are a grenadier's march to my heart! I believe courage must be catching! I certainly do feel a kind of valour rising as it were—a kind of courage, as I may say.—Odds flints, pans, and triggers! I'll challenge him directly.

Sir Luc. Ah, my little friend, if I had Blunderbuss Hall here, I could show you a range of ancestry, in the O'Trigger line, that would furnish the new room; every one of whom had killed his man!—For though the mansion-house and dirty acres have slipped through my fingers, I thank heaven our honour and the family-pictures are as fresh as ever.

Acres. O, Sir Lucius! I have had ancestors too!—every man of 'em colonel or captain in the militia!—Odds balls and barrels! say no more—I'm braced for it. The thunder of your words has soured the milk of human kindness in my breast;—Zounds! as the man in the play says, *I could do such deeds!*

Sir Luc. Come, come, there must be no passion at all in the case—these things should always be done civilly

Acres. I must be in a passion, Sir Lucius—I must be in a rage.—Dear Sir Lucius, let me be in a rage, if you love me. Come, here's pen and paper.—[*Sits down to write.*] I would the ink were red!—Indite, I say indite!—How shall I be-

gin? Odds bullets and blades! I 'll write a good bold hand,
however.

Sir Luc. Pray compose yourself.

Acres. Come—now, shall I begin with an oath? Do, Sir
Lucius, let me begin with a damme.

Sir Luc. Pho! pho! do the thing decently, and like a
Christian. Begin now—*Sir*——

Acres. That 's too civil by half.

Sir Luc. To prevent the confusion that might arise——

Acres. Well——

Sir Luc. From our both addressing the same lady——

Acres. Ay, there 's the reason—*same lady*—well——

Sir Luc. I shall expect the honour of your company——

Acres. Zounds! I 'm not asking him to dinner.

Sir Luc. Pray be easy.

Acres. Well then, *honour of your company*——

Sir Luc. To settle our pretensions——

Acres. Well.

Sir Luc. Let me see, ay, King's-Mead-Field will do—*in
King's-Mead-Fields.*

Acres. So, that 's done—Well, I 'll fold it up presently;
my own crest—a hand and dagger shall be the seal.

Sir Luc. You see now this little explanation will put a stop
at once to all confusion or misunderstanding that might arise
between you.

Acres. Ay, we fight to prevent any misunderstanding.

Sir Luc. Now, I 'll leave you to fix your own time.—Take
my advice, and you 'll decide it this evening if you can; then
let the worst come of it, 'twill be off your mind to-morrow.

Acres. Very true.

Sir Luc. So I shall see nothing more of you, unless it be by
letter, till the evening.—I would do myself the honour to
carry your message; but, to tell you a secret, I believe I shall
have just such another affair on my own hands. There is a
gay captain here, who put a jest on me lately, at the expense
of my country, and I only want to fall in with the gentleman,
to call him out.

Acres. By my valour, I should like to see you fight first!
Odds life! I should like to see you kill him if it was only
to get a little lesson.

Sir Luc. I shall be very proud of instructing you.—Well for the present—but remember now, when you meet your antagonist, do everything in a mild and agreeable manner.— Let your courage be as keen, but at the same time as polished, as your sword.   [*Exeunt severally.*

ACT IV.

Scene I.—Acres' *Lodgings.*

Acres *and* David.

Dav. Then, by the mass, sir! I would do no such thing —ne'er a Sir Lucius O'Trigger in the kingdom should make me fight, when I wa'n't so minded. Oons! what will the old lady say, when she hears o't?

Acres. Ah! David, if you had heard Sir Lucius!—Odds sparks and flames! he would have roused your valour.

Dav. Not he, indeed. I hate such bloodthirsty cormorants. Look'ee, master, if you'd wanted a bout at boxing, quarter-staff, or short-staff, I should never be the man to bid you cry off: but for your curst sharps and snaps, I never knew any good come of 'em.

Acres. But my honour, David, my honour! I must be very careful of my honour.

Dav. Ay, by the mass! and I would be very careful of it; and I think in return my honour couldn't do less than to be very careful of me.

Acres. Odds blades! David, no gentleman will ever risk the loss of his honour!

Dav. I say then, it would be but civil in honour never to risk the loss of a gentleman.—Look'ee, master, this honour seems to me to be a marvellous false friend: ay, truly, a very courtier-like servant.—Put the case, I was a gentleman (which, thank God, no one can say of me;) well—my honour makes me quarrel with another gentleman of my acquaintance.—So —we fight. (Pleasant enough that!) Boh!—I kill him— (the more's my luck!) now, pray who gets the profit of it?— Why, my honour. But put the case that he kills me!—by the mass! I go to the worms, and my honour whips over to my enemy.

Acres. No, David—in that case!—Odds crowns and laurels! your honour follows you to the grave.

E

Dav. Now, that's just the place where I could make a shift
to do without it.

Acres. Zounds! David, you are a coward!—It doesn't become my valour to listen to you.—What, shall I disgrace my
ancestors?—Think of that, David—think what it would be to
disgrace my ancestors!

Dav. Under favour, the surest way of not disgracing them,
is to keep as long as you can out of their company. Look'ee
now, master, to go to them in such haste—with an ounce of
lead in your brains—I should think might as well be let
alone. Our ancestors are very good kind of folks; but they
are the last people I should choose to have a visiting acquaintance with.

Acres. But, David, now, you don't think there is such
very, very, very great danger, hey?—Odds life! people often
fight without any mischief done!

Dav. By the mass, I think 'tis ten to one against you!—
Oons! here to meet some lion-headed fellow, I warrant,
with his damned double-barrelled swords, and cut-and-thrust
pistols!—Lord bless us! it makes me tremble to think o't!
—Those be such desperate bloody-minded weapons! Well, I
never could abide 'em—from a child I never could fancy 'em!
—I suppose there a'nt been so merciless a beast in the world
as your loaded pistol!

Acres. Zounds! I won't be afraid!—Odds fire and fury!
you shan't make me afraid.—Here is the challenge, and I
have sent for my dear friend Jack Absolute to carry it for me

Dav. Ay, i'the name of mischief, let him be the mes-
senger.—For my part, I wouldn't lend a hand to it for the
best horse in your stable. By the mass! it don't look like
another letter! It is, as I may say, a designing and mali-
cious-looking letter; and I warrant smells of gunpowder like a
soldier's pouch!—Oons! I wouldn't swear it mayn't go off!

Acres. Out, you poltroon! you ha'nt the valour of a grasshopper.

Dav. Well, I say no more—'twill be sad news, to be sure,
at Clod-Hall! but I ha' done.—How Phillis will howl when
she hears of it!—Ay, poor bitch, she little thinks what shoot-
ing her master's going after! And I warrant old Crop, who
has carried your honour, field and road, these ten years, will
curse the hour he was born.   [*Whimpering.*

Acres. It won't do, David—I am determined to fight—so get along you coward, while I 'm in the mind.

Enter SERVANT.

Ser. Captain Absolute, sir

Acres. Oh! show him up.   [*Exit* SERVANT

Dav. Well, Heaven send we be all alive this time to morrow

Acres. What 's that?—Don't provoke me, David!

Dav. Good-bye, master.   [*Whimpering.*

Acres. Get along, you cowardly, dastardly, croaking raven!
[*Exit* DAVID.

Enter CAPTAIN ABSOLUTE.

Abs. What 's the matter, Bob?

Acres. A vile, sheep-hearted blockhead! If I hadn't the valour of St. George and the dragon to boot——

Abs. But what did you want with me, Bob?

Acres. Oh!—There——   [*Gives him the challenge.*

Abs. [*Aside.*] *To Ensign Beverley.*—So, what 's going on now!—[*Aloud.*] Well, what 's this?

Acres. A challenge!

Abs. Indeed! Why, you won't fight him; will you, Bob?

Acres. Egad, but I will, Jack. Sir Lucius has wrought me to it. He has left me full of rage—and I 'll fight this evening, that so much good passion mayn't be wasted.

Abs. But what have I to do with this?

Acres. Why, as I think you know something of this fellow, I want you to find him out for me, and give him this mortal defiance.

Abs. Well, give it to me, and trust me he gets it.

Acres. Thank you, my dear friend, my dear Jack; but it is giving you a great deal of trouble

Abs. Not in the least—I beg you won 't mention it.—No trouble in the world, I assure you.

Acres. You are very kind.—What it is to have a friend!—You couldn't be my second, could you, Jack?

Abs. Why no, Bob—not in this affair—it would not be quite so proper.

Acres. Well, then, I must get my friend Sir Lucius I shall have your good wishes, however, Jack?

E 2

Abs. Whenever he meets you, believe me.

Re-enter SERVANT.

Ser. Sir Anthony Absolute is below, inquiring for the captain.

Abs. I'll come instantly.—[*Exit* SERVANT.] Well, my little hero, success attend you. [*Going.*

Acres.—Stay—stay, Jack.—If Beverley should ask you what kind of a man your friend Acres is, do tell him I am a devil of a fellow—will you, Jack?

Abs. To be sure I shall. I'll say you are a determined dog—hey, Bob!

Acres. Ay, do, do—and if that frightens him, egad, perhaps he mayn't come. So tell him I generally kill a man a week; will you, Jack?

Abs. I will, I will; I'll say you are called in the country Fighting Bob.

Acres. Right—right—'tis all to prevent mischief; for I don't want to take his life if I clear my honour.

Abs. No!—that's very kind of you.

Acres. Why, you don't wish me to kill him—do you, Jack?

Abs. No, upon my soul, I do not. But a devil of a fellow, hey? [*Going.*

Acres. True, true—but stay—stay, Jack—you may add, that you never saw me in such a rage before—a most devouring rage!

Abs. I will, I will.

Acres. Remember, Jack—a determined dog!

Abs. Ay, ay, Fighting Bob! [*Exeunt severally*

SCENE. II.—MRS MALAPROP'S *Lodgings.*

MRS. MALAPROP *and* LYDIA.

Mrs Mal. Why, thou perverse one!—tell me what you can object to him? Isn't he a handsome man?—tell me that. A genteel man? a pretty figure of a man?

Lyd. [*Aside.*] She little thinks whom she is praising!—[*Aloud.*] So is Beverley, ma'am.

Mrs Mal. No caparisons, miss, if you please. Caparisons don't become a young woman. No! Captain Absolute is indeed a fine gentleman!

Lyd. Ay, the Captain Absolute you have seen.   [*Aside*

Mrs. Mal. Then he's so well bred;—so full of alacrity, and adulation!—and has so much to say for himself:—in such good language too! His physiognomy so grammatical! Then his presence is so noble! I protest, when I saw him, I thought of what Hamlet says in the play:—

> "Hesperian curls—the front of Job himself!—
> An eye, like March, to threaten at command!—
> A station, like Harry Mercury, new—"

Something about kissing—on a hill—however, the similitude struck me directly.

Lyd. How enraged she'll be presently, when she discovers her mistake!   [*Aside.*

Enter SERVANT.

Ser. Sir Anthony and Captain Absolute are below, ma'am.

Mrs. Mal. Show them up here.—[*Exit* SERVANT.] Now, Lydia, I insist on your behaving as becomes a young woman. Show your good breeding, at least, though you have forgot your duty.

Lyd. Madam, I have told you my resolution!—I shall not only give him no encouragement, but I won't even speak to, or look at him.

[*Flings herself into a chair, with her face from the door.*

Enter SIR ANTHONY ABSOLUTE *and* CAPTAIN ABSOLUTE.

Sir Anth. Here we are, Mrs. Malaprop; come to mitigate the frowns of unrelenting beauty,—and difficulty enough I had to bring this fellow.—I don't know what's the matter;* but if I had not held him by force, he'd have given me the slip.

Mrs. Mal. You have infinite trouble, Sir Anthony, in the affair   I am ashamed for the cause!—[*Aside to* LYDIA.] Lydia, Lydia, rise, I beseech you!—pay your respects!

Sir Anth. I hope, madam, that Miss Languish has reflected on the worth of this gentleman, and the regard due to her aunt's choice, and my alliance.—[*Aside to* CAPTAIN ABSOLUTE.] Now, Jack, speak to her.

Abs. [*Aside.*] What the devil shall I do!—[*Aside to* SIR ANTHONY.] You see, sir, she won't even look at me whilst

you are here. I knew she wouldn't! I told you so. Let
me entreat you, sir, to leave us together!

> [*Seems to expostulate with his father*

Lyd. [*Aside.*] I wonder I ha'n't heard my aunt exclaim
yet! sure she can't have looked at him!—perhaps their regimentals are alike, and she is something blind.

Sir Anth. I say, sir, I won't stir a foot yet!

Mrs. Mal. I am sorry to say, Sir Anthony, that my affluence over my niece is very small.—[*Aside to* LYDIA.] Turn
round, Lydia: I blush for you!

Sir Anth. May I not flatter myself, that Miss Languish
will assign what cause of dislike she can have to my son!—
[*Aside to* CAPTAIN ABSOLUTE.] Why don't you begin, Jack?—
Speak, you puppy—speak!

Mrs. Mal. It is impossible, Sir Anthony, she can have any.
She will not say she has.—[*Aside to* LYDIA.] Answer, hussy!
why don't you answer?

Sir Anth. Then, madam, I trust that a childish and hasty
predilection will be no bar to Jack's happiness.—[*Aside to*
CAPTAIN ABSOLUTE.]—Zounds! sirrah! why don't you speak!

Lyd. [*Aside.*] I think my lover seems as little inclined to
conversation as myself.—How strangely blind my aunt must
be!

Abs. Hem! hem! madam—hem!—[*Attempts to speak, then
returns to* SIR ANTHONY.] Faith! sir, I am so confounded! -
and—so—so—confused!—I told you I should be so, sir—I
knew it.—The—the—tremor of my passion entirely takes
away my presence of mind.

Sir Anth. But it don't take away your voice, fool, does it?
—Go up, and speak to her directly!

> [CAPTAIN ABSOLUTE *makes signs to* MRS. MALAPROP *to
> leave them together.*

Mrs. Mal. Sir Anthony, shall we leave them together?—
[*Aside to* LYDIA.] Ah! you stubborn little vixen!

Sir Anth. Not yet, ma'am, not yet!—[*Aside to* CAPTAIN
ABSOLUTE.] What the devil are you at? unlock your jaws,
sirrah, or——

Abs. [*Aside.*] Now Heaven send she may be too sullen to
look round!—I must disguise my voice.—[*Draws near* LYDIA,
and speaks in a low hoarse tone.] Will not Miss Languish
lend an ear to the mild accents of true love? Will not——

Sir Anth. What the devil ails the fellow? Why don't you speak out?—not stand croaking like a frog in a quinsy!

Abs. The—the—excess of my awe, and my—my—my mo desty, quite choke me!

Sir Anth. Ah! your modesty again!—I 'll tell you what, Jack; if you don't speak out directly, and glibly too, I shall be in such a rage!—Mrs. Malaprop, I wish the lady would favour us with something more than a side-front.

[Mrs MALAPROP *seems to chide* LYDIA.

Abs. [*Aside.*] So all will out, I see!—[*Goes up to* LYDIA, *speaks softly.*] Be not surprised, my Lydia, suppress all sup prise at present.

Lyd. [*Aside.*] Heavens! 'tis Beverley's voice! Sure he can't have imposed on Sir Anthony too!—[*Looks round by degrees, then starts up.*] Is this possible!—my Beverley!— how can this be?—my Beverley?

Abs. Ah! 'tis all over.　　　　　　　　　　　　　[*Aside*

Sir Anth. Beverley!—the devil—Beverley!—What can the girl mean?—This is my son, Jack Absolute.

Mrs. Mal. For shame, hussy! for shame! your head runs so on that fellow, that you have him always in your eyes!— beg Captain Absolute's pardon directly.

Lyd. I see no Captain Absolute, but my loved Beverley!

Sir Anth. Zounds! the girl's mad!—her brain 's turned by reading.

Mrs. Mal. O' my conscience, I believe so!—What do you mean by Beverley, hussy?—You saw Captain Absolute before to-day; there he is—your husband that shall be.

Lyd. With all my soul, ma'am—when I refuse my Bever ley——

Sir Anth. Oh! she 's as mad as Bedlam!—or has this fel low been playing us a rogue's trick!—Come here, sirrah, who the devil are you?

Abs. Faith, sir, I am not quite clear myself; but I 'll en deavour to recollect.

Sir Anth. Are you my son or not?—answer for your mo ther, you dog, if you won't for me.

Mrs. Mal. Ay, sir, who are you? O mercy! I begin to suspect!—

Abs. [*Aside.*] Ye powers of impudence, befriend me!— [*Aloud.*] Sir Anthony, most assuredly I am your wife's son

and that I sincerely believe myself to be your's also, I hope
my duty has always shown.—Mrs. Malaprop, I am your most
respectful admirer, and shall be proud to add affectionate
nephew.—I need not tell my Lydia, that she sees her faithful
Beverley, who, knowing the singular generosity of her temper,
assumed that name and station, which has proved a test of the
most disinterested love, which he now hopes to enjoy in a more
elevated character.

Lyd. So!—there will be no elopement after all! [*Sullenly.*

Sir Anth. Upon my soul, Jack, thou art a very impudent
fellow! to do you justice, I think I never saw a piece of more
consummate assurance!

Abs. Oh, you flatter me, sir—you compliment—'tis my
modesty you know, sir,—my modesty that has stood in my
way.

Sir Anth. Well, I am glad you are not the dull, insensible
varlet you pretended to be, however!—I'm glad you have
made a fool of your father, you dog—I am.   So this was your
penitence, your *duty* and *obedience!*—I thought it was damned
sudden!—*You never heard their names before,* not you!—*what
the Languishes of Worcestershire,* hey?—*if you could please me
in the affair it was all you desired!*—Ah! you dissembling
villain!—What!—[*Pointing to* LYDIA] *she squints, don't she?*
—*a little red-haired girl!*—hey?—Why, you hypocritical
young rascal!—I wonder you an't ashamed to hold up your
head!

Abs. 'Tis with difficulty, sir.—I am confused—very much
confused, as you must perceive.

Mrs. Mal. O Lud! Sir Anthony!—a new light breaks in
upon me!—hey!—how! what! captain, did you write the
letters then?—What—am I to thank you for the elegant com-
pilation of *an old weather-beaten she-dragon*—hey!—O mercy!
-was it you that reflected on my parts of speech?

Abs. Dear sir! my modesty will be overpowered at last, if
you don't assist me—I shall certainly not be able to stand
it!

Sir Anth. Come, come, Mrs. Malaprop, we must forget and
forgive;—odds life! matters have taken so clever a turn all of
a sudden, that I could find in my heart to be so good-hu-
moured! and so gallant! hey! Mrs. Malaprop!

Mrs Mal. Well, sir Anthony, since you desire it, we will

not anticipate the past!—so mind, young people—our retro-
spection will be all to the future.

Sir Anth. Come, we must leave them together; Mrs. Malaprop, they long to fly into each other's arms, I warrant!—
Jack—isn't the cheek as I said, hey?—and the eye, you
rogue!—and the lip—hey? Come, Mrs. Malaprop, we'll not
disturb their tenderness—theirs is the time of life for happiness!—*Youth's the season made for joy*—[*Sings*]—hey!—Odds
life! I'm in such spirits,—I don't know what I could not do!
—Permit me, ma'am—[*Gives his hand to* Mrs. MALAPROP.]
Tol-de-rol—'gad, I should like to have a little fooling myself
—Tol-de-rol! de-rol.

> [*Exit, singing and handing* Mrs. MALAPROP.—LYDIA *sits
> sullenly in her chair.*

Abs. [*Aside.*] So much thought bodes me no good.—[*Aloud.*]
So grave, Lydia!

Lyd. Sir!

Abs. [*Aside.*] So!—egad! I thought as much!—that
damned monosyllable has froze me!—[*Aloud.*] What, Lydia,
now that we are as happy in our friends' consent, as in our
mutual vows——

Lyd Friends' consent indeed!   [*Peevishly*

Abs. Come, come, we must lay aside some of our romance
—a little wealth and comfort may be endured after all. And
for your fortune, the lawyers shall make such settlements
as——

Lyd. Lawyers! I hate lawyers!

Abs. Nay, then, we will not wait for their lingering forms,
but instantly procure the licence, and——

Lyd. The licence!—I hate licence!

Abs. Oh my love! be not so unkind!—thus let me entreat——   [*Kneeling.*

Lyd. Psha!—what signifies kneeling, when you know I
must have you?

Abs. [*Rising.*] Nay, madam, there shall be no constraint
upon your inclinations, I promise you.—If I have lost your
heart—I resign the rest—[*Aside.*] 'Gad, I must try what a
little spirit will do.

Lyd. [*Rising.*] Then, sir, let me tell you, the interest you
had there was acquired by a mean, unmanly imposition, and
deserves the punishment of fraud.—What, you have been

treating me like a child!—humouring my romance! and
laughing, I suppose, at your success!

Abs. You wrong me, Lydia, you wrong me—only hear——

Lyd. So, while I fondly imagined we were deceiving my
relations, and flattered myself that I should outwit and incense
them all—behold my hopes are to be crushed at once, by my
aunt's consent and approbation—and I am myself the only
dupe at last!—[*Walking about in a heat.*]   But here, sir,
here is the picture—Beverley's picture! [*taking a miniature
from her bosom*] which I have worn, night and day, in spite of
threats and entreaties!—There, sir; [*flings it to him*] and be
assured I throw the original from my heart as easily.

Abs. Nay, nay, ma'am, we will not differ as to that.—Here,
[*taking out a picture*] here is Miss Lydia Languish.—What a
difference!—ay, there is the heavenly assenting smile that
first gave soul and spirit to my hopes!—those are the lips
which sealed a vow, as yet scarce dry in Cupid's calendar!
and there the half-resentful blush, that would have checked
the ardour of my thanks!—Well, all that's past!—all over
indeed!—There, madam—in beauty, that copy is not equal
to you, but in my mind its merit over the original, in being
still the same, is such—that—I cannot find in my heart to
part with it.   [*Puts it up again.*

Lyd. [*Softening.*] 'Tis your own doing, sir—I, I, I suppose
you are perfectly satisfied.

Abs. O, most certainly—sure, now, this is much better than
being in love!—ha! ha! ha!—there's some spirit in this!—
What signifies breaking some scores of solemn promises:—all
that's of no consequence, you know.—To be sure people will
say, that miss don't know her own mind—but never mind
that!   Or, perhaps, they may be ill-natured enough to hint,
that the gentleman grew tired of the lady and forsook her—
but don't let that fret you.

Lyd. There is no bearing his insolence   [*Bursts into tears*

Re-enter Mrs. MALAPROP *and* SIR ANTHONY ABSOLUTE.

Mrs. Mal. Come, we must interrupt your billing and cooing
awhile.

Lyd. This is worse than your treachery and deceit, you base
ingrate!   [*Sobbing.*

Sir Anth. What the devil's the matter now!—Zounds,

Mrs. Malaprop, this is the oddest billing and cooing I ever heard!—but what the deuce is the meaning of it?—I am quite astonished!

Abs. Ask the lady, sir.

Mrs. Mal. Oh mercy!—I'm quite analysed, for my part!—Why, Lydia, what is the reason of this?

Lyd. Ask the gentleman, ma'am.

Sir Anth. Zounds! I shall be in a frenzy!—Why, Jack, you are not come out to be any one else, are you?

Mrs. Mal. Ay, sir, there's no more trick, is there?—you are not like Cerberus, three gentlemen at once, are you?

Abs. You'll not let me speak—I say the lady can account for this much better than I can.

Lyd. Ma'am, you once commanded me never to think of Beverley again—there is the man—I now obey you: for, from this moment, I renounce him for ever.   [*Exit.*

Mrs. Mal. O mercy! and miracles! what a turn here is—why sure, captain, you haven't behaved disrespectfully to my niece.

Sir Anth. Ha! ha! ha!—ha! ha! ha!—now I see it. Ha! ha! ha!—now I see it—you have been too lively, Jack.

Abs. Nay, sir, upon my word——

Sir Anth. Come, no lying, Jack—I'm sure 'twas so.

Mrs. Mal. O Lud! Sir Anthony!—O fy, captain!

Abs. Upon my soul, ma'am——

Sir Anth. Come, no excuses, Jack; why, your father, you rogue, was so before you:—the blood of the Absolutes was always impatient.—Ha! ha! ha! poor little Lydia! why, you've frightened her, you dog, you have.

Abs. By all that's good, sir——

Sir Anth. Zounds! say no more, I tell you—Mrs. Malaprop shall make your peace.—You must make his peace, Mrs. Malaprop:—you must tell her 'tis Jack's way—tell her 'tis all our ways—it runs in the blood of our family!—Come away, Jack —Ha! ha! ha! Mrs. Malaprop—a young villain!

[*Pushing him out.*

Mrs. Mal. O! Sir Anthony!—O fy, captain!

[*Exeunt severally.*

Scene III.—*The North Parade.*

Enter Sir Lucius O'Trigger.

Sir Luc I wonder where this Captain Absolute hides him

Abs. Very well, sir; I shall certainly not balk your inclina·
tions.—But I should be glad you would please to explain
your motives.

Sir Luc. Pray sir, be easy; the quarrel is a very pretty
quarrel as it stands; we should only spoil it by trying to ex·
plain it.   However, your memory is very short, or you could
not have forgot an affront you passed on me within this week.
So, no more, but name your time and place.

Abs. Well, sir, since you are so bent on it, the sooner the
better; let it be this evening—here, by the Spring Gardens.
We shall scarcely be interrupted.

Sir Luc. Faith! that same interruption in affairs of this
nature shows very great ill-breeding.   I don't know what's
the reason, but in England, if a thing of this kind gets
wind, people make such a pother, that a gentleman can never
fight in peace and quietness.   However, if it's the same to
you, captain, I should take it as a particular kindness if you'd
let us meet in King's-Mead-Fields, as a little business will
call me there about six o'clock, and I may despatch both matters at once.

Abs. 'Tis the same to me exactly.   A little after six, then,
we will discuss this matter more seriously.

Sir Luc If you please, sir; there will be very pretty small·
sword light, though it won't do for a long shot.   So that matter's settled, and my mind's at ease!   [*Exit.*

Enter FAULKLAND.

Abs. Well met! I was going to look for you.   O Faulkland! all the demons of spite and disappointment have con·
spired against me!   I'm so vexed, that if I had not the
prospect of a resource in being knocked o' the head by-and-
by, I should scarce have spirits to tell you the cause.

Faulk. What can you mean?—Has Lydia changed her
mind?—I should have thought her duty and inclination would
now have pointed to the same object.

Abs. Ay, just as the eyes do of a person who squints:
when her love-eye was fixed on me, t'other, her eye of duty,
was finely obliqued: but when duty bid her point that the
same way, off t'other turned on a swivel, and secured its re·
treat with a frown!

Faulk. But what's the resource you——

Abs. Oh, to wind up the whole, a good-natured Irishman here has—[*Mimicking* SIR LUCIUS]—begged leave to have the pleasure of cutting my throat; and I mean to indulge him—that's all.

Faulk. Prithee, be serious!

Abs. 'Tis fact, upon my soul! Sir Lucius O'Trigger—you know him by sight—for some affront, which I am sure I never intended, has obliged me to meet him this evening at six o'clock: 'tis on that account I wished to see you; you must go with me.

Faulk. Nay, there must be some mistake, sure Sir Lucius shall explain himself, and I dare say matters may be accommodated. But this evening did you say? I wish it had been any other time.

Abs. Why? there will be light enough: there will (as Sir Lucius says) be very pretty small-sword light, though it will not do for a long shot. Confound his long shots.

Faulk. But I am myself a good deal ruffled by a difference I have had with Julia. My vile tormenting temper has made me treat her so cruelly, that I shall not be myself till we are reconciled.

Abs. By heavens! Faulkland, you don't deserve her!

Enter SERVANT, *gives* FAULKLAND *a letter, and exit.*

Faulk. Oh, Jack! this is from Julia. I dread to open it! I fear it may be to take a last leave!—perhaps to bid me return her letters, and restore——Oh, how I suffer for my folly!

Abs. Here, let me see.—[*Takes the letter and opens it.*] Ay. a final sentence, indeed!—'tis all over with you, faith!

Faulk. Nay, Jack, don't keep me in suspense!

Abs. Hear then.—[*Reads.*] *As I am convinced that my dear Faulkland's own reflections have already upbraided him for his last unkindness to me, I will not add a word on the subject. I wish to speak with you as soon as possible. Yours ever and truly,* JULIA. There's stubbornness and resentment for you!—[*Gives him the letter.*] Why, man, you don't seem one whit the happier at this!

Faulk. O yes, I am; but—but——

Abs. Confound your buts! you never hear any thing that

would make another man bless himself, but you immediately
damn it with a but!

Faulk. Now, Jack, as you are my friend, own honestly—
don't you think there is something forward, something indelicate, in this haste to forgive?   Women should never sue for
reconciliation : that should always come from us.   They
should retain their coldness till wooed to kindness ; and their
pardon, like their love, should "not unsought be won."

Abs. I have not patience to listen to you! thou 'rt incorrigible! so say no more on the subject.   I must go to settle
a few matters.   Let me see you before six, remember, at my
lodgings.   A poor industrious devil like me, who have toiled,
and drudged, and plotted to gain my ends, and am at last
disappointed by other people's folly, may in pity be allowed
to swear and grumble a little ; but a captious sceptic in love,
a slave to fretfulness and whim, who has no difficulties but of
his own creating, is a subject more fit for ridicule than compassion !   [*Exit.*

Faulk. I feel his reproaches ; yet I would not change this
too exquisite nicety for the gross content with which he
tramples on the thorns of love!   His engaging me in this
duel has started an idea in my head, which I will instantly
pursue.   I 'll use it as the touchstone of Julia's sincerity and
disinterestedness.   If her love prove pure and sterling ore,
my name will rest on it with honour; and once I 've stamped
it there, I lay aside my doubts for ever!   But if the dross of
selfishness, the alloy of pride, predominate, 'twill be best to
leave her as a toy for some less cautious fool to sigh for!

                                                                 [*Exit.*

ACT V.

Scene I.—Julia's *Dressing-Room.*

Julia *discovered alone*

Jul. How this message has alarmed me! what dreadful
accident can he mean? why such charge to be alone?—O
Faulkland!—how many unhappy moments—how many tears
have you cost me.

Enter FAULKLAND.

Jul. What means this?—why this caution, Faulkland?

Faulk. Alas! Julia, I am come to take a long farewell.

Jul. Heavens! what do you mean?

Faulk. You see before you a wretch, whose life is forfeited. Nay, start not!—the infirmity of my temper has drawn all this misery on me. I left you fretful and passionate—an untoward accident drew me into a quarrel—the event is, that I must fly this kingdom instantly. O Julia, had I been so fortunate as to have called you mine entirely, before this mischance had fallen on me, I should not so deeply dread my banishment!

Jul. My soul is oppressed with sorrow at the nature of your misfortune: had these adverse circumstances arisen from a less fatal cause, I should have felt strong comfort in the thought that I could now chase from your bosom every doubt of the warm sincerity of my love. My heart has long known no other guardian—I now entrust my person to your honour —we will fly together. When safe from pursuit, my father's will may be fulfilled—and I receive a legal claim to be the partner of your sorrows, and tenderest comforter. Then on the bosom of your wedded Julia, you may lull your keen regret to slumbering; while virtuous love, with a cherub's hand, shall smooth the brow of upbraiding thought, and pluck the thorn from compunction.

Faulk. O Julia! I am bankrupt in gratitude! but the time is so pressing, it calls on you for so hasty a resolution.— Would you not wish some hours to weigh the advantages you forego, and what little compensation poor Faulkland can make you beside his solitary love?

Jul. I ask not a moment. No, Faulkland, I have loved you for yourself: and if I now, more than ever, prize the solemn engagement which so long has pledged us to each other, it is because it leaves no room for hard aspersions on my fame, and puts the seal of duty to an act of love. But let us not linger. Perhaps this delay——

Faulk. 'Twill be better I should not venture out again till dark. Yet am I grieved to think what numberless distresses will press heavy on your gentle disposition!

Jul. Perhaps your fortune may be forfeited by this unhappy act.—I know not whether 'tis so; but sure that alone
can never make us unhappy.   The little I have will be
sufficient to support us; and exile never should be splendid.

Faulk. Ay, but in such an abject state of life, my wounded
pride perhaps may increase the natural fretfulness of my
temper, till I become a rude, morose companion, beyond your
patience to endure.   Perhaps the recollection of a deed my
conscience cannot justify may haunt me in such gloomy and
unsocial fits, that I shall hate the tenderness that would
relieve me, break from your arms, and quarrel with your
fondness!

Jul. If your thoughts should assume so unhappy a bent,
you will the more want some mild and affectionate spirit to
watch over and console you: one who, by bearing your infirmities with gentleness and resignation, may teach you so to
bear the evils of your fortune.

Faulk. Julia, I have proved you to the quick! and with
this useless device I throw away all my doubts.   How shall
I plead to be forgiven this last unworthy effect of my restless,
unsatisfied disposition?

Jul. Has no such disaster happened as you related?

Faulk. I am ashamed to own that it was pretended; yet
in pity, Julia, do not kill me with resenting a fault which
never can be repeated: but sealing, this once, my pardon, let
me to-morrow, in the face of Heaven, receive my future guide
and monitress, and expiate my past folly by years of tender
adoration.

Jul. Hold, Faulkland!—that you are free from a crime,
which I before feared to name, Heaven knows how sincerely
I rejoice!   These are tears of thankfulness for that!   But
that your cruel doubts should have urged you to an imposition
that has wrung my heart, gives me now a pang more keen
than I can express!

Faulk. By Heavens! Julia——

Jul. Yet hear me.—My father loved you, Faulkland! and
you preserved the life that tender parent gave me; in his
presence I pledged my hand—joyfully pledged it—where
before I had given my heart.   When, soon after, I lost that
parent, it seemed to me that Providence had, in Faulkland,
shown me whither to transfer without a pause, my grateful

F

duty, as well as my affection: hence I have been content to bear from you what pride and delicacy would have forbid me from another. I will not upbraid you, by repeating how you have trifled with my sincerity——

Faulk. I confess it all! yet hear——

Jul. A'ter such a year of trial, I might have flattered myself tha. I should not have been insulted with a new probation of my sincerity, as cruel as unnecessary! I now see it is not in your nature to be content or confident in love. With this conviction—I never will be yours. While I had hopes that my persevering attention, and unreproaching kindness, might in time reform your temper, I should have been happy to have gained a dearer influence over you; but I will not furnish you with a licensed power to keep alive an incorrigible fault, at the expense of one who never would contend with you.

Faulk. Nay, but, Julia, by my soul and honour, if after this——

Jul. But one word more.—As my faith has once been given to you, I never will barter it with another.—I shall pray for your happiness with the truest sincerity; and the dearest blessing I can ask of Heaven to send you will be to charm you from that unhappy temper, which alone has prevented the performance of our solemn engagement. All I request of you is, that you will yourself reflect upon this infirmity, and when you number up the many true delights it has deprived you of, let it not be your least regret, that it lost you the love of one who would have followed you in beggary through the world!   [*Exit.*

Faulk. She's gone—for ever!—There was an awful resolution in her manner, that riveted me to my place.—O fool! —dolt!—barbarian! Cursed as I am, with more imperfections than my fellow wretches, kind Fortune sent a heaven-gifted cherub to my aid, and, like a ruffian, I have driven her from my side!—I must now haste to my appointment. Well, my mind is tuned for such a scene. I shall wish only to become a principal in it, and reverse the tale my cursed folly put me upon forging here.—O Love!—tormentor!—fiend!— whose influence, like the moon's, acting on men of dull souls, makes idiots of them, but meeting subtler spirits, betrays their course, and urges sensibility to madness!   [*Exit.*

Maid. My mistress, ma'am, I know, was here just now—perhaps she is only in the next room.   [*Exit.*

Lyd. Heigh-ho! Though he has used me so, this fellow runs strangely in my head. I believe one lecture from my grave cousin will make me recall him.   [*Re-enter* JULIA.] O Julia, I am come to you with such an appetite for consolation.—Lud! child, what 's the matter with you? You have been crying!—I 'll be hanged if that Faulkland has not been tormenting you!

Jul. You mistake the cause of my uneasiness!—Something has flurried me a little. Nothing that you can guess at.— [*Aside.*] I would not accuse Faulkland to a sister!

Lyd. Ah! whatever vexations you may have, I can assure you mine surpass them. You know who Beverley proves to be?

Jul. I will now own to you, Lydia, that Mr. Faulkland had before informed me of the whole affair. Had young Absolute been the person you took him for, I should not have accepted your confidence on the subject, without a serious endeavour to counteract your caprice.

Lyd. So, then, I see I have been deceived by every one! But I don't care—I 'll never have him.

Jul. Nay, Lydia——

Lyd. Why, is it not provoking? when I thought we were coming to the prettiest distress imaginable, to find myself made a mere Smithfield bargain of at last! There, had I projected one of the most sentimental elopements!—so becoming a disguise!—so amiable a ladder of ropes!—Conscious moon—four horses—Scotch parson—with such surprise to Mrs. Malaprop—and such paragraphs in the newspapers!— Oh, I shall die with disappointment!

Jul. I don't wonder at it!

Lyd. Now—sad reverse!—what have I to expect, but, after a deal of flimsy preparation with a bishop's licence, and my aunt's blessing, to go simpering up to the altar; or perhaps be cried three times in a country church, and have an un-mannerly fat clerk ask the consent of every butcher in the parish to join John Absolute and Lydia Languish, spinster! Oh that I should live to hear myself called spinster!

F 2

Jul. Melancholy indeed!

Lyd. How mortifying, to remember the dear delicious shifts
I used to be put to, to gain half a minute's conversation with
this fellow! How often have I stole forth, in the coldest night
in January, and found him in the garden, stuck like a dripping
statue! There would he kneel to me in the snow, and sneeze
and cough so pathetically! he shivering with cold and I with
apprehension! and while the freezing blast numbed our joints,
how warmly would he press me to pity his flame, and glow
with mutual ardour!—Ah, Julia, that was something like being
in love.

Jul. If I were in spirits, Lydia, I should chide you only
by laughing heartily at you; but it suits more the situation of
my mind, at present, earnestly to entreat you not to let a man,
who loves you with sincerity, suffer that unhappiness from
your caprice, which I know too well caprice can inflict.

Lyd. O Lud! what has brought my aunt here?

Enter MRS MALAPROP, FAG, *and* DAVID.

Mrs. Mal. So! so! here's fine work!—here's fine suicide,
parricide, and simulation, going on in the fields! and Sir Anthony not to be found to prevent the antistrophe!

Jul. For Heaven's sake, madam, what's the meaning of
this?

Mrs. Mal. That gentleman can tell you—'twas he enveloped
the affair to me.

Lyd. Do, sir, will you, inform us?   [*To* FAG.

Fag. Ma'am, I should hold myself very deficient in every
requisite that forms the man of breeding, if I delayed a moment to give all the information in my power to a lady so
deeply interested in the affair as you are.

Lyd. But quick! quick sir!

Fag. True, ma'am, as you say, one should be quick in di-
vulging matters of this nature; for should we be tedious,
perhaps while we are flourishing on the subject, two or three
lives may be lost!

Lyd. O patience!—Do, ma'am, for Heaven's sake! tell us
what is the matter?

Mrs. Mal. Why, murder's the matter! slaughter's the
matter! killing's the matter!—but he can tell you the per-
pendiculars.

Lyd. Then, prithee, sir, be brief.

Fag. Why then, ma'am, as to murder—I cannot take upon me to say—and as to slaughter, or manslaughter, that will be as the jury finds it.

Lyd. But who, sir—who are engaged in this?

Fag. Faith, ma'am, one is a young gentleman whom I should be very sorry any thing was to happen to—a very pretty behaved gentleman! We have lived much together, and always on terms.

Lyd. But who is this? who! who! who?

Fag. My master, ma'am—my master—I speak of my master.

Lyd. Heavens! What, Captain Absolute!

Mrs. Mal. Oh, to be sure, you are frightened now!

Jul. But who are with him, sir?

Fag. As to the rest, ma'am, this gentleman can inform you better than I.

Jul. Do speak, friend.   [*To* DAVID

Dav. Look'ee, my lady—by the mass! there's mischief going on. Folks don't use to meet for amusement with fire-arms, firelocks, fire-engines, fire-screens, fire-office, and the devil knows what other crackers beside!—This, my lady, I say, has an angry favour

Jul. But who is there beside Captain Absolute, friend?

Dav. My poor master—under favour for mentioning him first. You know me, my lady—I am David—and my master of course is, or was, Squire Acres. Then comes Squire Faulk-land.

Jul. Do, ma'am, let us instantly endeavour to prevent mischief.

Mrs. Mal. O fy!—it would be very inelegant in us:—we should only participate things.

Dav. Ah! do, Mrs. Aunt, save a few lives—they are desperately given, believe me.—Above all, there is that blood-thirsty Philistine, Sir Lucius O'Trigger.

Mrs. Mal. Sir Lucius O'Trigger? O mercy! have they drawn poor little dear Sir Lucius into the scrape?—Why, how you stand, girl! you have no more feeling than one of the Derbyshire petrifactions!

Lyd. What are we to do, madam?

Mrs. Mal. Why fly with the utmost felicity, to be sure, to prevent mischief!—Here, friend, you can show us the place?

Fag. If you please, ma'am, I will conduct you.—David, do you look for Sir Anthony.   [*Exit* DAVID.

Mrs. Mal. Come. girls! this gentleman will exhort us.—Come, sir, you're our envoy—lead the way, and we'll precede.

Fag. Not a step before the ladies for the world!

Mrs. Mal. You're sure you know the spot?

Fag. I think I can find it, ma'am; and one good thing is, we shall hear the report of the pistols as we draw near, so we can't well miss them;—never fear, ma'am, never fear.

[*Exeunt, he talking.*

SCENE II.—*The South Parade*

Enter CAPTAIN ABSOLUTE, *putting his sword under his great coat.*

Abs. A sword seen in the streets of Bath would raise as great an alarm as a mad dog.—How provoking this is in Faulkland!- never punctual! I shall be obliged to go without him at last.—Oh, the devil! here's Sir Anthony! how shall I escape him?

[*Muffles up his face, and takes a circle to go off.*

Enter SIR ANTHONY ABSOLUTE.

Sir. Anth. How one may be deceived at a little distance! only that I see he don't know me, I could have sworn that was Jack!—Hey! Gad's life! it is.—Why, Jack, what are you afraid of? hey!—sure I'm right.—Why Jack, Jack Absolute!

[*Goes up to him.*

Abs. Really, sir, you have the advantage of me:—I don't remember ever to have had the honour—my name is Saunderson, at your service.

Sir Anth. Sir, I beg your pardon—I took you—hey?—why, zounds! it is—Stay—[*Looks up to his face.*] So, so—your humble servant, Mr. Saunderson! Why, you scoundrel, what tricks are you after now?

Abs. Oh, a joke, sir, a joke! I came here on purpose to look for you, sir.

Sir Anth. You did! well, I am glad you were so lucky:—but what are you muffled up so for?—what's this for?—hey!

Abs. 'Tis cool, sir; isn't?—rather chilly somehow—but I shall be late—I have a particular engagement.

Sir Anth. Stay!—Why, I thought you were looking for me?—Pray, Jack, where is't you are going?

Abs. Going, sir!

Sir Anth. Ay, where are you going?

Abs. Where am I going?

Sir Anth. You unmannerly puppy!

Abs. I was going, sir, to—to—to—to Lydia—sir, to Lydia —to make matters up if I could;—and I was looking for you, sir, to—to—

Sir Anth. To go with you, I suppose.—Well, come along.

Abs. Oh! zounds! no, sir, not for the world!—I wished to meet with you, sir,—to—to—to—You find it cool, I'm sure, sir—you'd better not stay out.

Sir Anth. Cool!—not at all.—Well, Jack—and what will you say to Lydia?

Abs. Oh, sir, beg her pardon, humour her—promise and vow: but I detain you, sir—consider the cold air on your gout.

Sir Anth. Oh, not at all!—not at all! I'm in no hurry.— Ah! Jack, you youngsters, when once you are wounded here [*Putting his hand to* CAPTAIN ABSOLUTE's *breast.*] Hey! what the deuce have you got here?

Abs. Nothing, sir—nothing;

Sir Anth. What's this?—here's something damned hard

Abs. Oh, trinkets, sir! trinkets!—a bauble for Lydia!

Sir Anth. Nay, let me see your taste.—[*Pulls his coat open, the sword falls.*] Trinkets!—a bauble for Lydia!—Zounds! sirrah, you are not going to cut her throat, are you?

Abs. Ha! ha! ha!—I thought it would divert you, sir, though I didn't mean to tell you till afterwards.

Sir Anth. You didn't?—Yes, this is a very diverting trinket, truly!

Abs. Sir, I'll explain to you.—You know, sir, Lydia is ro-mantic, devilish romantic, and very absurd of course: now, sir, I intend, if she refuses to forgive me, to unsheath this sword, and swear—I'll fall upon its point, and expire at her feet!

Sir Anth. Fall upon a fiddlestick's end!—why, I suppose it is the very thing that would please her.—Get along, you fool!

Abs. Well, sir, you shall hear of my success—you shall hear.—*O Lydia!—forgive me, or this pointed steel*—says I.

Sir Anth. O, booby! stab away and welcome—says she.—Get along! and damn your trinkets! [*Exit* CAPTAIN ABSOLUTE.

Enter DAVID, *running.*

Dav. Stop him! stop him! Murder! Thief! Fire!—Stop fire! Stop fire!—O Sir Anthony—call! call! bid 'm stop! Murder! Fire!

Sir Anth. Fire! Murder!—Where?

Dav. Oons i he's out of sight! and I'm out of breath! for my part! O Sir Anthony, why didn't you stop him? why didn't you stop him?

Sir Anth. Zounds! the fellow's mad!—Stop whom? stop Jack?

Dav. Ay, the captain, sir!—there's murder and slaughter——

Sir Anth. Murder!

Dav. Ay, please you, Sir Anthony, there's all kinds of murder, all sorts of slaughter to be seen in the fields: there's fighting going on, sir—bloody sword-and-gun fighting!

Sir Anth. Who are going to fight, dunce?

Dav. Every body that I know of, Sir Anthony:—every body is going to fight, my poor master, Sir Lucius O'Trigger, your son, the captain——

Sir Anth. Oh, the dog! I see his tricks.—Do you know the place?

Dav. King's-Mead-Fields.

Sir Anth. You know the way?

Dav. Not an inch; but I'll call the mayor—aldermen—constables—churchwardens—and beadles—we can't be too many to part them.

Sir Anth. Come along—give me your shoulder! we'll get assistance as we go—the lying villain!—Well, I shall be in such a frenzy!—So—this was the history of his trinkets! I'll bauble him! [*Exeunt*

SCENE III.—*King's-Mead-Fields.*

Enter Sir Lucius O'Trigger *and* Acres, *with pistols.*

Acres. By my valour! then, Sir Lucius, forty yards is a good distance. Odds levels and aims!—I say it is a good distance.

Sir Luc. Is it for muskets or small field-pieces? Upon my conscience, Mr. Acres, you must leave those things to me.— Stay now—I 'll show you.—[*Measures paces along the stage.*] There now, that is a very pretty distance—a pretty gentleman's distance.

Acres. Zounds! we might as well fight in a sentry-box! I tell you, Sir Lucius, the farther he is off, the cooler I shall take my aim.

Sir Luc. Faith! then I suppose you would aim at him best of all if he was out of sight!

Acres. No, Sir Lucius; but I should think forty or eight-and-thirty yards——

Sir Luc. Pho! pho! nonsense! three or four feet between the mouths of your pistols is as good as a mile

Acres. Odds bullets, no!—by my valour! there is no merit in killing him so near: do, my dear Sir Lucius, let me bring him down at a long shot:—a long shot, Sir Lucius, if you love me!

Sir Luc. Well, the gentleman's friend and I must settle that.—But tell me now, Mr. Acres, in case of an accident, is there any little will or commission I could execute for you?

Acres. I am much obliged to you, Sir Lucius—but I don't understand——

Sir Luc. Why, you may think there 's no being shot at without a little risk—and if an unlucky bullet should carry a quietus with it—I say it will be no time then to be bothering you about family matters.

Acres. A quietus!

Sir Luc. For instance, now—if that should be the case— would you choose to be pickled and sent home?—or would it bo the same to you to lie here in the Abbey?—I 'm told there is very snug lying in the Abbey.

Acres. Pickled!—Snug lying in the Abbey!—Odds tremors! Sir Lucius, don't talk so!

Sir Luc. I suppose, Mr. Acres, you never were engaged in an affair of this kind before?

Acres. No, Sir Lucius, never before.

Sir Luc. Ah! that 's a pity!—there 's nothing like being used to a thing.—Pray now, how would you receive the gentleman's shot?

Acres. Odds files!—I 've practised that—there, Sir Lucius

—there.—[*Puts himself in an attitude.*] A side-front, hey? Odd! I'll make myself small enough: I'll stand edgeways.

Sir Luc. Now—you're quite out—for if you stand so when I take my aim——   [*Levelling at him.*

Acres. Zounds! Sir Lucius—are you sure it is not cocked?

Sir Luc. Never fear.

Acres. But—but—you don't know—it may go off of its own head!

Sir Luc. Pho! be easy.—Well, now if I hit you in the body, my bullet has a double chance—for if it misses a vital part of your right side—'twill be very hard if it don't succeed on the left!

Acres. A vital part!

Sir Luc. But, there—fix yourself so—[*Placing him*]—let him see the broad-side of your full front—there—now a ball or two may pass clean through your body, and never do any harm at all.

Acres. Clean through me!—a ball or two clean through me!

Sir Luc. Ay—may they—and it is much the genteelest attitude into the bargain.

Acres. Look'ee! Sir Lucius—I'd just as lieve be shot in an awkward posture as a genteel one; so, by my valour! I will stand edgeways.

Sir Luc. [*Looking at his watch.*] Sure they don't mean to disappoint us—Hah!—no, faith—I think I see them coming.

Acres. Hey!—what!—coming!——

Sir Luc. Ay.—Who are those yonder getting over the stile?

Acres. There are two of them indeed!—well—let them come—hey, Sir Lucius!—we—we—we—we—won't run.

Sir Luc. Run!

Acres. No—I say—we won't run, by my valour!

Sir Luc. What the devil's the matter with you?

Acres. Nothing—nothing—my dear friend—my dear Sir Lucius—but I—I—I don't feel quite so bold, somehow, as I did.

Sir Luc. O fy!—consider your honour.

Acres. Ay—true—my honour. Do, Sir Lucius, edge in a word or two every now and then about my honour.

Sir Luc. Well, here they're coming.   [*Looking.*

Acres. Sir Lucius—if I wa'n't with you, I should almost

think I was afraid.—If my valour should leave me!—Valour will come and go.

Sir Luc. Then pray keep it fast, while you have it.

Acres. Sir Lucius—I doubt it is going—yes—my valour is certainly going!—it is sneaking off!—I feel it oozing out as it were at the palms of my hands!

Sir Luc. Your honour—your honour.—Here they are.

Acres. O mercy!—now—that I was safe at Clod-Hall! or could be shot before I was aware!

Enter FAULKLAND *and* CAPTAIN ABSOLUTE

Sir Luc. Gentlemen, your most obedient. — Hah!—what, Captain Absolute!—So, I suppose, sir, you are come here, just like myself—to do a kind office, first for your friend – then to proceed to business on your own account.

Acres. What, Jack!—my dear Jack!—my dear friend!

Abs. Hark'ee, Bob, Beverley's at hand.

Sir Luc. Well, Mr. Acres—I don't blame your saluting the gentleman civilly.—[*To* FAULKLAND.] So, Mr. Beverley, if you 'll choose your weapons, the captain and I will measure the ground.

Faulk. My weapons, sir!

Acres. Odds life! Sir Lucius, I 'm not going to fight Mr. Faulkland; these are my particular friends.

Sir Luc. What, sir, did you not come here to fight Mr. Acres?

Faulk. Not I, upon my word, sir.

Sir Luc. Well, now, that 's mighty provoking! But I hope, Mr. Faulkland, as there are three of us come on purpose for the game, you won't be so cantanckerous as to spoil the party by sitting out.

Abs. O pray, Faulkland, fight to oblige Sir Lucius.

Faulk. Nay, if Mr. Acres is so bent on the matter——

Acres. No, no, Mr. Faulkland;—I 'll bear my disappointment like a Christian.—Look'ee, Sir Lucius, there 's no occasion at all for me to fight; and if it is the same to you, I 'd as lieve let it alone.

Sir Luc. Observe me, Mr. Acres—I must not be trifled with. You have certainly challenged somebody—and you came here to fight him. Now, if that gentleman is willing to represent him—I can't see, for my soul, why it isn't just the same thing.

Acres. Why no—Sir Lucius—I tell you, 'tis one Beverley
I 've challenged—a fellow, you see, that dare not show his
face!—If he were here, I 'd make him give up his pretensions
directly!

Abs. Hold, Bob—let me set you right—there is no such man
as Beverley in the case.—The person who assumed that name
is before you; and as his pretensions are the same in both
characters, he is ready to support them in whatever way you
please.

Sir Luc. Well, this is lucky.—Now you have an opportunity——

Acres What, quarrel with my dear friend Jack Absolute?—
not if he were fifty Beverleys! Zounds! Sir Lucius, you would
not have me so unnatural.

Sir Luc. Upon my conscience, Mr Acres, your valour has
oozed away with a vengeance!

Acres. Not in the least! Odds backs and abettors! I 'll be
your second with all my heart—and if you should get a quietus,
you may command me entirely. I 'll get you snug lying in
the Abbey here; or pickle you, and send you over to Blun-
derbuss-hall, or any thing of the kind, with the greatest
pleasure.

Sir Luc. Pho! pho! you are little better than a coward.

Acres. Mind, gentlemen, he calls me a coward; coward was
the word, by my valour!

Sir Luc. Well, sir?

Acres. Look 'ee, Sir Lucius, 'tisn't that I mind the word
coward—coward may be said in joke—But if you had called
me a poltroon, odds daggers and balls——

Sir Luc. Well, sir?

Acres. I should have thought you a very ill-bred man.

Sir Luc. Pho! you are beneath my notice.

Abs. Nay, Sir Lucius, you can't have a better second than
my friend Acres —He is a most determined dog—called in
the country, Fighting Bob.—He generally kills a man a week
—don't you, Bob?

Acres. Ay—at home!

Sir Luc. Well, then, captain, 'tis we must begin—so come
out, my little counsellor—[*Draws his sword*]—and ask the gentleman, whether he will resign the lady, without forcing you
to proceed against him?

Abs. Come on then, sir—[*Draws*]; since you won't let it be an amicable suit, here's my reply.

Enter SIR ANTHONY ABSOLUTE, DAVID, MRS. MALAPROP,
LYDIA, *and* JULIA.

Dav. Knock 'em all down, sweet Sir Anthony; knock down my master in particular; and bind his hands over to their good behaviour!

Sir Anth. Put up, Jack, put up, or I shall be in a frenzy—how came you in a duel, sir?

Abs. Faith, sir, that gentleman can tell you better than I; 'twas he called on me, and you know, sir, I serve his majesty.

Sir Anth. Here's a pretty fellow; I catch him going to cut a man's throat, and he tells me, he serves his majesty!—Zounds! sirrah, then how durst you draw the king's sword against one of his subjects?

Abs. Sir, I tell you! that gentleman called me out, without explaining his reasons.

Sir Anth. Gad! sir, how came you to call my son out, without explaining your reasons?

Sir Luc. Your son, sir, insulted me in a manner which my honour could not brook.

Sir Anth. Zounds! Jack, how durst you insult the gentleman in a manner which his honour could not brook?

Mrs. Mal. Come, come, let's have no honour before ladies—Captain Absolute, come here—How could you intimidate us so?—Here's Lydia has been terrified to death for you.

Abs. For fear I should be killed, or escape, ma'am?

Mrs. Mal. Nay, no delusions to the past—Lydia is convinced; speak, child.

Sir Luc. With your leave, ma'am, I must put in a word here: I believe I could interpret the young lady's silence. Now mark——

Lyd. What is it you mean, sir?

Sir Luc. Come, come, Delia, we must be serious now—this is no time for trifling.

Lyd. 'Tis true, sir; and your reproof bids me offer this gentleman my hand, and solicit the return of his affections.

Abs. O! my little angel, say you so!—Sir Lucius—I perceive there must be some mistake here, with regard to the affront which you affirm I have given you. I can only say,

that it could not have been intentional. And as you must be
convinced, that I should not fear to support a real injury—you
shall now see that I am not ashamed to atone for an inadver-
tency—I ask your pardon.—But for this lady, while honoured
with her approbation, I will support my claim against any man
whatever.

Sir Anth. Well said, Jack, and I 'll stand by you, my boy.

Acres. Mind, I give up all my claim—I make no preten
sions to any thing in the world; and if I can't get a wife with
out fighting for her, by my valour! I 'll live a bachelor.

Sir Luc. Captain, give me your hand: an affront hand
somely acknowledged becomes an obligation; and as for the
lady, if she chooses to deny her own hand-writing, here——

[*Takes out letters.*

Mrs. Mal. O, he will dissolve my mystery!—Sir Lucius,
perhaps there 's some mistake—perhaps I can illuminate——

Sir Luc. Pray, old gentlewoman, do'nt interfere where you
have no business.—Miss Languish, are you my Delia, or not?

Lyd. Indeed, Sir Lucius, I am not.

[*Walks aside with* CAPTAIN ABSOLUTE.

Mrs. Mal. Sir Lucius O'Trigger—ungrateful as you are—I
own the soft impeachment—pardon my blushes, I am Delia.

Sir Luc. You Delia—pho! pho! be easy.

Mrs. Mal. Why, thou barbarous Vandyke—those letters are
mine—When you are more sensible of my benignity—perhaps
I may be brought to encourage your addresses.

Sir Luc. Mrs. Malaprop, I am extremely sensible of your
condescension; and whether you or Lucy have put this trick
on me, I am equally beholden to you.—And, to show you I am
not ungrateful, Captain Absolute, since you have taken that
lady from me, I 'll give you my Delia into the bargain.

Abs. I am much obliged to you, Sir Lucius; but here 's my
friend, Fighting Bob, unprovided for.

Sir Luc. Hah! little Valour—here, will you make your fortune?

Acres. Odds wrinkles! No.—But give me your hand, Sir
Lucius, forget and forgive; but if ever I give you a chance of
pickling me again, say Bob Acres is a dunce, that 's all

Sir Anth. Come, Mrs. Malaprop, don't be cast down—you
are in your bloom yet.

Mrs. Mal. O Sir Anthony—men are all barbarians.

[*All retire but* JULIA *and* FAULKLAND.

Jul. [*Aside.*] He seems dejected and unhappy—not sullen; there was some foundation, however, for the tale he told me— O woman! how true should be your judgment, when your resolution is so weak!

Faulk. Julia!—how can I sue for what I so little deserve? I dare not presume—yet Hope is the child of Penitence.

Jul. Oh! Faulkland, you have not been more faulty in your unkind treatment of me, than I am now in wanting inclination to resent it. As my heart honestly bids me place my weakness to the account of love, I should be ungenerous not to admit the same plea for yours.

Faulk. Now I shall be blest indeed!

Sir Anth. [*Coming forward.*] What's going on here?—So you have been quarrelling too, I warrant! Come, Julia, I never interfered before; but let me have a hand in the matter at last.—All the faults I have ever seen in my friend Faulkland seemed to proceed from what he calls the delicacy and warmth of his affection for you—There, marry him directly, Julia; you'll find he'll mend surprisingly!

[*The rest come forward.*

Sir Luc. Come, now, I hope there is no dissatisfied person, but what is content; for as I have been disappointed myself, it will be very hard if I have not the satisfaction of seeing other people succeed better.

Acres. You are right, Sir Lucius.—So Jack, I wish you joy— Mr. Faulkland the same.—Ladies,—come now, to show you I'm neither vexed nor angry, odds tabors and pipes! I'll order the fiddles in half an hour to the New Rooms—and I insist on your all meeting me there.

Sir Anth. 'Gad! sir, I like your spirit; and at night we single lads will drink a health to the young couples, and a husband to Mrs. Malaprop.

Faulk. Our partners are stolen from us, Jack—I hope to be congratulated by each other—yours for having checked in time the errors of an ill-directed imagination, which might have betrayed an innocent heart; and mine, for having, by her gentleness and candour, reformed the unhappy temper of one, who by it made wretched whom he loved most, and tortured the heart he ought to have adored.

Abs. Well, Jack, we have both tasted the bitters, as well as

the sweets of love ; with this difference only, that you always
prepared the bitter cup for yourself, while I——

Lyd. Was always obliged to me for it, hey! Mr. Modesty?
——-But, come, no more of that—our happiness is now as
unalloyed as general.

Jul. Then let us study to preserve it so: and while Hope
pictures to us a flattering scene of future bliss, let us deny its
pencil those colours which are too bright to be lasting.—When
hearts deserving happiness would unite their fortunes, Virtue
would crown them with an unfading garland of modest hurt-
less flowers; but ill-judging Passion will force the gaudier rose
into the wreath, whose thorn offends them when its leaves are
dropped!   [*Exeunt omnes.*

EPILOGUE.

BY THE AUTHOR.

SPOKEN BY MRS. BULKLEY.

LADIES, for you—I heard our poet say—
He 'd try to coax some moral from his play:
" One moral's plain," cried I, " without more fuss;
Man's social happiness all rests on us:
Through all the drama—whether damn'd or not—
Love gilds the scene, and women guide the plot.
From every rank obedience is our due—
D' ye doubt?—The world's great stage shall prove it true.'
    The cit, well skill'd to shun domestic strife,
Will sup abroad; but first he 'll ask his wife:
John Trot, his friend, for once will do the same,
But then—he 'll just step home to tell his dame.
    The surly squire at noon resolves to rule,
And half the day—Zounds! madam is a fool!
Convinced at night, the vanquish'd victor says,
Ah, Kate! you women have such coaxing ways
    The jolly toper chides each tardy blade,
Till reeling Bacchus calls on Love for aid:
Then with each toast he sees fair bumpers swim,
And kisses Chloe on the sparkling brim!

Nay, I have heard that statesmen—great and wise--
Will sometimes counsel with a lady's eyes!
The servile suitors watch her various face,
She smiles preferment, or she frowns disgrace,
Curtsies a pension here—there nods a place.
 Nor with less awe, in scenes of humbler life,
Is view'd the mistress, or is heard the wife.
The poorest peasant of the poorest soil,
The child of poverty, and heir to toil,
Early from radiant Love's impartial light
Steals one small spark to cheer this world of night:
Dear spark! that oft through winter's chilling woes
Is all the warmth his little cottage knows!
 The wandering tar, who not for years has press'd,
The widow'd partner of his day of rest,
On the cold deck, far from her arms removed,
Still hums the ditty which his Susan loved;
And while around the cadence rude is blown,
The boatswain whistles in a softer tone.
 The soldier, fairly proud of wounds and toil,
Pants for the triumph of his Nancy's smile;
But ere the battle should he list her cries,
The lover trembles—and the hero dies!
That heart, by war and honour steel'd to fear,
Droops on a sigh, and sickens at a tear!
 But ye more cautious, ye nice-judging few,
Who give to beauty only beauty's due,
Though friends to love—ye view with deep regret
Our conquests marr'd, our triumphs incomplete,
Till polish'd wit more lasting charms disclose,
And judgment fix the darts which beauty throws!
In female breasts did sense and merit rule,
The lover's mind would ask no other school;
Shamed into sense, the scholars of our eyes,
Our beaux from gallantry would soon be wise;
Would gladly light, their homage to improve,
The lamp of knowledge at the torch of love!

THE SCHOOL FOR SCANDAL.

A COMEDY.

DRAMATIS PERSONÆ.

AS ORIGINALLY ACTED AT DRURY-LANE THEATRE IN 1777.

Sir Peter Teazle .	*Mr. King.*	Crabtree . . .	*Mr. Parsons.*
Sir Oliver Surface	*Mr. Yates.*	Rowley . . .	*Mr. Aickin.*
Sir Harry Bumper .	*Mr. Gawdry.*	Moses	*Mr. Baddeley.*
Sir Benjamin Back- BITE	*Mr. Dodd.*	Trip	*Mr. Lamash.*
		Lady Teazle .	*Mrs. Abington.*
Joseph Surface .	*Mr. Palmer.*	Lady Sneerwell	*Miss Sherry.*
Charles Surface .	*Mr. Smith.*	Mrs. Candour .	*Miss Pope.*
Careless	*Mr. Farren.*	Maria . . .	*Miss P. Hopkins.*
Snake	*Mr. Packer.*	Gentlemen, Maid, *and* Servants.

SCENE.—London.

A PORTRAIT;

ADDRESSED TO MRS. CREWE, WITH THE COMEDY OF THE SCHOOL FOR SCANDAL.

BY R. B. SHERIDAN, ESQ.

Tell me, ye prim adepts in Scandal's school,
Who rail by precept, and detract by rule,
Lives there no character, so tried, so known,
So deck'd with grace, and so unlike your own,
That even you assist her fame to raise,
Approve by envy, and by silence praise !
Attend !—a model shall attract your view—
Daughters of calumny, I summon you !
You shall decide if this a portrait prove,
Or fond creation of the Muse and Love.
Attend, ye virgin critics, shrewd and sage,
Ye matron censors of this childish age,
Whose peering eye and wrinkled front declare
A fix'd antipathy to young and fair ;
By cunning, cautious ; or by nature, cold,
In maiden madness, virulently bold !—
Attend, ye skill'd to coin the precious tale,
Creating proof, where inuendos fail !
Whose practised memories, cruelly exact,
Omit no circumstance, except the fact !—
Attend, all ye who boast,—or old or young,—
The living libel of a slanderous tongue !

So shall my theme as far contrasted be,
As saints by fiends, or hymns by calumny.
Come, gentle Amoret (for 'neath that name
In worthier verse is sung thy beauty's fame);
Come—for but thee who seeks the Muse? and whils
Celestial blushes check thy conscious smile,
With timid grace, and hesitating eye,
The perfect model, which I boast, supply:—
Vain Muse! couldst thou the humblest sketch create
Of her, or slightest charm couldst imitate—
Could thy blest strain in kindred colours trace
The faintest wonder of her form and face—
Poets would study the immortal line,
And Reynolds own his art subdued by thine;
That art, which well might added lustre give
To Nature's best, and Heaven's superlative:
On Granby's cheek might bid new glories rise,
Or point a purer beam from Devon's eyes!
Hard is the task to shape that beauty's praise,
Whose judgment scorns the homage flattery pays!
But praising Amoret we cannot err,
No tongue o'ervalues Heaven, or flatters her!
Yet she by fate's perverseness—she alone
Would doubt our truth, nor deem such praise her own
Adorning fashion, unadorn'd by dress,
Simple from taste, and not from carelessness;
Discreet in gesture, in deportment mild,
Not stiff with prudence, nor uncouthly wild:
No state has Amoret; no studied mien;
She frowns no goddess, and she moves no queen.
The softer charm that in her manner lies
Is framed to captivate, yet not surprise;
It justly suits the expression of her face,—
'Tis less than dignity, and more than grace!
On her pure cheek the native hue is such,
That, form'd by Heaven to be admired so much,
The hand divine, with a less partial care,
Might well have fix'd a fainter crimson there,
And bade the gentle inmate of her breast—
Inshrined Modesty—supply the rest.
But who the peril of her lips shall paint?
Strip them of smiles—still, still all words are fain
But moving Love himself appears to teach
Their action, though denied to rule her speech;
And thou who seest her speak, and dost not hear,
Mourn not her distant accents 'scape thine ear;
Viewing those lips, thou still may'st make pretence
To judge of what she says, and swear 'tis sense:
Clothed with such grace, with such expression fraught,
They move in meaning, and they pause in thought!

But dost thou farther watch, with charm'd surprise,
The mild irresolution of her eyes,
Curious to mark how frequent they repose,
In brief eclipse and momentary close—
Ah ! seest thou not an ambush'd Cupid there,
Too tim'rous of his charge, with jealous care
Veils and unveils those beams of heavenly light,
Too full, too fatal else, for mortal sight?
Nor yet, such pleasing vengeance fond to meet,
In pard'ning dimples hope a safe retreat.
What though her peaceful breast should ne'er allow
Subduing frowns to arm her alter'd brow,
By Love, I swear, and by his gentle wiles,
More fatal still the mercy of her smiles !
Thus lovely, thus adorn'd, possessing all
Of bright or fair that can to woman fall,
The height of vanity might well be thought
Prerogative in her, and Nature's fault.
Yet gentle Amoret, in mind supreme
As well as charms, rejects the vainer theme;
And, half mistrustful of her beauty's store,
She barbs with wit those darts too keen before:—
Read in all knowledge that her sex should reach,
Though Greville, or the Muse, should deign to teach,
Fond to improve, nor timorous to discern
How far it is a woman's grace to learn;
In Millar's dialect she would not prove
Apollo's priestess, but Apollo's love,
Graced by those signs which truth delights to own,
The timid blush, and mild submitted tone:
Whate'er she says, though sense appear throughout,
Displays the tender hue of female doubt;
Deck'd with that charm, how lovely wit appears,
How graceful science, when that robe she wears !
Such too her talents, and her bent of mind,
As speak a sprightly heart by thought refined:
A taste for mirth, by contemplation school'd,
A turn for ridicule, by candour ruled,
A scorn of folly, which she tries to hide;
An awe of talent, which she owns with pride !
      Peace, idle Muse ! no more thy strain prolong,
But yield a theme, thy warmest praises wrong;
Just to her merit, though thou canst not raise
Thy feeble verse, behold th' acknowledged praise
Has spread conviction through the envious train,
And cast a fatal gloom o'er Scandal's reign !
And lo ! each pallid hag, with blister'd tongue,
Mutters assent to all thy zeal has sung—
Owns all the colours just—the outline true·
Thee my inspirer, and my model—CREWE !

PROLOGUE

WRITTEN BY MR. GARRICK.

A SCHOOL for Scandal! tell me, I beseech you,
Needs there a school this modish art to teach you?
No need of lessons now, the knowing think;
We might as well be taught to eat and drink.
Caused by a dearth of scandal, should the vapours
Distress our fair ones—let them read the papers;
Their powerful mixtures such disorders hit;
Crave what you will—there's *quantum sufficit.*
"Lord !" cries my Lady Wormwood (who loves tattle,
And puts much salt and pepper in her prattle),
Just risen at noon, all night at cards when threshing
Strong tea and scandal—"Bless me, how refreshing!
Give me the papers, Lisp—how bold and free ! [*Sips.*
Last night Lord L. [*Sips*] *was caught with Lady D.*
For aching heads what charming sal volatile ! [*Sips.*
If Mrs. B. will still continue flirting,
We hope she'll DRAW, *or we'll* UNDRAW *the curtain.*
Fine satire, poz—in public all abuse it,
But, by ourselves [*Sips*], our praise we can't refuse it.
Now, Lisp, read you—there, at that dash and star *"*
"Yes, ma'am—*A certain lord had best beware,*
Who lives not twenty miles from Grosvenor Square;
For, should he Lady W. find willing,
Wormwood is bitter"——"Oh ! that's me ! the villain!
Throw it behind the fire, and never more
Let that vile paper come within my door."
Thus at our friends we laugh, who feel the dart;
To reach our feelings, we ourselves must smart.
Is our young bard so young, to think that he   ·
Can stop the full spring-tide of calumny?
Knows he the world so little, and its trade?
Alas ! the devil's sooner raised than laid.
So strong, so swift, the monster there's no gagging:
Cut Scandal's head off, still the tongue is wagging.
Proud of your smiles once lavishly bestow'd,
Again our young Don Quixote takes the road;
To show his gratitude he draws his pen,
And seeks this hydra, Scandal, in his den.
For your applause all perils he would through—
He'll fight—that's write—a cavalliero true,
Till every drop of blood—that's ink—is spilt for you.

ACT I.

SCENE I.—LADY SNEERWELL'S *Dressing-room.*

LADY SNEERWELL *discovered at her toilet;* SNAKE *drinking chocolate.*

Lady Sneer. The paragraphs, you say, Mr. Snake, were all inserted?

Snake. They were, madam; and, as I copied them myself in a feigned hand, there can be no suspicion whence they came.

Lady Sneer. Did you circulate the report of Lady Brittle's intrigue with Captain Boastall?

Snake. That's in as fine a train as your ladyship could wish. In the common course of things, I think it must reach Mrs. Clackitt's ears within four-and-twenty hours; and then, you know, the business is as good as done.

Lady Sneer. Why, truly, Mrs. Clackitt has a very pretty talent, and a great deal of industry.

Snake. True, madam, and has been tolerably successful in her day. To my knowledge, she has been the cause of six matches being broken off, and three sons being disinherited; of four forced elopements, and as many close confinements; nine separate maintenances, and two divorces. Nay, I have more than once traced her causing a *tête-à-tête* in the "Town and Country Magazine," when the parties, perhaps, had never seen each other's face before in the course of their lives.

Lady Sneer. She certainly has talents, but her manner is gross.

Snake. 'Tis very true. She generally designs well, has a free tongue and a bold invention; but her colouring is too dark, and her outlines often extravagant She wants that delicacy of tint, and mellowness of sneer, which distinguish your ladyship's scandal.

Lady Sneer. You are partial, Snake.

Snake. Not in the least; every body allows that Lady Sneerwell can do more with a word or look than many can with the most laboured detail, even when they happen to have a little truth on their side to support it.

Lady Sneer. Yes, my dear Snake; and I am no hypocrite to deny the satisfaction I reap from the success of my efforts. Wounded myself, in the early part of my life, by the en-venomed tongue of slander, I confess I have since known **no** pleasure equal to the reducing others to the level of my own reputation.

Snake. Nothing can be more natural. But, Lady Sneerwell, there is one affair in which you have lately employed me, wherein, I confess, I am at a loss to guess your motives.

Lady Sneer. I conceive you mean with respect to my neighbour, Sir Peter Teazle, and his family?

Snake. I do. Here are two young men, to whom Sir Peter has acted as a kind of guardian since their father's death; the eldest possessing the most amiable character, and universally well spoken of—the youngest, the most dissipated and extra vagant young fellow in the kingdom, without friends or character: the former an avowed admirer of your ladyship, and apparently your favourite; the latter attached to Maria, Sir Peter's ward, and confessedly beloved by her. Now, on the face of these circumstances, it is utterly unaccountable to me, why you, the widow of a city knight, with a good jointure, should not close with the passion of a man of such character and expectations as Mr. Surface; and more so why you should be so uncommonly earnest to destroy the mutual attachment subsisting between his brother Charles and Maria.

Lady Sneer. Then, at once to unravel this mystery, I must inform you that love has no share whatever in the intercourse between Mr. Surface and me.

Snake. No!

Lady Sneer. His real attachment is to Maria, or her fortune; but, finding in his brother a favoured rival, he has been obliged to mask his pretensions, and profit by my assistance.

Snake. Yet still I am more puzzled why you should interest yourself in his success.

Lady Sneer. Heavens! how dull you are! Cannot you surmise the weakness which I hitherto, through shame, have concealed even from you? Must I confess that Charles—that libertine, that extravagant, that bankrupt in fortune and reputation—that he it is for whom I am thus anxious and malicious, and to gain whom I would sacrifice every thing?

Snake. Now, indeed, your conduct appears consistent: but how came you and Mr. Surface so confidential?

Lady Sneer. For our mutual interest. I have found him out a long time since. I know him to be artful, selfish, and malicious—in short, a sentimental knave; while with Sir Peter, and indeed with all his acquaintance, he passes for a youthful miracle of prudence, good sense, and benevolence

Snake. Yes; yet Sir Peter vows he has not his equal in England; and, above all, he praises him as a man of sentiment.

Lady Sneer. True; and with the assistance of his sentiment and hypocrisy he has brought Sir Peter entirely into his interest with regard to Maria; while poor Charles has no friend in the house—though, I fear, he has a powerful one in Maria's heart, against whom we must direct our schemes.

Enter SERVANT.

Ser. Mr. Surface.

Lady Sneer. Show him up. [*Exit* SERVANT.] He generally calls about this time. I don't wonder at people giving him to me for a lover.

Enter JOSEPH SURFACE.

Jos. Surf. My dear Lady Sneerwell, how do you do to-day? Mr. Snake, your most obedient.

Lady Sneer. Snake has just been rallying me on our mutual attachment· but I have informed him of our real views. You know how useful he has been to us; and, believe me, the confidence is not ill placed.

Jos Surf. Madam, it is impossible for me to suspect a man of Mr. Snake's sensibility and discernment.

Lady Sneer. Well, well, no compliments now; but tell me when you saw your mistress, Maria—or, what is more material to me, your brother.

Jos. Surf. I have not seen either since I left you; but I can inform you that they never meet. Some of your stories have taken a good effect on Maria.

Lady Sneer. Ah, my dear Snake! the merit of this belongs to you. But do your brother's distresses increase?

Jos. Surf. Every hour. I am told he has had another execution in the house yesterday. In short, his dissipation and extravagance exceed any thing I have ever heard of.

Lady Sneer. Poor Charles!

Jos. Surf. True, madam; notwithstanding his vices, one can't help feeling for him. Poor Charles! I'm sure I wish it were in my power to be of any essential service to him; for the man who does not share in the distresses of a brother, even though merited by his own misconduct, deserves——

Lady Sneer. O Lud! you are going to be moral, and forget that you are among friends.

Jos. Surf. Egad, that's true! I'll keep that sentiment till I see Sir Peter. However, it is certainly a charity to rescue Maria from such a libertine, who, if he is to be reclaimed, can be so only by a person of your ladyship's superior accomplish ments and understanding.

Snake. I believe, Lady Sneerwell, here's company coming : I'll go and copy the letter I mentioned to you. Mr. Surface, your most obedient.

Jos. Surf. Sir, your very devoted.—[*Exit* Snake.] Lady Sneerwell, I am very sorry you have put any farther confidence in that fellow.

Lady Sneer. Why so?

Jos. Surf. I have lately detected him in frequent conference with old Rowley, who was formerly my father's steward, and has never, you know, been a friend of mine.

Lady Sneer. And do you think he would betray us?

Jos. Surf. Nothing more likely : take my word for 't, Lady Sneerwell, that fellow hasn't virtue enough to be faithful even to his own villany. Ah, Maria!

Enter MARIA.

Lady Sneer. Maria, my dear, how do you do? What's the matter?

Mar. Oh! there's that disagreeable lover of mine, Sir Benjamin Backbite, has just called at my guardian's, with his odious uncle, Crabtree ; so I slipped out, and ran hither to avoid them.

Lady Sneer. Is that all?

Jos. Surf. If my brother Charles had been of the party, madam, perhaps you would not have been so much alarmed.

Lady Sneer. Nay, now you are severe ; for I dare swear the truth of the matter is, Maria heard you were here. But, my dear, what has Sir Benjamin done, that you should avoid him so?

Mar. Oh, he has done nothing—but 'tis for what he has said : his conversation is a perpetual libel on all his acquaintance.

Jos. Surf. Ay, and the worst of it is, there is no advantage in not knowing him ; for he'll abuse a stranger just as soon as his best friend : and his uncle's as bad.

Lady Sneer. Nay, but we should make allowance ; Sir Benjamin is a wit and a poet

Mar. For my part, I own, madam, wit loses its respect with me, when I see it in company with malice. What do you think, Mr. Surface?

Jos. Surf. Certainly, madam; to smile at the jest which plants a thorn in another's breast is to become a principal in the mischief.

Lady Sneer. Psha! there's no possibility of being witty without a little ill nature: the malice of a good thing is the barb that makes it stick. What's your opinion, Mr. Surface?

Jos. Surf. To be sure, madam; that conversation, where the spirit of raillery is suppressed, will ever appear tedious and insipid.

Mar. Well, I'll not debate how far scandal may be allowable; but in a man, I am sure, it is always contemptible. We have pride, envy, rivalship, and a thousand motives to depreciate each other; but the male slanderer must have the cowardice of a woman before he can traduce one

Re-enter SERVANT.

Ser. Madam, Mrs. Candour is below, and, if your ladyship's at leisure, will leave her carriage.

Lady Sneer. Beg her to walk in.—[*Exit* SERVANT.]   Now, Maria, here is a character to your taste; for, though Mrs. Candour is a little talkative, every body allows her to be the best natured and best sort of woman.

Mar. Yes, with a very gross affectation of good nature and benevolence, she does more mischief than the direct malice of old Crabtree.

Jos. Surf. I' faith that's true, Lady Sneerwell: whenever I hear the current running against the characters of my friends, I never think them in such danger as when Candour undertakes their defence.

Lady Sneer. Hush!—here she is!

Enter MRS. CANDOUR.

Mrs. Can. My dear Lady Sneerwell, how have you been this century?—Mr. Surface, what news do you hear?—though indeed it is no matter, for I think one hears nothing else but scandal.

Jos. Surf. Just so, indeed, ma'am.

Mrs. Can. Oh, Maria! child,—what, is the whole affair

off between you and Charles? His extravagance, I presume —the town talks of nothing else.

Mar. I am very sorry, ma'am, the town has so little to do.

Mrs. Can. True, true, child: 'but there's no stopping people's tongues. I own I was hurt to hear it, as I indeed was to learn, from the same quarter, that your guardian, Sir Peter, and Lady Teazle have not agreed lately as well as could be wished.

Mar. 'Tis strangely impertinent for people to busy themselves so.

Mrs. Can. Very true, child: but what's to be done? People will talk—there's no preventing it. Why, it was but yesterday I was told that Miss Gadabout had eloped with Sir Filigree Flirt. But, Lord! there's no minding what one hears; though, to be sure, I had this from very good authority.

Mar. Such reports are highly scandalous.

Mrs. Can. So they are, child—shameful, shameful! But the world is so censorious, no character escapes. Lord, now who would have suspected your friend, Miss Prim, of an indiscretion? Yet such is the ill nature of people, that they say her uncle stopped her last week, just as she was stepping into the York Mail with her dancing-master.

Mar. I'll answer for 't there are no grounds for that report.

Mrs. Can. Ah, no foundation in the world, I dare swear: no more, probably, than for the story circulated last month, of Mrs. Festino's affair with Colonel Cassino—though, to be sure, that matter was never rightly cleared up.

Jos. Surf. The licence of invention some people take is monstrous indeed.

Mar. 'Tis so; but, in my opinion, those who report such things are equally culpable.

Mrs. Can. To be sure they are; tale-bearers are as bad as the tale-makers—'tis an old observation, and a very true one: but what's to be done, as I said before? how will you prevent people from talking? To-day, Mrs. Clackitt assured me, Mr. and Mrs. Honeymoon were at last become mere man and wife, like the rest of their acquaintance. She likewise hinted that a certain widow, in the next street, had got rid of her dropsy and recovered her shape in a most surprising manner. And at the same time Miss Tattle, who was by, affirmed, that Lord Buffalo had discovered his lady at a house of no extraordinary fame; and that Sir Harry Bouquet and Tom Saunter were to measure swords on a similar provocation. But, Lord, do you think I would report these things! No, no! tale-bearers, as I said before, are just as bad as the tale-makers.

Jos. Surf. Ah! Mrs. Candour, if every body had your forbearance and good nature!

Mrs. Can. I confess, Mr. Surface, I cannot bear to hear people attacked behind their backs; and when ugly circumstances come out against our acquaintance I own I always love to think the best. By the by, I hope 'tis not true that your brother is absolutely ruined?

Jos. Surf. I am afraid his circumstances are very bad indeed, ma'am.

Mrs. Can. Ah! I heard so—but you must tell him to keep up his spirits; every body almost is in the same way: Lord Spindle, Sir Thomas Splint, Captain Quinze, and Mr. Nickit —all up, I hear, within this week; so, if Charles is undone, he'll find half his acquaintance ruined too, and that, you know, is a consolation.

Jos. Surf. Doubtless, ma'am—a very great one.

Re-enter SERVANT.

Ser. Mr. Crabtree and Sir Benjamin Backbite   [*Exit.*
Lady Sneer. So, Maria, you see your lover pursues you; positively you sha'n't escape.

Enter CRABTREE *and* SIR BENJAMIN BACKBITE.

Crab. Lady Sneerwell, I kiss your hand. Mrs. Candour, I don't believe you are acquainted with my nephew, Sir Benjamin Backbite? Egad, ma'am, he has a pretty wit, and is a pretty poet too. Isn't he, Lady Sneerwell?

Sir Ben. Oh, fie, uncle!

Crab. Nay, egad it's true; I back him at a rebus or a charade against the best rhymer in the kingdom. Has your ladyship heard the epigram he wrote last week on Lady Frizzle's feather catching fire?—Do, Benjamin, repeat it, or the charade you made last night extempore at Mrs. Drowzie's conversazione. Come now; your first is the name of a fish, your second a great naval commander, and——

Sir Ben. Uncle. now—pr'ythee——

Crab. I'faith, ma'am, 'twould surprise you to hear how ready he is at all these sort of things.

Lady Sneer I wonder. Sir Benjamin, you never publish any thing.

Sir Ben. To say truth, ma'am, 'tis very vulgar to print: and as my little productions are mostly satires and lampoons on particular people, I find they circulate more by giving copies in confidence to the friends of the parties. However, I have some love elegies, which, when favoured with ths lady's smiles, I mean to give the public.   [*Pointing to* MARIA.

Crab. [*To* MARIA.] 'Fore heaven, ma'am, they 'll immortalize you!—you will be handed down to posterity, like Petrarch's Laura, or Waller's Sacharissa.

Sir Ben. [*To* MARIA.] Yes, madam, I think you will like them, when you shall see them on a beautiful quarto page, where a neat rivulet of text shall meander through a meadow of margin. 'Fore Gad they will be the most elegant things of their kind!

Crab. But, ladies, that's true—have you heard the news?

Mrs. Can. What, sir, do you mean the report of——

Crab. No, ma'am, that's not it.—Miss Nicely is going to be married to her own footman.

Mrs. Can. Impossible.

Crab. Ask Sir Benjamin.

Sir Ben. 'Tis very true, ma'am: every thing is fixed, and the wedding liveries bespoke.

Crab. Yes—and they do say there were pressing reasons for it.

Lady Sneer. Why, I have heard something of this before.

Mrs. Can. It can't be—and I wonder any one should believe such a story of so prudent a lady as Miss Nicely.

Sir Ben. O Lud! ma'am, that's the very reason 'twas believed at once. She has always been so cautious and so reserved, that every body was sure there was some reason for it at bottom.

Mrs. Can. Why, to be sure, a tale of scandal is as fatal to the credit of a prudent lady of her stamp as a fever is generally to those of the strongest constitutions. But there is a sort of puny sickly reputation, that is always ailing, yet will outlive the robuster characters of a hundred prudes.

Sir Ben. True, madam, there are valetudinarians in reputation as well as constitution, who, being conscious of their weak part, avoid the least breath of air, and supply their want of stamina by care and circumspection.

Mrs. Can. Well, but this may be all a mistake.   You know,
Sir Benjamin, very trifling circumstances often give rise to the
most injurious tales.

Crab. That they do, I 'll be sworn, ma'am.   Did you ever
hear how Miss Piper came to lose her lover and her character last summer at Tunbridge?—Sir Benjamin, you remember it?

Sir Ben. Oh, to be sure!—the most whimsical circumstance.

Lady Sneer How was it, pray?

Crab. Why, one evening, at Mrs. Ponto's assembly, the
conversation happened to turn on the breeding Nova Scotia
sheep in this country.   Says a young lady in company, I have
known instances of it; for Miss Letitia Piper, a first cousin
of mine, had a Nova Scotia sheep that produced her twins.
"What!" cries the Lady Dowager Dundizzy (who you know is
as deaf as a post), "has Miss Piper had twins?" This mistake,
as you may imagine, threw the whole company into a fit of
laughter.   However, 'twas the next morning every where re-
ported, and in a few days believed by the whole town, that
Miss Letitia Piper had actually been brought to bed of a fine
boy and a girl: and in less than a week there were some
people who could name the father, and the farm-house where
the babies were put to nurse.

Lady Sneer. Strange, indeed!

Crab. Matter of fact, I assure you.   O Lud! Mr. Surface,
pray is it true that your uncle, Sir Oliver, is coming home?

Jos. Surf. Not that I know of, indeed, sir

Crab. He has been in the East Indies a long time.   You
can scarcely remember him, I believe?   Sad comfort, whenever he returns, to hear how your brother has gone on!

Jos. Surf. Charles has been imprudent, sir, to be sure; but
I hope no busy people have already prejudiced Sir Oliver
against him.   He may reform.

Sir Ben. To be sure he may: for my part, I never believed
him to be so utterly void of principle as people say; and,
though he has lost all his friends, I am told nobody is better
spoken of by the Jews.

Crab. That's true, egad, nephew   If the Old Jewry was
a ward, I believe Charles would be an alderman : no man
more popular there, 'fore God! I hear he pays as many an
nuities as the Irish tontine ; and that, whenever he is sick,

they have prayers for the recovery of his health in all the synagogues.

Sir Ben. Yet no man lives in greater splendour. They tell me, when he entertains his friends he will sit down to dinner with a dozen of his own securities ; have a score of tradesmen waiting in the antechamber, and an officer behind every guest's chair.

Jos. Surf. This may be entertainment to you, gentlemen, but you pay very little regard to the feelings of a brother.

Mar. [*Aside.*] Their malice is intolerable!—[*Aloud.*] Lady Sneerwell, I must wish you a good morning : I'm not very well. [*Exit*

Mrs. Can. O dear! she changes colour very much.

Lady Sneer. Do, Mrs. Candour, follow her : she may want your assistance.

Mrs. Can. That I will, with all my soul, ma'am.—Poor dear girl, who knows what her situation may be ! [*Exit*

Lady Sneer. 'Twas nothing but that she could not bear to hear Charles reflected on, notwithstanding their difference.

Sir Ben. The young lady's *penchant* is obvious.

Crab. But, Benjamin, you must not give up the pursuit for that: follow her, and put her into good humour. Repeat her some of your own verses. Come, I'll assist you.

Sir Ben. Mr. Surface, I did not mean to hurt you ; but depend on 't your brother is utterly undone.

Crab. O Lud, ay ! undone as ever man was—can't raise a guinea !

Sir Ben. And every thing sold, I'm told, that was movable.

Crab. I have seen one that was at his house. Not a thing left but some empty bottles that were overlooked, and the family pictures, which I believe are framed in the wainscots.

Sir Ben. And I'm very sorry also to hear some bad stories against him. [*Going.*

Crab. Oh, he has done many mean things, that's certain.

Sir Ben. But, however, as he's your brother—— [*Going.*

Crab We'll tell you all another opportunity.

[*Exeunt* CRABTREE *and* SIR BENJAMIN.

Lady Sneer. Ha! ha! 'tis very hard for them to leave a subject they have not quite run down.

Jos. Surf. And I believe the abuse was no more acceptable to your ladyship than Maria.

Lady Sneer. I doubt her affections are farther engaged than we imagine. But the family are to be here this evening, so you may as well dine where you are, and we shall have an opportunity of observing farther; in the meantime, I 'll go and plot mischief, and you shall study sentiment.   [*Exeunt*

SCENE II.—*A Room in* SIR PETER TEAZLE's *House.*

Enter SIR PETER TEAZLE

Sir Pet. When an old bachelor marries a young wife, what is he to expect? 'Tis now six months since Lady Teazle made me the happiest of men—and I have been the most miserable dog ever since! We tift a little going to church, and fairly quarrelled before the bells had done ringing. I was more than once nearly choked with gall during the honeymoon, and had lost all comfort in life before my friends had done wishing me joy. Yet I chose with caution—a girl bred wholly in the country, who never knew luxury beyond one silk gown, nor dissipation above the annual gala of a race ball. Yet she now plays her part in all the extravagant fopperies of fashion and the town, with as ready a grace as if she never had seen a bush or a grass-plot out of Grosvenor Square! I am sneered at by all my acquaintance, and paragraphed in the newspapers. She dissipates my fortune, and contradicts all my humours; yet the worst of it is, I doubt I love her, or I should never bear all this. However, I 'll never be weak enough to own it.

Enter ROWLEY

Row. Oh! Sir Peter, your servant: how is it with you, sir?

Sir Pet. Very bad, Master Rowley, very bad. I meet with nothing but crosses and vexations.

Row. What can have happened since yesterday?

Sir Pet. A good question to a married man!

Row. Nay, I 'm sure, Sir Peter, your lady can't be the cause of your uneasiness.

Sir Pet. Why, has any body told you she was dead?

Row. Come, come, Sir Peter you love her, notwithstanding your tempers don't exactly agree

Sir Pet. But the fault is entirely hers, Master Rowley. I am, myself, the sweetest-tempered man alive, and hate a teasing temper; and so I tell her a hundred times a day.

Row. Indeed!

Sir Pet. Ay; and what is very extraordinary, in all our dis putes she is always in the wrong! But Lady Sneerwell, and the set she meets at her house, encourage the perverseness of her disposition. Then, to complete my vexation, Maria, my ward, whom I ought to have the power of a father over, is determined to turn rebel too, and absolutely refuses the man whom I have long resolved on for her husband; meaning, I suppose, to bestow herself on his profligate brother.

Row You know, Sir Peter, I have always taken the liberty to differ with you on the subject of these two young gentlemen. I only wish you may not be deceived in your opinion of the elder. For Charles, my life on 't! he will retrieve his errors yet. Their worthy father, once my honoured master, was, at his years, nearly as wild a spark; yet, when he died, he did not leave a more benevolent heart to lament his loss.

Sir Pet. You are wrong, Master Rowley. On their father's death, you know, I acted as a kind of guardian to them both, till their uncle Sir Oliver's liberality gave them an early independence: of course, no person could have more opportuni· ties of judging of their hearts, and I was never mistaken in my life. Joseph is indeed a model for the young men of the age. He is a man of sentiment, and acts up to the sentiments he professes; but, for the other, take my word for 't, if he had any grain of virtue by descent, he has dissipated it with the rest of his inheritance. Ah! my old friend, Sir Oliver, will be deeply mortified when he finds how part of his bounty has been misapplied.

Row. I am sorry to find you so violent against the young man, because this may be the most critical period of his fortune. I came hither with news that will surprise you

Sir Pet. What! let me hear.

Row. Sir Oliver is arrived, and at this moment in town.

Sir Pet. How! you astonish me! I thought you did not expect him this month.

Row. I did not: but his passage has been remarkably quick.

Sir Pet. Egad, I shall rejoice to see my old friend. 'Tis sixteen years since we met. We have had many a day together:—but does he still enjoin us not to inform his nephews of his arrival?

Row. Most strictly. He means, before it is known, to make some trial of their dispositions.

Sir Pet. Ah! there needs no art to discover their merits

—however he shall have his way; but, pray, does he know I am married?

Row. Yes, and will soon wish you joy.

Sir Pet. What, as we drink health to a friend in a consumption! Ah! Oliver will laugh at me. We used to rail at matrimony together, but he has been steady to his text. Well, he must be soon at my house, though—I 'll instantly give orders for his reception. But, Master Rowley, don't drop a word that Lady Teazle and I ever disagree

Row. By no means.

Sir Pet. For I should never be able to stand Noll's jokes; so I 'll have him think, Lord forgive me! that we are a very happy couple.

Row. I understand you :—but then you must be very careful not to differ while he is in the house with you.

Sir Pet Egad, and so we must—and that 's impossible. Ah! Master Rowley, when an old bachelor marries a young wife, he deserves—no—the crime carries its punishment along with it   [*Exeunt*

ACT II.

Scene I.—*A Room in* Sir Peter Teazle's *House*
Enter Sir Peter *and* Lady Teazle.

Sir Pet. Lady Teazle, Lady Teazle, I 'll not bear it!

Lady Teaz. Sir Peter, Sir Peter, you may bear it or not, as you please; but I ought to have my own way in every thing, and, what 's more, I will too. What! though I was educated in the country, I know very well that women of fashion in London are accountable to nobody after they are married.

Sir Pet. Very well, ma'am, very well; so a husband is to have no influence, no authority?

Lady Teaz. Authority! No, to be sure :—if you wanted authority over me, you should have adopted me, and not married me: I am sure you were old enough.

Sir Pet. Old enough!—ay, there it is. Well, well, Lady Teazle, though my life may be made unhappy by your temper, I 'll not be ruined by your extravagance!

Lady Teaz. My extravagance! I 'm sure I 'm not more extravagant than a woman of fashion ought to be.

Sir Pet. No, no, madam, you shall throw away no more sums on such unmeaning luxury. 'Slife! to spend as much to furnish your dressing-room with flowers in winter as would suffice to turn the Pantheon into a greenhouse, and give a *fête champêtre* at Christmas.

Lady Teaz. And am I to blame, Sir Peter, because flowers are dear in cold weather? You should find fault with the climate, and not with me. For my part, I 'm sure I wish it was spring all the year round, and that roses grew under our feet!

Sir Pet. Oons! madam—if you had been born to this, I should'nt wonder at your talking thus; but you forget what your situation was when I married you.

Lady Teaz. No, no, I don't; 'twas a very disagreeable one, or I should never have married you.

Sir Pet. Yes, yes, madam, you were then in somewhat a humbler style—the daughter of a plain country squire. Recollect, Lady Teazle, when I saw you first sitting at your tambour, in a pretty figured linen gown, with a bunch of keys at your side, your hair combed smooth over a roll, and your apartment hung round with fruits in worsted, of your own working.

Lady Teaz. Oh, yes! I remember it very well, and a curious life I led. My daily occupation to inspect the dairy, superintend the poultry, make extracts from the family receipt-book, and comb my aunt Deborah's lapdog.

Sir Pet. Yes, yes, ma'am, 'twas so indeed.

Lady Teaz. And then you know, my evening amusements! To draw patterns for ruffles, which I had not materials to make up; to play Pope Joan with the curate; to read a sermon to my aunt; or to be stuck down to an old spinet to strum my father to sleep after a fox-chase.

Sir Pet. I am glad you have so good a memory. Yes, madam, these were the recreations I took you from; but now you must have your coach—*vis-à-vis*—and three powdered footmen before your chair; and, in the summer, a pair of white cats to draw you to Kensington Gardens. No recollection, I suppose, when you were content to ride double, behind the butler, on a docked coach-horse

Lady Teaz. No—I swear I never did that: I deny the butler and the coach-horse.

Sir Pet. This, madam, was your situation; and what have I done for you? I have made you a woman of fashion, of fortune, of rank—in short, I have made you my wife.

Lady Teaz. Well, then, and there is but one thing **more** you can make me to add to the obligation, that is——

Sir Pet. My widow, I suppose?

Lady Teaz. Hem! hem!

Sir Pet. I thank you, madam—but don't flatter yourself; for, though your ill conduct may disturb my peace of mind, it shall never break my heart, I promise you: however, I am equally óbliged to you for the hint.

Lady Teaz. Then why will you endeavour to make yourself so disagreeable to me, and thwart me in every little elegant expense?

Sir Pet. 'Slife, madam, I say, had you any of these little elegant expenses when you married me?

Lady Teaz. Lud, Sir Peter! would you have me be out of the fashion?

Sir Pet. The fashion, indeed! what had you to do with the fashion before you married me?

Lady Teaz. For my part, I should think you would like to have your wife thought a woman of taste.

Sir Pet. Ay—there again—taste! Zounds! madam, you had no taste when you married me!

Lady Teaz. That's very true, indeed, Sir Peter! and, after having married you, I should never pretend to taste again, I allow. But now, Sir Peter, since we have finished our daily jangle, I presume I may go to my engagement at Lady Sneerwell's.

Sir Pet. Ay, there's another precious circumstance—a charming set of acquaintance you have made there!

Lady Teaz. Nay, Sir Peter, they are all people of rank and fortune, and remarkably tenacious of reputation.

Sir Pet. Yes, egad, they are tenacious of reputation with a vengeance; for they don't choose any body should have a character but themselves! Such a crew! Ah! many a wretch has rid on a hurdle who has done less mischief than these utterers of forged tales, coiners of scandal, and clippers of reputation.

Lady Teaz. What, would you restrain the freedom of speech?

Sir Pet. Ah! they have made you just as bad as any one of the society.

Lady Teaz. Why, I believe I do bear a part with a toler-able grace.

Sir Pet. Grace indeed!

Lady Teaz. But I vow I bear no malice against the people I abuse: when I say an ill-natured thing, 'tis out of pure good humour; and I take it for granted they deal exactly in the same manner with me. But, Sir Peter, you know you promised to come to Lady Sneerwell's too.

Sir Pet. Well, well, I 'll call in, just to look after my own character.

Lady Teaz. Then, indeed, you must make haste after me, or you 'll be too late. So good by to ye. [*Exit.*

Sir Pet. So—I have gained much by my intended expostulation! Yet with what a charming air she contradicts every thing I say, and how pleasantly she shows her contempt for my authority! Well, though I can't make her love me, there is great satisfaction in quarrelling with her; and I think she never appears to such advantage as when she is doing every thing in her power to plague me. [*Exit.*

SCENE II.—*A Room in* LADY SNEERWELL'S *House.*

LADY SNEERWELL, MRS. CANDOUR, CRABTREE, SIR BENJAMIN BACKBITE, *and* JOSEPH SURFACE, *discovered.*

Lady Sneer. Nay, positively, we will hear it.

Jos. Surf. Yes, yes, the epigram, by all means.

Sir Ben. O plague on 't, uncle! 'tis mere nonsense.

Crab. No, no; 'fore Gad, very clever for an extempore!

Sir Ben. But, ladies, you should be acquainted with the circumstance. You must know, that one day last week, as Lady Betty Curricle was taking the dust in Hyde Park, in a sort of duodecimo phaeton, she desired me to write some verses on her ponies; upon which, I took out my pocket-book, and in one moment produced the following:—

> Sure never were seen two such beautiful ponies;
> Other horses are clowns, but these macaronies:
> To give them this title I 'm sure can't be wrong,
> Their legs are so slim, and their tails are so long.

Crab. There, ladies, done in the smack of a whip, and on horseback too.

Jos. Surf. A very Phœbus, mounted—indeed, Sir Benjamin!

Sir Ben. Oh dear, sir! trifles—trifles.

Enter LADY TEAZLE *and* MARIA.

Mrs. Can. I must have a copy.

Lady Sneer. Lady Teazle, I hope we shall see Sir Peter?

Lady Teaz. I believe he 'll wait on your ladyship presently.

Lady Sneer. Maria, my love, you look grave. Come, you shall sit down to piquet with Mr. Surface.

Mar. I take very little pleasure in cards—however, I 'll do as your ladyship pleases

Lady Teaz. I am surprised Mr. Surface should sit down with her; I thought he would have embraced this opportunity of speaking to me before Sir Peter came   [*Aside*

Mrs. Can. Now, I'll die; but you are so scandalous, I'll forswear your society.

Lady Teaz. What's the matter, Mrs. Candour?

Mrs. Can. They'll not allow our friend Miss Vermilion to be handsome.

Lady Sneer. Oh, surely she is a pretty woman

Crab. I am very glad you think so, ma'am

Mrs. Can. She has a charming fresh colour

Lady Teaz. Yes, when it is fresh put on.

Mrs. Can. Oh, fie! I'll swear her colour is natural: I have seen it come and go!

Lady Teaz. I dare swear you have, ma'am: it goes off at night, and comes again in the morning.

Sir Ben. True, ma'am, it not only comes and goes; but, what's more, egad, her maid can fetch and carry it!

Mrs. Can. Ha! ha! ha! how I hate to hear you talk so! But surely, now, her sister is, or was, very handsome.

Crab. Who? Mrs. Evergreen? O Lord! she's six-and-fifty if she's an hour!

Mrs. Can. Now positively you wrong her; fifty-two or fifty-three is the utmost—and I don't think she looks more.

Sir Ben. Ah! there's no judging by her looks, unless one could see her face.

Lady Sneer. Well, well, if Mrs. Evergreen does take some pains to repair the ravages of time, you must allow she effects it with great ingenuity; and surely that's better than the careless manner in which the widow Ochre caulks her wrinkles.

Sir Ben. Nay, now, Lady Sneerwell, you are severe upon the widow. Come, come, 'tis not that she paints so ill—but, when she has finished her face, she joins it on so badly to her neck, that she looks like a mended statue, in which the connoisseur may see at once that the head is modern, though the trunk's antique.

Crab. Ha! ha! ha! Well said, nephew!

Mrs. Can. Ha! ha! ha! Well, you make me laugh; but I vow I hate you for it. What do you think of Miss Simper?

Sir Ben. Why, she has very pretty teeth.

Lady Teaz. Yes; and on that account, when she is neither

speaking nor laughing (which very seldom happens), she never absolutely shuts her mouth, but leaves it always on a-jar, as it were—thus.   [*Shows her teeth.*

Mrs. Can. How can you be so ill-natured?

Lady Teaz. Nay, I allow even that's better than the pains Mrs. Prim takes to conceal her losses in front. She draws her mouth till it positively resembles the aperture of a poor's-box, and all her words appear to slide out edgewise, as it were—thus: *How do you do, madam? Yes, madam.*   [*Mimics.*

Lady Sneer. Very well, Lady Teazle; I see you can be a little severe.

Lady Teaz. In defence of a friend it is but justice   But here comes Sir Peter to spoil our pleasantry.

Enter SIR PETER TEAZLE.

Sir Pet. Ladies, your most obedient.—[*Aside.*]   Mercy on me, here is the whole set! a character dead at every word, I suppose.

Mrs. Can. I am rejoiced you are come. Sir Peter. They have been so censorious—and Lady Teazle as bad as any one

Sir Pet. That must be very distressing to you, indeed, Mrs. Candour.

Mrs. Can. Oh, they will allow good qualities to nobody; not even good nature to our friend Mrs. Pursy.

Lady Teaz. What, the fat dowager who was at Mrs. Quadrille's last night?

Mrs Can. Nay, her bulk is her misfortune: and, when she takes so much pains to get rid of it, you ought not to reflect on her.

Lady Sneer That's very true, indeed

Lady Teaz. Yes, I know she almost lives on acids and small whey; laces herself by pulleys; and often, in the hottest noon in summer, you may see her on a little squat pony, with her hair plaited up behind like a drummer's and puffing round the Ring on a full trot.

Mrs. Can. I thank you, Lady Teazle, for defending her

Sir Pet. Yes, a good defence, truly.

Mrs. Can. Truly, Lady Teazle is as censorious as Miss Sallow.

Crab. Yes, and she is a curious being to pretend to be cen

sorious—an awkward gawky, without any one good point under
heaven.

Mrs. Can. Positively you shall not be so very severe. Miss
Sallow is a near relation of mine by marriage, and, as for her
person, great allowance is to be made; for, let me tell you, a
woman labours under many disadvantages who tries to pass
for a girl of six-and-thirty.

Lady Sneer. Though, surely, she is handsome still—and
for the weakness in her eyes, considering how much she reads
by candlelight, it is not to be wondered at.

Mrs. Can True, and then as to her manner; upon my word
I think it is particularly graceful, considering she never had
the least education : for you know her mother was a Welsh
milliner, and her father a sugar-baker at Bristol.

Sir Ben. Ah! you are both of you too good-natured!

Sir Pet. Yes, damned good-natured! This their own relation! mercy on me!   [*Aside.*

Mrs. Can. For my part, I own I cannot bear to hear a
friend ill spoken of.

Sir Pet. No, to be sure!

Sir Ben. Oh! you are of a moral turn. Mrs. Candour and
I can sit for an hour and hear Lady Stucco talk sentiment.

Lady Teaz. Nay, I vow Lady Stucco is very well with the
dessert after dinner; for she's just like the French fruit one
cracks for mottoes—made up of paint and proverb.

Mrs. Can. Well, I will never join in ridiculing a friend;
and so I constantly tell my cousin Ogle, and you all know
what pretensions she has to be critical on beauty.

Crab. Oh, to be sure! she has herself the oddest countenance that ever was seen; 'tis a collection of features from all
the different countries of the globe.

Sir Ben. So she has, indeed—an Irish front——

Crab. Caledonian locks——

Sir Ben. Dutch nose——

Crab. Austrian lips——

Sir Ben. Complexion of a Spaniard——

Crab. And teeth *à la Chinoise*——

Sir Ben. In short, her face resembles a *table d'hôte* at Spa
—where no two guests are of a nation——

Crab. Or a congress at the close of a general war—wherein
all the members, even to her eyes, appear to have a different

interest, and her nose and chin are the only parties likely to
join issue.

Mrs. Can. Ha! ha! ha!

Sir Pet. Mercy on my life!—a person they dine with twice
a week!   [*Aside*

Mrs. Can. Nay, but I vow you shall not carry the laugh off
so—for give me leave to say, that Mrs. Ogle——

Sir Pet. Madam, madam, I beg your pardon—there 's no
stopping these good gentlemen's tongues.   But when I
tell you, Mrs. Candour, that the lady they are abusing is
a particular friend of mine, I hope you 'll not take her part.

Lady Sneer. Ha! ha! ha! well said, Sir Peter! but you are
a cruel creature—too phlegmatic yourself for a jest, and too
peevish to allow wit in others

Sir Pet. Ah, madam, true wit is more nearly allied to
good nature than your ladyship is aware of.

Lady Teaz. True, Sir Peter: I believe they are so near
akin that they can never be united.

Sir Ben. Or rather, suppose them man and wife, because
one seldom sees them together.

Lady Teaz. But Sir Peter is such an enemy to scandal, I
believe he would have it put down by parliament.

Sir Pet. 'Fore heaven, madam, if they were to consider the
sporting with reputation of as much importance as poach-
ing on manors, and pass an act for the preservation of
fame, as well as game, I believe many would thank them for
the bill.

Lady Sneer O Lud! Sir Peter; would you deprive us of
our privileges?

Sir Pet. Ay, madam; and then no person should be per-
mitted to kill characters and run down reputations, but qua-
lified old maids and disappointed widows.

Lady Sneer. Go, you monster!

Mrs. Can. But, surely, you would not be quite so severe
on those who only report what they hear?

Sir Pet. Yes, madam, I would have law merchant for them
too; and in all cases of slander currency, whenever the drawer
of the lie was not to be found, the injured parties should have
a right to come on any of the indorsers.

Crab. Well, for my part, I believe there never was a scandalous tale without some foundation.

Lady Sneer. Come, ladies, shall we sit down to cards in the next room?

Enter SERVANT, *who whispers* SIR PETER.

Sir Pet. I'll be with them directly.—[*Exit* SERVANT.] I'll get away unperceived.   [*Aside.*

Lady Sneer. Sir Peter, you are not going to leave us?

Sir Pet. Your ladyship must excuse me; I'm called away by particular business. But I leave my character behind me.
                                                        [*Exit.*

Sir Ben. Well—certainly, Lady Teazle, that lord of yours is a strange being: I could tell you some storie of him would make you laugh heartily if he were not your husband.

Lady Teaz. Oh, pray don't mind that; come, do let's hear them.   [*Exeunt all but* JOSEPH SURFACE *and* MARIA.

Jos. Surf. Maria, I see you have no satisfaction in this society.

Mar. How is it possible I should? If to raise malicious smiles at the infirmities or misfortunes of those who have never injured us be the province of wit or humour, Heaven grant me a double portion of dulness!

Jos. Surf. Yet they appear more ill-natured than they are; they have no malice at heart.

Mar. Then is their conduct still more contemptible; for, in my opinion, nothing could excuse the intemperance of their tongues but a natural and uncontrollable bitterness of mind.

Jos. Surf. Undoubtedly, madam; and it has always been a sentiment of mine, that to propagate a malicious truth wantonly is more despicable than to falsify from revenge. But can you, Maria, feel thus for others, and be unkind to me alone? Is hope to be denied the tenderest passion?

Mar. Why will you distress me by renewing this subject?

Jos. Surf. Ah, Maria! you would not treat me thus, and oppose your guardian, Sir Peter's will, but that I see that profligate Charles is still a favoured rival.

Mar. Ungenerously urged! But, whatever my sentiments are for that unfortunate young man, be assured I shall not feel more bound to give him up, because his distresses have lost him the regard even of a brother.

Jos. Surf. Nay, but, Maria, do not leave me with a frown: by all that's honest, I swear——   [*Kneels*

Re-enter LADY TEAZLE *behind.*

Aside.] Gad's life, here's Lady Teazle.—[*Aloud to* MARIA.] You must not—no, you shall not—for, though I have the greatest regard for Lady Teazle——

Mar. Lady Teazle!

Jos. Surf. Yet were Sir Peter to suspect——

Lady Teaz. [*Coming forward.*] What is this, pray? Does he take her for me?—Child, you are wanted in the next room.—[*Exit* MARIA.] What is all this, pray?

Jos. Surf Oh, the most unlucky circumstance in nature! Maria has somehow suspected the tender concern I have for your happiness, and threatened to acquaint Sir Peter with her suspicions, and I was just endeavouring to reason with her when you came in.

Lady Teaz. Indeed! but you seemed to adopt a very tender mode of reasoning—do you usually argue on your knees?

Jos. Surf. Oh, she's a child, and I thought a little bombast——But, Lady Teazle, when are you to give me your judgment on my library, as you promised?

Lady Teaz No, no; I begin to think it would be imprudent, and you know I admit you as a lover no farther than fashion requires.

Jos. Surf. True—a mere Platonic cicisbeo, what every wife is entitled to

Lady Teaz Certainly, one must not be out of the fashion. However, I have so many of my country prejudices left, that, though Sir Peter's ill humour may vex me ever so, it never shall provoke me to——

Jos. Surf. The only revenge in your power. Well, I applaud your moderation.

Lady Teaz Go—you are an insinuating wretch! But we shall be missed—let us join the company.

Jos. Surf. But we had best not return together.

Lady Teaz Well, don't stay; for Maria sha'n't come to hear any more of your reasoning, I promise you.   [*Exit.*

Jos. Surf. A curious dilemma, truly, my politics have run me into! I wanted, at first, only to ingratiate myself with Lady Teazle, that she might not be my enemy with Maria; and I have, I don't know how, become her serious lover. Sincerely I begin to wish I had never made such a point of gaining so

very good a character, for it has led me into so many cursed
rogueries that I doubt I shall be exposed at last.   [*Exit.*

SCENE III.—*A Room in* SIR PETER TEAZLE's *House.*

Enter SIR OLIVER SURFACE *and* ROWLEY.

Sir Oliv. Ha! ha! ha! so my old friend is married, hey?
—a young wife out of the country. Ha! ha! ha! that he
should have stood bluff to old bachelor so long, and sink into
a husband at last!

Row. But you must not rally him on the subject, Sir
Oliver; 'tis a tender point, I assure you, though he has been
married only seven months.

Sir Oliv. Then he has been just half a year on the stool of
repentance!—Poor Peter! But you say he has entirely given
up Charles—never sees him, hey?

Row. His prejudice against him is astonishing, and I am
sure greatly increased by a jealousy of him with Lady Teazle,
which he has industriously been led into by a scandalous
society in the neighbourhood, who have contributed not a
little to Charles's ill name. Whereas the truth is, I believe,
if the lady is partial to either of them, his brother is the
favourite.

Sir Oliv. Ay, I know there are a set of malicious, prating,
prudent gossips, both male and female, who murder characters to kill time, and will rob a young fellow of his good
name before he has years to know the value of it. But I am
not to be prejudiced against my nephew by such, I promise
you! No, no: if Charles has done nothing false or mean, I
shall compound for his extravagance.

Row. Then, my life on 't, you will reclaim him. Ah, sir,
it gives me new life to find that your heart is not turned
against him, and that the son of my good old master has one
friend, however, left.

Sir Oliv. What! shall I forget, Master Rowley, when I was
at his years myself? Egad, my brother and I were neither
of us very prudent youths; and yet, I believe, you have not
seen many better men than your old master was?

Row. Sir, 'tis this reflection gives me assurance that
Charles may yet be a credit to his family. But here comes
Sir Peter.

Sir Oliv. Egad, so he does! Mercy on me! he's greatly

altered, and seems to have a settled married look ! One may read husband in his face at this distance !

Enter SIR PETER TEAZLE.

Sir Pet. Ha! Sir Oliver—my old friend! Welcome to England a thousand times!

Sir Oliv. Thank you, thank you, Sir Peter! and i' faith I am glad to find you well, believe me !

Sir Pet. Oh! 'tis a long time since we met—fifteen years, I doubt, Sir Oliver, and many a cross accident in the time.

Sir Oliv. Ay, I have had my share. But, what! I find you are married, hey, my old boy? Well, well, it can't be helped ; and so—I wish you joy with all my heart!

Sir Pet. Thank you, thank you, Sir Oliver.—Yes, I have entered into—the happy state; but we'll not talk of that now.

Sir Oliv. True, true, Sir Peter; old friends should not begin on grievances at first meeting. No, no, no.

Row. [*Aside to* SIR OLIVER.] Take care, pray, sir.

Sir Oliv. Well, so one of my nephews is a wild rogue hey?

Sir Pet. Wild! Ah! my old friend, I grieve for your disappointment there ; he's a lost young man, indeed. However, his brother will make you amends ; Joseph is, indeed, what a youth should be—every body in the world speaks well of him.

Sir Oliv. I am sorry to hear it; he has too good a character to be an honest fellow. Every body speaks well of him ! Psha! then he has bowed as low to knaves and fools as to the honest dignity of genius and virtue.

Sir Pet. What, Sir Oliver! do you blame him for not making enemies ?

Sir Oliv. Yes, if he has merit enough to deserve them.

Sir Pet. Well, well—you'll be convinced when you know him. 'Tis edification to hear him converse ; he professes the noblest sentiments.

Sir Oliv. Oh, plague of his sentiments! If he salutes me with a scrap of morality in his mouth, I shall be sick directly. But, however, don't mistake me, Sir Peter; I don't mean to defend Charles's errors: but, before I form my judgment of either of them, I intend to make a trial of their hearts;

and my friend Rowley and I have planned something for the purpose.

Row. And Sir Peter shall own for once he has been mis-taken.

Sir Pet. Oh, my life on Joseph's honour!

Sir Oliv. Well—come, give us a bottle of good wine, and we'll drink the lads' health, and tell you our scheme

Sir Pet. *Allons,* then!

Sir Oliv. And don't, Sir Peter, be so severe against your old friend's son. Odds my life! I am not sorry that he has run out of the course a little: for my part, I hate to see prudence clinging to the green suckers of youth; 'tis like ivy round a sapling, and spoils the growth of the tree.

[Exeunt.

ACT III.

Scene I.—*A Room in* Sir Peter Teazle's *House.*

Enter Sir Peter Teazle, Sir Oliver Surface, *and* Rowley

Sir Pet. Well, then, we will see this fellow first, and have our wine afterwards But how is this, Master Rowley? I don't see the jet of your scheme.

Row. Why, sir, this Mr. Stanley, whom I was speaking of, is nearly related to them by their mother. He was once a mer-chant in Dublin, but has been ruined by a series of unde-served misfortunes. He has applied, by letter, since his con-finement, both to Mr. Surface and Charles: from the former he has received nothing but evasive promises of future service, while Charles has done all that his extravagance has left him power to do; and he is, at this time, endeavouring to raise a sum of money, part of which, in the midst of his own dis-tresses, I know he intends for the service of poor Stanley.

Sir Oliv. Ah! he is my brother's son.

Sir Pet. Well, but how is Sir Oliver personally to——

Row. Why, sir, I will inform Charles and his brother that Stanley has obtained permission to apply personally to his friends; and, as they have neither of them ever seen him, let Sir Oliver assume his character, and he will have a fair oppor-tunity of judging, at least, of the benevolence of their dispo-sitions: and believe me, sir, you will find in the youngest brother one who, in the midst of folly and dissipation, has still, as our immortal bard expresses it,—

> "a heart to pity, and a hand,
> Open as day, for melting charity."

Sir Pet Psha! What signifies his having an open hand or purse either, when he has nothing left to give? Well, well, make the trial, if you please. But where is the fellow whom you brought for Sir Oliver to examine, relative to Charles's affairs?

Row. Below, waiting his commands, and no one can give him better intelligence.—This, Sir Oliver, is a friendly Jew, who, to do him justice, has done every thing in his power to bring your nephew to a proper sense of his extravagance.

Sir Pet. Pray let us have him in.

Row. Desire Mr. Moses to walk up stairs.

　　　　　　　　　　　　　　　[Calls to SERVANT.

Sir Pet. But, pray, why should you suppose he will speak the truth?

Row. Oh, I have convinced him that he has no chance of recovering certain sums advanced to Charles but through the bounty of Sir Oliver, who he knows is arrived; so that you may depend on his fidelity to his own interests. I have also another evidence in my power, one Snake, whom I have de-tected in a matter little short of forgery, and shall shortly produce to remove some of your prejudices, Sir Peter, relative to Charles and Lady Teazle.

Sir Pet. I have heard too much on that subject.

Row. Here comes the honest Israelite.

Enter MOSES

—This is Sir Oliver.

Sir Oliv. Sir, I understand you have lately had great deal-ings with my nephew Charles.

Mos. Yes, Sir Oliver, I have done all I could for him; but he was ruined before he came to me for assistance.

Sir Oliv. That was unlucky, truly; for you have had no opportunity of showing your talents.

Mos. None at all; I hadn't the pleasure of knowing his distresses till he was some thousands worse than nothing.

Sir Oliv. Unfortunate, indeed! But I suppose you have done all in your power for him, honest Moses?

Mos. Yes, he knows that. This very evening I was to have

brought him a gentleman from the city, who does not know him, and will, I believe, advance him some money.

Sir Pet. What, one Charles has never had money from before?

Mos. Yes, Mr. Premium, of Crutched Friars, formerly a broker.

Sir Pet. Egad, Sir Oliver, a thought strikes me!—Charles, you say, does not know Mr. Premium?

Mos. Not at all.

Sir Pet. Now then, Sir Oliver, you may have a better opportunity of satisfying yourself than by an old romancing tale of a poor relation: go with my friend Moses, and represent Premium, and then, I'll answer for it, you'll see your nephew in all his glory.

Sir Oliv. Egad, I like this idea better than the other, and I may visit Joseph afterwards as old Stanley.

Sir Pet. True—so you may.

Row. Well, this is taking Charles rather at a disadvantage, to be sure. However, Moses, you understand Sir Peter, and will be faithful?

Mos. You may depend upon me.—[*Looks at his watch.*] This is near the time I was to have gone.

Sir Oliv. I'll accompany you as soon as you please, Moses ——But hold! I have forgot one thing—how the plague shall I be able to pass for a Jew?

Mos. There's no need—the principal is Christian.

Sir Oliv. Is he? I'm very sorry to hear it. But, then again, an't I rather too smartly dressed to look like a money lender?

Sir Pet. Not at all; 'twould not be out of character, if you went in your own carriage—would it, Moses?

Mos. Not in the least.

Sir Oliv. Well, but how must I talk? there's certainly some cant of usury and mode of treating that I ought to know

Sir Pet. Oh, there's not much to learn. The great point, as I take it, is to be exorbitant enough in your demands. Hey, Moses?

Mos. Yes, that's a very great point.

Sir Oliv. I'll answer for't I'll not be wanting in that I'll ask him eight or ten per cent. on the loan, at least.

Mos. If you ask him no more than that, you'll be discovered immediately.

Sir Oliv. Hey! what, the plague! how much then?

Mos. That depends upon the circumstances. If he appears not very anxious for the supply, you should require only forty or fifty per cent.; but if you find him in great distress, and want the moneys very bad, you may ask double.

Sir Pet. A good honest trade you 're learning, Sir Oliver!

Sir Oliv. Truly, I think so—and not unprofitable.

Mos. Then, you know, you haven't the moneys yourself, but are forced to borrow them for him of a friend.

Sir Oliv. Oh! I borrow it of a friend, do I?

Mos. And your friend is an unconscionable dog: but you can't help that.

Sir Oliv. My friend an unconscionable dog, is he?

Mos. Yes, and he himself has not the moneys by him, but is forced to sell stock at a great loss.

Sir Oliv. He is forced to sell stock at a great loss, is he? Well, that 's very kind of him.

Sir Pet. I' faith, Sir Oliver—Mr. Premium, I mean—you 'll soon be master of the trade. But, Moses! would not you have him run out a little against the annuity bill? That would be in character, I should think.

Mos. Very much.

Row. And lament that a young man now must be at years of discretion before he is suffered to ruin himself?

Mos. Ay, great pity!

Sir Pet. And abuse the public for allowing merit to an act whose only object is to snatch misfortune and imprudence from the rapacious gripe of usury, and give the minor a chance of inheriting his estate without being undone by coming into possession.

Sir Oliv. So, so—Moses shall give me farther instructions as we go together.

Sir Pet. You will not have much time, for your nephew lives hard by.

Sir Oliv. Oh, never fear! my tutor appears so able, that though Charles lived in the next street, it must be my own fault if I am not a complete rogue before I turn the corner.

[*Exit with* MOSES.

Sir Pet. So, now, I think Sir Oliver will be convinced: you are partial, Rowley, and would have prepared Charles for the other plot.

Row No, upon my word, Sir Peter

I

Sir Pet. Well, go bring me this Snake, and I 'll hear what he has to say presently. I see Maria, and want to speak with her.—[*Exit* ROWLEY.] I should be glad to be convinced my suspicions of Lady Teazle and Charles were unjust. I have never yet opened my mind on this subject to my friend Joseph —I am determined I will do it—he will give me his opinion sincerely.

Enter MARIA.

So, child, has Mr. Surface returned with you?

Mar. No, sir; he was engaged.

Sir Pet. Well, Maria, do you not reflect, the more you converse with that amiable young man, what return his partiality for you deserves?

Mar. Indeed, Sir Peter, your frequent importunity on this subject distresses me extremely—you compel me to declare, that I know no man who has ever paid me a particular attention whom I would not prefer to Mr. Surface.

Sir Pet. So—here's perverseness! No, no, Maria, 'tis Charles only whom you would prefer. 'Tis evident his vices and follies have won your heart.

Mar. This is unkind, sir. You know I have obeyed you in neither seeing nor corresponding with him: I have heard enough to convince me that he is unworthy my regard. Yet I cannot think it culpable, if, while my understanding severely condemns his vices, my heart suggests some pity for his distresses.

Sir Pet. Well, well, pity him as much as you please; but give your heart and hand to a worthier object.

Mar. Never to his brother!

Sir Pet. Go, perverse and obstinate! But take care, madam; you have never yet known what the authority of a guardian is: don't compel me to inform you of it.

Mar. I can only say, you shall not have just reason. 'Tis true, by my father's will, I am for a short period bound to regard you as his substitute; but must cease to think you so, when you would compel me to be miserable. [*Exit.*

Sir Pet. Was ever man so crossed as I am, every thing conspiring to fret me! I had not been involved in matrimony a fortnight, before her father, a hale and hearty man, died, on purpose, I believe, for the pleasure of plaguing me with the care of his daughter.—[*Lady Teazle sings without.*] But here comes my helpmate! She appears in great good humour

How happy I should be if I could tease her into loving me, though but a little!

Enter LADY TEAZLE.

Lady Teaz. Lud! Sir Peter, I hope you haven't been quarrelling with Maria? It is not using me well to be ill-humoured when I am not by.

Sir Pet. Ah, Lady Teazle, you might have the power to make me good humoured at all times.

Lady Teaz. I am sure I wish I had; for I want you to be in a charming sweet temper at this moment. Do be good humoured now, and let me have two hundred pounds, will you?

Sir Pet. Two hundred pounds; what an't I to be in a good humour without paying for it! But speak to me thus, and i'faith there's nothing I could refuse you. You shall have it; but seal me a bond for the repayment.

Lady Teaz. Oh, no—there—my note of hand will do as well

[*Offering her hand.*

Sir Pet. And you shall no longer reproach me with not giving you an independent settlement. I mean shortly to surprise you: but shall we always live thus, hey?

Lady Teaz. If you please. I'm sure I don't care how soon we leave off quarrelling, provided you'll own you were tired first.

Sir Pet. Well—then let our future contest be, who shall be most obliging.

Lady Teaz. I assure you, Sir Peter, good nature becomes you. You look now as you did before we were married, when you used to walk with me under the elms, and tell me stories of what a gallant you were in your youth, and chuck me under the chin, you would; and ask me if I thought I could love an old fellow, who would deny me nothing—didn't you?

Sir Pet. Yes, yes, and you were as kind and attentive——

Lady Teaz. Ay, so I was, and would always take your part, when my acquaintance used to abuse you, and turn you into ridicule.

Sir Pet. Indeed!

Lady Teaz. Ay, and when my cousin Sophy has called you a stiff, peevish old bachelor, and laughed at me for thinking of marrying one who might be my father, I have always defended you, and said, I didn't think you so ugly by any means.

Sir Pet. Thank you.

Lady Teaz. And I dared say you'd make a very good sort of a husband.

Sir Pet. And you prophesied right; and we shall now be the happiest couple——

Lady Teaz. And never differ again?

Sir Pet. No, never!—though at the same time, indeed, my dear Lady Teazle, you must watch your temper very seriously; for in all our little quarrels, my dear, if you recollect, my love, you always began first.

Lady Teaz. I beg your pardon, my dear Sir Peter: indeed, you always gave the provocation.

Sir Pet. Now see, my angel! take care—contradicting isn't the way to keep friends.

Lady Teaz. Then don't you begin it, my love!

Sir Pet. There, now! you—you are going on. You don't perceive, my life, that you are just doing the very thing which you know always makes me angry.

Lady Teaz. Nay, you know if you will be angry without any reason, my dear——

Sir Pet. There! now you want to quarrel again.

Lady Teaz. No, I'm sure I don't: but, if you will be so peevish——

Sir Pet. There now! who begins first?

Lady Teaz. Why, you, to be sure. I said nothing—but there's no bearing your temper.

Sir Pet. No, no, madam: the fault's in your own temper.

Lady Teaz. Ay, you are just what my cousin Sophy said you would be.

Sir Pet. Your cousin Sophy is a forward, impertinent gipsy.

Lady Teaz. You are a great bear, I'm sure, to abuse my relations.

Sir Pet. Now may all the plagues of marriage be doubled on me, if ever I try to be friends with you any more!

Lady Teaz. So much the better.

Sir Pet. No, no, madam: 'tis evident you never cared a pin for me, and I was a madman to marry you—a pert, rural coquette, that had refused half the honest 'squires in the neighbourhood!

Lady Teaz. And I am sure I was a fool to marry you—an old dangling bachelor, who was single at fifty, only because he never could meet with any one who would have him.

Sir Pet. Ay, ay, madam; but you were pleased enough to listen to me: you never had such an offer before.

Lady Teaz. No! didn't I refuse Sir Tivy Terrier, who every body said would have been a better match? for his estate is just as good as yours, and he has broke his neck since we have been married.

Sir Pet. I have done with you, madam! You are an unfeeling, ungrateful—but there's an end of every thing. I believe you capable of every thing that is bad. Yes, madam, I now believe the reports relative to you and Charles, madam. Yes, madam, you and Charles are, not without grounds——

Lady Teaz. Take care, Sir Peter! you had better not insinuate any such thing! I'll not be suspected without cause, I promise you.

Sir Pet. Very well, madam! very well! A separate maintenance as soon as you please. Yes, madam, or a divoore! I'll make an example of myself for the benefit of all old bachelors. Let us separate, madam.

Lady Teaz. Agreed! agreed! And now, my dear Sir Peter, we are of a mind once more, we may be the happiest couple, and never differ again, you know: ha! ha! ha! Well, you are going to be in a passion, I see, and I shall only interrupt you—so, bye! bye! *Exit.*

Sir Pet. Plagues and tortures! can't I make her angry either! Oh, I am the most miserable fellow! But I'll not bear her presuming to keep her temper: no! she may break my heart, but she shan't keep her temper *[Exit*

SCENE II.—*A Room in* CHARLES SURFACE's *House.*

Enter TRIP, MOSES, *and* SIR OLIVER SURFACE.

Trip. Here, Master Moses! if you'll stay a moment, I'll try whether—what's the gentleman's name?

Sir Oliv. Mr. Moses, what is my name? [*Aside to* MOSES

Mos. Mr. Premium.

Trip. Premium—very well. [*Exit, taking snuff.*

Sir Oliv. To judge by the servants, one wouldn't believe the master was ruined. But what!—sure, this was my brother's house?

Mos. Yes, sir; Mr. Charles bought it of Mr. Joseph, with the furniture, pictures, &c., just as the old gentleman left it. Sir Peter thought it a piece of extravagance in him.

Sir Oliv. In my mind, the other's economy in selling it to him was more reprehensible by half.

Re-enter TRIP.

Trip. My master says you must wait, gentlemen: he has company, and can't speak with you yet.

Sir Oliv. If he knew who it was wanted to see him, perhaps he would not send such a message?

Trip. Yes, yes, sir; he knows you are here—I did not forget little Premium: no, no, no.

Sir Oliv. Very well; and I pray, sir, what may be your name?

Trip. Trip, sir; my name is Trip, at your service.

Sir Oliv. Well, then, Mr. Trip, you have a pleasant sort of place here, I guess?

Trip. Why, yes—here are three or four of us pass our time agreeably enough; but then our wages are sometimes a little in arrear—and not very great either—but fifty pounds a year, and find our own bags and bouquets.

Sir Oliv. Bags and bouquets! halters and bastinadoes!
                                    [*Aside.*

Trip. And *à propos*, Moses, have you been able to get me that little bill discounted?

Sir Oliv. Wants to raise money too!—mercy on me! Has his distresses too, I warrant, like a lord, and affects creditors and duns.   [*Aside*

Mos. 'Twas not to be done, indeed, Mr. Trip.

Trip. Good lack, you surprise me! My friend Brush has indorsed it, and I thought when he put his name at the back of a bill 'twas the same as cash.

Mos. No, 'twouldn't do.

Trip. A small sum—but twenty pounds. Hark'ee, Moses, do you think you couldn't get it me by way of annuity?

Sir Oliv. An annuity! ha! ha! a footman raise money by way of annuity! Well done, luxury, egad!   [*Aside.*

Mos. Well, but you must insure your place.

Trip. Oh, with all my heart! I'll insure my place, and my life too, if you please.

Sir Oliv. It's more than I would your neck.   [*Aside.*

Mos. But is there nothing you could deposit?

Trip. Why, nothing capital of my master's wardrobe has dropped lately; but I could give you a mortgage on some of his winter clothes, with equity of redemption before November —or you shall have the reversion of the French velvet, or a post-obit on the blue and silver;—these, I should think, Moses, with a few pair of point ruffles, as a collateral security—hey, my little fellow?

Mos. Well, well.   [*Bell rings.*

Trip. Egad, I heard the bell! I believe, gentlemen, I can now introduce you. Don't forget the annuity, little Moses! This way, gentlemen, I'll insure my place, you know.

Sir Oliv. [*Aside.*] If the man be a shadow of the master, this is the temple of dissipation indeed!   [*Exeunt.*

SCENE III.—*Another Room in the same.*

CHARLES SURFACE, SIR HARRY BUMPER, CARELESS, *and* GEN-TLEMEN, *discovered drinking.*

Chas. Surf. 'Fore heaven, 'tis true!—there's the great de-generacy of the age. Many of our acquaintance have taste, spirit, and politeness; but, plague on't, they won't drink.

Care. It is so, indeed, Charles! they give into all the sub-stantial luxuries of the table, and abstain from nothing but wine and wit. Oh, certainly society suffers by it intolerably! for now, instead of the social spirit of raillery that used to mantle over a glass of bright Burgundy, their conversation is be-come just like the Spa-water they drink, which has all the pert-ness and flatulency of champagne, without its spirit or flavour.

1 Gent. But what are they to do who love play better than wine?

Care. True! there's Sir Harry diets himself for gaming, and is now under a hazard regimen.

Chas. Surf. Then he'll have the worst of it. What! you wouldn't train a horse for the course by keeping him from corn? For my part, egad, I am never so successful as when I am a little merry: let me throw on a bottle of champagne, and I never lose.

All. Hey, what?

Care At least I never feel my losses, which is exactly the same thing.

2 Gent. Ay, that I believe.

Chas. Surf. And then, what man can pretend to be a be-liever in love, who is an abjurer of wine? 'Tis the test by which the lover knows his own heart. Fill a dozen bumpers to a dozen beauties, and she that floats at the top is the maid that has bewitched you.

Care. Now then, Charles, be honest, and give us your real favourite.

Chas. Surf. Why, I have withheld her only in compassion

to you.   If I toast her, you must give a round of her peers,
which is impossible—on earth.

Care. Oh! then we'll find some canonised vestals or heathen
goddesses that will do, I warrant!

Chas. Surf. Here then, bumpers, you rogues! bumpers!
Maria! Maria!——

Sir Har. Maria who?

Chas. Surf. Oh, damn the surname!—'tis too formal to be
registered in Love's calendar—Maria!

All. Maria!

Chas. Surf. But now, Sir Harry, beware, we must have
beauty superlative.

Care. Nay, never study, Sir Harry: we'll stand to the
toast, though your mistress should want an eye, and you know
you have a song will excuse you.

Sir Har. Egad, so I have! and I'll give him the song instead of the lady.   [*Sings*

> Here's to the maiden of bashful fifteen;
>   Here's to the widow of fifty;
> Here's to the flaunting extravagant quean,
>   And here's to the housewife that's thrifty.
>
> *Chorus.*   Let the toast pass,—
>   Drink to the lass,
> I'll warrant she'll prove an excuse for the glass.
>
> Here's to the charmer whose dimples we prize;
>   Now to the maid who has none, sir:
> Here's to the girl with a pair of blue eyes,
>   And here's to the nymph with but one, sir.
>
> *Chorus.*   Let the toast pass, &c.
>
> Here's to the maid with a bosom of snow:
>   Now to her that's as brown as a berry:
> Here's to the wife with a face full of woe,
>   And now to the damsel that's merry.
>
> *Chorus.*   Let the toast pass, &c.
>
> For let 'em be clumsy, or let 'em be slim,
>   Young or ancient, I care not a feather;
> So fill a pint bumper quite up to the brim,
> So fill up your glasses, nay, fill to the brim,
>   And let us e'en toast them together.
>
> *Chorus.*   Let the toast pass, &c.

All. Bravo! bravo!

Enter TRIP, *and whispers* CHARLES SURFACE.

Chas. Surf. Gentlemen, you must excuse me a little.—
Careless, take the chair, will you?

Care. Nay, pr'ythee, Charles, what now? This is one of
your peerless beauties, I suppose, has dropped in by chance?

Chas. Surf. No, faith! To tell you the truth, 'tis a Jew and a broker, who are come by appointment.

Care. Oh, damn it! let's have the Jew in.

1 Gent. Ay, and the broker too, by all means.

2 Gent. Yes, yes, the Jew and the broker.

Chas. Surf. Egad, with all my heart!—Trip, bid the gentlemen walk in.—[*Exit* TRIP.] Though there's one of them a stranger, I can tell you.

Care. Charles, let us give them some generous Burgundy, and perhaps they'll grow conscientious.

Chas. Surf. Oh, hang 'em, no! wine does but draw forth a man's natural qualities; and to make them drink would only be to whet their knavery.

Re-enter TRIP, *with* SIR OLIVER SURFACE *and* MOSES.

Chas. Surf. So, honest Moses; walk in, pray, Mr. Premium —that's the gentleman's name, isn't it, Moses?

Mos. Yes, sir.

Chas. Surf. Set chairs, Trip.—Sit down, Mr. Premium.— Glasses, Trip.—[TRIP *gives chairs and glasses, and exit.*] Sit down, Moses.—Come, Mr. Premium, I'll give you a sentiment; here's *Success to usury!*—Moses, fill the gentleman a bumper.

Mos. Success to usury!   [*Drinks*

Care. Right, Moses—usury is prudence and industry, and deserves to succeed.

Sir Oliv. Then here's—All the success it deserves! [*Drinks*

Care. No, no, that won't do! Mr. Premium, you have demurred at the toast, and must drink it in a pint bumper.

1 Gent. A pint bumper, at least.

Mos. Oh, pray, sir, consider—Mr. Premium's a gentleman.

Care. And therefore loves good wine.

2 Gent. Give Moses a quart glass—this is mutiny, and a high contempt for the chair.

Care. Here, now for't! I'll see justice done, to the last drop of my bottle.

Sir Oliv. Nay, pray, gentlemen—I did not expect this usage.

Chas. Surf. No, hang it, you shan't; Mr. Premium's a stranger.

Sir Oliv. Odd! I wish I was well out of their company.
                                                          [*Aside.*

Care. Plague on 'em then! if they won't drink, we'll not sit down with them. Come, Harry, the dice are in the next room.—Charles, you'll join us when you have finished your business with the gentlemen?

Chas. Surf. I will! I will!—[*Exeunt* SIR HARRY BUMPER *and* GENTLEMEN; CARELESS *following.*] Careless!

Care. [*Returning.*] Well!

Chas. Surf. Perhaps I may want you.

Care. Oh, you know I am always ready: word, note, or bond, 'tis all the same to me.   [*Exit.*

Mos. Sir, this is Mr. Premium, a gentleman of the strictest honour and secrecy; and always performs what he undertakes. Mr. Premium, this is——

Chas. Surf. Psha! have done. Sir, my friend Moses is a very honest fellow, but a little slow at expression: he'll be an hour giving us our titles. Mr. Premium, the plain state of the matter is this: I am an extravagant young fellow who wants to borrow money; you I take to be a prudent old fellow, who have got money to lend. I am blockhead enough to give fifty per cent. sooner than not have it; and you, I presume, are rogue enough to take a hundred if you can get it. Now, sir, you see we are acquainted at once, and may proceed to business without farther ceremony

Sir Oliv. Exceeding frank, upon my word. I see, sir, you are not a man of many compliments.

Chas. Surf. Oh, no, sir! plain dealing in business I always think best.

Sir Oliv. Sir, I like you the better for it. However, you are mistaken in one thing; I have no money to lend, but I believe I could procure some of a friend; but then he's an unconscionable dog. Isn't he, Moses? And must sell stock to accommodate you. Mustn't he, Moses?

Mos. Yes, indeed! You know I always speak the truth, and scorn to tell a lie!

Chas. Surf. Right. People that speak truth generally do. But these are trifles, Mr. Premium. What! I know money isn't to be bought without paying for 't!

Sir Oliv. Well, but what security could you give? You have no land, I suppose?

Chas. Surf. Not a mole-hill, nor a twig, but what's in the bough-pots out of the window!

Sir Oliv. Nor any stock, I presume?

Chas. Surf. Nothing but live stock—and that's only a few pointers and ponies. But pray, Mr. Premium, are you acquainted at all with any of my connexions?

Sir Oliv. Why, to say truth, I am.

Chas. Surf. Then you must know that I have a devilish rich uncle in the East Indies, Sir Oliver Surface, from whom I have the greatest expectations?

Sir Oliv. That you have a wealthy uncle, I have heard; but how your expectations will turn out is more, I believe, than you can tell.

Chas. Surf. Oh, no!—there can be no doubt. They tell me I'm a prodigious favourite, and that he talks of leaving me every thing.

Sir Oliv. Indeed! this is the first I've heard of it.

Chas. Surf. Yes, yes, 'tis just so. Moses knows 'tis true; don't you, Moses?

Mos. Oh, yes! I'll swear to 't.

Sir Oliv. Egad, they'll persuade me presently I'm at Bengal.   [*Aside.*

Chas. Surf. Now I propose, Mr. Premium, if it's agreeable to you, a post-obit on Sir Oliver's life: though at the same time the old fellow has been so liberal to me, that I give you my word, I should be very sorry to hear that any thing had happened to him.

Sir Oliv. Not more than I should, I assure you. But the bond you mention happens to be just the worst security you could offer me—for I might live to a hundred and never see the principal.

Chas. Surf. Oh, yes, you would! the moment Sir Oliver dies, you know, you would come on me for the money.

Sir Oliv. Then I believe I should be the most unwelcome dun you ever had in your life.

Chas. Surf. What! I suppose you're afraid that Sir Oliver is too good a life?

Sir Oliv. No, indeed I am not; though I have heard he is as hale and healthy as any man of his years in Christendom.

Chas. Surf. There again, now, you are misinformed. No, no, the climate has hurt him considerably, poor uncle Oliver. Yes, yes, he breaks apace, I'm told—and is so much altered lately that his nearest relations would not know him

Sir Oliv. No! Ha! ha! ha! so much altered lately that his nearest relations would not know him! Ha! ha! ha! egad—ha! ha! ha!

Chas. Surf. Ha! ha!—you're glad to hear that, little Premium?

Sir Oliv. No, no, I'm not.

Chas. Surf. Yes, yes, you are—ha! ha! ha!—you know that mends your chance.

Sir Oliv. But I'm told Sir Oliver is coming over; nay, some say he is actually arrived.

Chas. Surf. Psha! sure I must know better than you whether he's come or not. No, no, rely on't he's at this moment at Calcutta. Isn't he, Moses?

Mos. Oh, yes, certainly.

Sir Oliv. Very true, as you say, you must know better than I, though I have it from pretty good authority Haven't I, Moses?

Mos. Yes, most undoubted!

Sir Oliv. But, sir, as I understand you want a few hundreds immediately, is there nothing you could dispose of?

Chas. Surf. How do you mean?

Sir Oliv. For instance, now, I have heard that your father left behind him a great quantity of massy old plate.

Chas. Surf O Lud! that's gone long ago. Moses can tell you how better than I can.

Sir Oliv. [*Aside.*] Good lack! all the family race-cups and corporation-bowls!—[*Aloud.*] Then it was also supposed that his library was one of the most valuable and compact.

Chas. Surf. Yes, yes, so it was—vastly too much so for a private gentleman. For my part, I was always of a communicative disposition, so I thought it a shame to keep so much knowledge to myself.

Sir Oliv. [*Aside.*] Mercy upon me! learning that had run in the family like an heir-loom!—[*Aloud.*] Pray, what are become of the books?

Chas. Surf. You must inquire of the auctioneer, Master Premium, for I don't believe even Moses can direct you

Mos. I know nothing of books.

Sir Oliv. So, so, nothing of the family property left, I suppose?

Chas. Surf. Not much, indeed; unless you have a mind to the family pictures. I have got a room full of ancestors above: and if you have a taste for old paintings, egad, you shall have 'em a bargain!

Sir Oliv. Hey! what the devil! sure, you wouldn't sell your forefathers, would you?

Chas. Surf. Every man of them, to the best bidder.

Sir Oliv. What! your great-uncles and aunts?

Chas. Surf. Ay, and my great-grandfathers and grand-mothers too.

Sir Oliv. [*Aside.*] Now I give him up!—[*Aloud.*] What the plague, have you no bowels for your own kindred? Odd's life! do you take me for Shylock in the play, that you would raise money of me on your own flesh and blood?

Chas. Surf. Nay, my little broker, don't be angry: what need you care, if you have your money's worth?

Sir Oliv Well, I'll be the purchaser: I think I can dispose of the family canvas.—[*Aside.*] Oh, I'll never forgive him this! never!

Re-enter CARELESS.

Care. Come, Charles, what keeps you?

Chas. Surf. I can't come yet. I'faith, we are going to have a sale above stairs; here's little Premium will buy all my ancestors!

Care. Oh, burn your ancestors!

Chas. Surf. No, he may do that afterwards, if he pleases. Stay, Careless, we want you: egad, you shall be auctioneer—so come along with us.

Care. Oh, have with you, if that's the case. I can handle a hammer as well as a dice-box! Going! going!

Sir Oliv. Oh, the profligates! [*Aside.*

Chas. Surf. Come, Moses, you shall be appraiser, if we want one. Gad's life, little Premium, you don't seem to like the business?

Sir Oliv. Oh, yes, I do, vastly! Ha! ha! ha! yes, yes, I think it a rare joke to sell one's family by auction—ha! ha!— [*Aside.*] Oh, the prodigal!

Chas. Surf. To be sure! when a man wants money, where the plague should he get assistance, if he can't make free with his own relations? [*Exeunt.*

Sir Oliv. I'll never forgive him; never! never!

ACT IV.

SCENE I.—*A Picture Room in* CHARLES SURFACE's *House.*

Enter CHARLES SURFACE, SIR OLIVER SURFACE, MOSES, *and* CARELESS.

Chas. Surf. Walk in, gentlemen, pray walk in;—here they are, the family of the Surfaces, up to the Conquest.

Sir Oliv And, in my opinion, a goodly collection.

Chas. Surf. Ay, ay, these are done in the true spirit of portrait-painting; no *volontière grace* or expression. Not like the works of your modern Raphaels, who give you the strongest resemblance, yet contrive to make your portrait independent of you; so that you may sink the original and not hurt the picture. No, no; the merit of these is the inveterate likeness—all stiff and awkward as the originals, and like nothing in human nature besides.

Sir Oliv. Ah! we shall never see such figures of men again.

Chas. Surf. I hope not Well, you see, Master Premium, what a domestic character I am; here I sit of an evening surrounded by my family. But come, get to your pulpit, Mr. Auctioneer; here's an old gouty chair of my grandfather's will answer the purpose.

Care. Ay, ay, this will do. But, Charles, I haven't a hammer; and what's an auctioneer without his hammer?

Chas. Surf. Egad, that's true. What parchment have we here? Oh, our genealogy in full. [*Taking pedigree down.*] Here, Careless, you shall have no common bit of mahogany, here's the family tree for you, you rogue! This shall be your hammer, and now you may knock down my ancestors with their own pedigree.

Sir Oliv. What an unnatural rogue!—an *ex post facto* parricide! [*Aside.*

Care. Yes, yes, here's a list of your generation indeed;—faith, Charles, this is the most convenient thing you could have found for the business, for 'twill not only serve as a hammer, but a catalogue into the bargain. Come, begin—A-going, a-going, a-going!

Chas. Surf. Bravo, Careless! Well, here's my great-uncle, Sir Richard Raveline, a marvellous good general in his day. I assure you. He served in all the Duke of Marlborough's wars, and got that cut over his eye at the battle of Malplaquet. What say you, Mr. Premium? look at him—there's a hero! not cut out of his feathers, as your modern clipped captains are, but enveloped in wig and regimentals, as a general should be.   What do you bid?

Sir Oliv. [*Aside to Moses.*] Bid him speak.

Mos. Mr. Premium would have you speak.

Chas. Surf. Why, then, he shall have him for ten pounds, and I 'm sure that 's not dear for a staff-officer.

Sir Oliv. [*Aside.*] Heaven deliver me! his famous uncle Richard for ten pounds!—[*Aloud.*] Very well, sir, I take him at that.

Chas. Surf. Careless, knock down my uncle Richard.— Here, now, is a maiden sister of his, my great-aunt Deborah, done by Kneller, in his best manner, and esteemed a very formidable likeness.   There she is, you see, a shepherdess feeding her flock.   You shall have her for five pounds ten— the sheep are worth the money.

Sir Oliv. [*Aside.*] Ah! poor Deborah! a woman who set such a value on herself!—[*Aloud.*] Five pounds ten—she 's mine

Chas. Surf. Knock down my aunt Deborah!   Here, now, are two that were a sort of cousins of theirs.—You see, Moses, these pictures were done some time ago, when beaux wore wigs, and the ladies their own hair.

Sir Oliv. Yes, truly, head-dresses appear to have been a little lower in those days.

Chas. Surf Well, take that couple for the same.

Mos. 'Tis a good bargain.

Chas. Surf. Careless!—This, now, is a grandfather of my mother's, a learned judge, well known on the western circuit.—What do you rate him at, Moses?

Mos. Four guineas.

Chas. Surf. Four guineas!   Gad's life, you don't bid me the price of his wig.—Mr. Premium, you have more respect for the woolsack; do let us knock his lordship down at fifteen.

Sir Oliv. By all means.

Care. Gone!

Chas. Surf. And there are two brothers of his, William and Walter Blunt, Esquires, both members of parliament, and noted speakers; and, what 's very extraordinary, I believe, this is the first time they were ever bought or sold.

Sir Oliv. That is very extraordinary, indeed!   I 'll take them at your own price, for the honour of parliament.

Care. Well said, little Premium! I'll knock them down at forty.

Chas. Surf. Here's a jolly fellow—I don't know what relation, but he was mayor of Norwich: take him at eight pounds.

Sir Oliv. No, no; six will do for the mayor.

Chas. Surf. Come, make it guineas, and I'll throw you the two aldermen there into the bargain.

Sir Oliv. They're mine.

Chas. Surf. Careless, knock down the mayor and alder men. But, plague on't! we shall be all day retailing in this manner; do let us deal wholesale: what say you, little Premium? Give me three hundred pounds for the rest of the family in the lump.

Care. Ay, ay, that will be the best way.

Sir Oliv. Well, well, any thing to accommodate you; they are mine. But there is one portrait which you have always passed over.

Care. What, that ill-looking little fellow over the settee?

Sir Oliv. Yes, sir, I mean that; though I don't think him so ill-looking a little fellow, by any means.

Chas. Surf. What, that? Oh; that's my uncle Oliver! 'twas done before he went to India.

Care. Your uncle Oliver! Gad, then you'll never be friends, Charles. That, now, to me, is as stern a looking rogue as ever I saw; an unforgiving eye, and a damned disinheriting countenance! an inveterate knave, depend on't. Don't you think so, little Premium?

Sir Oliv. Upon my soul, sir, I do not; I think it is as honest a looking face as any in the room, dead or alive. But I suppose uncle Oliver goes with the rest of the lumber?

Chas. Surf. No, hang it! I'll not part with poor Noll. The old fellow has been very good to me, and, egad, I'll keep his picture while I've a room to put it in

Sir Oliv. [*Aside.*] The rogue's my nephew after all!—[*Aloud.*] But, sir, I have somehow taken a fancy to that picture.

Chas. Surf. I'm sorry for't, for you certainly will not have it. Oons, haven't you got enough of them?

Sir Oliv. [*Aside.*] I forgive him every thing!—[*Aloud.*] But, sir, when I take a whim in my head, I don't value money. I'll give you as much for that as for all the rest.

Chas. Surf. Don't tease me, master broker; I tell you I'll not part with it, and there's an end of it.

Sir Oliv. [*Aside.*] How like his father the dog is!—[*Aloud.*] Well, well, I have done.—[*Aside.*] I did not perceive it before, but I think I never saw such a striking resemblance.—[*Aloud.*] Here is a draught for your sum.

Chas. Surf. Why, 'tis for eight hundred pounds!

Sir Oliv. You will not let Sir Oliver go?

Chas. Surf. Zounds! no! I tell you, once more.

Sir Oliv. Then never mind the difference, we'll balance that another time. But give me your hand on the bargain; you are an honest fellow, Charles—I beg pardon, sir, for being so free.—Come, Moses.

Chas. Surf. Egad, this is a whimsical old fellow!—But hark'ee, Premium, you'll prepare lodgings for these gentlemen.

Sir Oliv. Yes, yes, I'll send for them in a day or two.

Chas. Surf. But hold; do now send a genteel conveyance for them, for, I assure you, they were most of them used to ride in their own carriages.

Sir Oliv. I will, I will—for all but Oliver

Chas. Surf. Ay, all but the little nabob.

Sir Oliv. You're fixed on that?

Chas. Surf. Peremptorily.

Sir Oliv. [*Aside.*] A dear extravagant rogue!—[*Aloud.*] Good day!—Come, Moses.—[*Aside.*] Let me hear now who dares call him profligate!   [*Exit with* MOSES.

Care. Why, this is the oddest genius of the sort I ever met with!

Chas. Surf. Egad, he's the prince of brokers, I think. I wonder how the devil Moses got acquainted with so honest a fellow.—Ha! here's Rowley.—Do, Careless, say I'll join the company in a few moments.

Care. I will—but don't let that old blockhead persuade you to squander any of that money on old musty debts, or any such nonsense; for tradesmen, Charles, are the most exorbitant fellows.

Chas. Surf. Very true, and paying them is only encouraging them.

Care. Nothing else.

Chas. Surf. Ay, ay, never fear.—[*Exit* CARELESS.] So! this was an odd old fellow, indeed. Let me see, two-thirds of these

K

five hundred and thirty odd pounds are mine by right   'Fore
Heaven! I find one's ancestors are more valuable relations
than I took them for!—Ladies and gentlemen, your most
obedient and very grateful servant.

[*Bows ceremoniously to the pictures.*

Enter ROWLEY.

Ha! old Rowley! egad, you are just come in time to take
leave of your old acquaintance.

Row. Yes, I heard they were a-going.   But I wonder you
can have such spirits under so many distresses.

Chas. Surf. Why, there's the point! my distresses are so
many, that I can't afford to part with my spirits; but I shall
be rich and splenetic, all in good time.   However, I suppose
you are surprised that I am not more sorrowful at parting
with so many near relations; to be sure, 'tis very affecting,
but you see they never move a muscle, so why should I?

Row. There's no making you serious a moment.

Chas Surf. Yes, faith, I am so now.   Here, my honest
Rowley, here, get me this changed directly, and take a hundred pounds of it immediately to old Stanley.

Row. A hundred pounds!   Consider only——

Chas. Surf. Gad's life, don't talk about it! poor Stanley's
wants are pressing, and, if you don't make haste, we shall have
some one call that has a better right to the money.

Row. Ah! there's the point!   I never will cease dunning
you with the old proverb——

Chas. Surf. Be just before you're generous.—Why, so I
would if I could; but Justice is an old, hobbling beldame,
and I can't get her to keep pace with Generosity, for the soul
of me.

Row. Yet, Charles, believe me, one hour's reflection——

Chas. Surf. Ay, ay, it's very true; but, hark'ee, Rowley,
while I have, by Heaven I'll give; so, damn your economy!
and now for hazard   [*Exeunt*

SCENE II.—*Another room in the same.*

Enter SIR OLIVER SURFACE *and* MOSES.

Mos. Well, sir, I think, as Sir Peter said, you have seen
Mr. Charles in high glory; 'tis great pity he's so extravagant.

Sir Oliv. True, but he would not sell my picture

Mos. And loves wine and women so much.

Sir Oliv. But he would not sell my picture

Mos. And games so deep.

Sir Oliv. But he would not sell my picture. Oh, here's Rowley

Enter ROWLEY.

Row. So, Sir Oliver, I find you have made a purchase——

Sir Oliv. Yes, yes, our young rake has parted with his ancestors like old tapestry.

Row. And here has he commissioned me to re-deliver you part of the purchase money—I mean, though, in your necessitous character of old Stanley.

Mos. Ah! there is the pity of all; he is so damned chari·table.

Row. And I left a hosier and two tailors in the hall, who, I'm sure, won't be paid, and this hundred would satisfy them.

Sir Oliv. Well, well, I'll pay his debts, and his benevolence too. But now I am no more a broker, and you shall introduce me to the elder brother as old Stanley.

Row. Not yet awhile; Sir Peter, I know, means to call there about this time.

Enter TRIP.

Trip. Oh, gentlemen, I beg pardon for not showing you out: this way—Moses, a word.   [*Exit with* MOSES.

Sir Oliv. There's a fellow for you! Would you believe it, that puppy intercepted the Jew on our coming, and wanted to raise money before he got to his master!

Row. Indeed!

Sir Oliv. Yes, they are now planning an annuity business. Ah, Master Rowley, in my days servants were content with the follies of their masters, when they were worn a little threadbare; but now they have their vices, like their birth-day clothes, with the gloss on.   [*Exeunt*

SCENE III.—*A Library in* JOSEPH SURFACE's *House.*

Enter JOSEPH SURFACE *and* SERVANT.

Jos. Surf. No letter from Lady Teazle?

Ser. No, sir.

Jos. Surf. [*Aside.*] I am surprised she has not sent, if she is prevented from coming. Sir Peter certainly does not suspect me Yet I wish I may not lose the heiress, through the scrape I have drawn myself into with the wife; however, Charles's imprudence and bad character are great points in my favour.   [*Knocking without.*

Ser. Sir, I believe that must be Lady Teazle.

Jos. Surf. Hold! See whether it is or not, before you go to the door: I have a particular message for you if it should be my brother.

Ser. 'Tis her ladyship, sir; she always leaves her chair at the milliner's in the next street.

Jos. Surf. Stay, stay; draw that screen before the window —that will do;—my opposite neighbour is a maiden lady of so curious a temper.—[SERVANT *draws the screen, and exit.*] I have a difficult hand to play in this affair. Lady Teazle has lately suspected my views on Maria; but she must by no means be let into that secret,—at least, till I have her more in my power.

Enter LADY TEAZLE.

Lady Teaz. What, sentiment in soliloquy now? Have you been very impatient? O Lud! don't pretend to look grave. I vow I couldn't come before.

Jos. Surf. O madam, punctuality is a species of constancy very unfashionable in a lady of quality.

                [*Places chairs, and sits after* LADY TEAZLE *is seated.*

Lady Teaz. Upon my word, you ought to pity me. Do you know Sir Peter is grown so ill-natured to me of late, and so jealous of Charles too—that 's the best of the story, isn't it ?

Jos. Surf. I am glad my scandalous friends keep that up.

                                                    [*Aside*

Lady Teaz. I am sure I wish he would let Maria marry him, and then perhaps he would be convinced; don 't you, Mr. Surface?

Jos. Surf. [*Aside.*] Indeed I do not.—[*Aloud.*] Oh, certainly I do! for then my dear Lady Teazle would also be convinced how wrong her suspicions were of my having any design on the silly girl.

Lady Teaz. Well, well, I 'm inclined to believe you. But isn't it provoking, to have the most ill-natured things said of one? And there's my friend Lady Sneerwell has circulated I don't know how many scandalous tales of me, and all without any foundation too; that 's what vexes me.

Jos. Surf. Ay, madam, to be sure, that is the provoking

circumstance — without foundation; yes, yes, there's the mortification, indeed; for, when a scandalous story is believed against one, there certainly is no comfort like the consciousness of having deserved it.

Lady Teaz. No, to be sure, then I'd forgive their malice; but to attack me, who am really so innocent, and who never say an ill-natured thing of any body—that is, of any friend; and then Sir Peter, too, to have him so peevish, and so suspicious, when I know the integrity of my own heart—indeed 'tis monstrous!

Jos. Surf. But, my dear Lady Teazle, 'tis your own fault if you suffer it. When a husband entertains a groundless suspicion of his wife, and withdraws his confidence from her, the original compact is broken, and she owes it to the honour of her sex to endeavour to outwit him.

Lady Teaz. Indeed! So that, if he suspects me without cause, it follows, that the best way of curing his jealousy is to give him reason for 't?

Jos. Surf. Undoubtedly—for your husband should never be deceived in you: and in that case it becomes you to be frail in compliment to his discernment.

Lady Teaz. To be sure, what you say is very reasonable, and when the consciousness of my innocence——

Jos. Surf. Ah, my dear madam, there is the great mistake! 'tis this very conscious innocence that is of the greatest prejudice to you. What is it makes you negligent of forms, and careless of the world's opinion? why, the consciousness of your own innocence. What makes you thoughtless in your conduct, and apt to run into a thousand little imprudences? why, the consciousness of your own innocence. What makes you impatient of Sir Peter's temper, and outrageous at his suspicions? why, the consciousness of your innocence.

Lady Teaz. 'Tis very true!

Jos. Surf. Now, my dear Lady Teazle, if you would but once make a trifling *faux pas*, you can't conceive how cautious you would grow, and how ready to humour and agree with your husband.

Lady Teaz. Do you think so?

Jos. Surf. Oh, I am sure on 't; and then you would find all scandal would cease at once, for—in short, your character at present is like a person in a plethora, absolutely dying from too much health.

Lady Teaz. So, so; then I perceive your prescription is, that I must sin in my own defence, and part with my virtue to preserve my reputation?

Jos. Surf. Exactly so, upon my credit, ma'am.

Lady Teaz. Well, certainly this is the oddest doctrine, and the newest receipt for avoiding calumny!

Jos. Surf. An infallible one, believe me. Prudence, like experience, must be paid for.

Lady Teaz. Why, if my understanding were once convinced——

Jos. Surf. Oh, certainly, madam, your understanding should be convinced. Yes, yes—Heaven forbid I should persuade you to do any thing you thought wrong. No, no, I have too much honour to desire it.

Lady Teaz. Don't you think we may as well leave honour out of the argument?   [*Rises.*

Jos. Surf. Ah, the ill effects of your country education, I see, still remain with you

Lady Teaz. I doubt they do indeed; and I will fairly own to you, that if I could be persuaded to do wrong, it would be by Sir Peter's ill usage sooner than your honourable logic, after all.

Jos. Surf. Then, by this hand, which he is unworthy of——
          [*Taking her hand*

Re-enter SERVANT.

'Sdeath, you blockhead—what do you want?

Ser. I beg your pardon, sir, but I thought you would not choose Sir Peter to come up without announcing him.

Jos. Surf. Sir Peter!—Oons—the devil!

Lady Teaz. Sir Peter! O Lud! I'm ruined! I'm ruined!

Ser. Sir, 'twasn't I let him in.

Lady Teaz. Oh! I'm quite undone! What will become of me? Now, Mr. Logic—Oh! mercy, sir, he's on the stairs—I'll get behind here—and if ever I'm so imprudent again——
          [*Goes behind the screen.*

Jos. Surf. Give me that book.
          [*Sits down.* SERVANT *pretends to adjust his chair.*

Enter SIR PETER TEAZLE.

Sir Pet. Ay, ever improving himself—Mr. Surface, Mr. Surface——   [*Pats* JOSEPH *on the shoulder.*

Jos. Surf. Oh, my dear Sir Peter, I beg your pardon—

[*Gaping, throws away the book.*] I have been dozing over a stupid book. Well, I am much obliged to you for this call. You haven't been here, I believe, since I fitted up this room. Books, you know, are the only things I am a coxcomb in.

Sir Pet. 'Tis very neat indeed. Well, well, that's proper; and you can make even your screen a source of knowledge—hung, I perceive, with maps.

Jos. Surf. Oh, yes, I find great use in that screen.

Sir Pet. I dare say you must, certainly, when you want to find any thing in a hurry.

Jos. Surf. Ay, or to hide any thing in a hurry either.
                                                      [*Aside.*

Sir Pet. Well, I have a little private business——

Jos. Surf. You need not stay.   [*To* SERVANT.

Ser. No, sir.   [*Exit.*

Jos. Surf. Here's a chair, Sir Peter—I beg——

Sir Pet. Well, now we are alone, there is a subject, my dear friend, on which I wish to unburden my mind to you—a point of the greatest moment to my peace; in short, my good friend, Lady Teazle's conduct of late has made me very unhappy.

Jos. Surf. Indeed! I am very sorry to hear it.

Sir Pet. Yes, 'tis but too plain she has not the least regard for me; but, what's worse, I have pretty good authority to suppose she has formed an attachment to another.

Jos. Surf. Indeed! you astonish me!

Sir Pet. Yes! and, between ourselves, I think I've discovered the person.

Jos. Surf. How! you alarm me exceedingly.

Sir Pet. Ay, my dear friend, I knew you would sympathise with me!

Jos. Surf. Yes, believe me, Sir Peter, such a discovery would hurt me just as much as it would you.

Sir Pet. I am convinced of it. Ah! it is a happiness to have a friend whom we can trust even with one's family secrets. But have you no guess who I mean?

Jos. Surf. I haven't the most distant idea. It can't be Sir Benjamin Backbite!

Sir Pet. Oh, no! What say you to Charles?

Jos. Surf. My brother! impossible!

Sir Pet. Oh, my dear friend, the goodness of your own heart misleads you. You judge of others by yourself.

Jos. Surf. Certainly, Sir Peter, the heart that is conscious of its own integrity is ever slow to credit another's treachery.

Sir Pet. True; but your brother has no sentiment—you never hear him talk so.

Jos. Surf. Yet I can't but think Lady Teazle herself has too much principle.

Sir Pet. Ay; but what is principle against the flattery of a handsome, lively young fellow?

Jos. Surf. That's very true.

Sir Pet. And then, you know, the difference o: our ages makes it very improbable that she should have any great affection for me; and if she were to be frail, and I were to make it public, why the town would only laugh at me, the foolish old bachelor, who had married a girl.

Jos. Surf. That's true, to be sure—they would laugh.

Sir Pet. Laugh! ay, and make ballads, and paragraphs, and the devil knows what of me.

Jos. Surf. No, you must never make it public.

Sir Pet. But then again—that the nephew of my old friend, Sir Oliver, should be the person to attempt such a wrong, hurts me more nearly.

Jos. Surf. Ay, there's the point. When ingratitude barbs the dart of injury, the wound has double danger in it.

Sir Pet. Ay—I, that was, in a manner, left his guardian: in whose house he had been so often entertained; who never in my life denied him—my advice!

Jos. Surf. Oh, 'tis not to be credited! There may be a man capable of such baseness, to be sure; but, for my part, till you can give me positive proofs, I cannot but doubt it. However, if it should be proved on him, he is no longer a brother of mine—I disclaim kindred with him: for the man who can break the laws of hospitality, and tempt the wife of his friend, deserves to be branded as the pest of society.

Sir Pet. What a difference there is between you! What noble sentiments!

Jos. Surf. Yet I cannot suspect Lady Teazle's honour.

Sir Pet. I am sure I wish to think well of her, and to remove all ground of quarrel between us. She has lately reproached me more than once with having made no settlement on her; and, in our last quarrel, she almost hinted that she should not break her heart if I was dead. Now, as we seem to differ in our ideas of expense, I have resolved she shall

have her own way, and be her own mistress in that respect
for the future; and, if I were to die, she will find I have not
been inattentive to her interest while living.   Here, my friend,
are the drafts of two deeds, which I wish to have your opinion
on.   By one, she will enjoy eight hundred a year independent while I live; and, by the other, the bulk of my fortune at
my death.

Jos. Surf. This conduct, Sir Peter, is indeed truly gene-
ous.—[*Aside.*] I wish it may not corrupt my pupil.

Sir Pet. Yes, I am determined she shall have no cause to
complain, though I would not have her acquainted with the
latter instance of my affection yet awhile.

Jos. Surf. Nor I, if I could help it.   [*Aside.*

Sir Pet. And now, my dear friend, if you please, we will
talk over the situation of your hopes with Maria.

Jos. Surf. [*Softly.*] Oh, no, Sir Peter; another time, if you
please.

Sir Pet. I am sensibly chagrined at the little progress you
seem to make in her affections.

Jos. Surf. [*Softly.*] I beg you will not mention it.   What
are my disappointments when your happiness is in debate!—
[*Aside.*] 'Sdeath, I shall be ruined every way!   .

Sir Pet. And though you are averse to my acquainting Lady
Teazle with your passion, I 'm sure she 's not your enemy in
the affair.

Jos. Surf. Pray, Sir Peter, now oblige me.   I am really
too much affected by the subject we have been speaking of to
bestow a thought on my own concerns.   The man who is entrusted with his friend's distresses can never——

Re-enter SERVANT.

Well, sir?

Ser. Your brother, sir, is speaking to a gentleman in the
street, and says he knows you are within.

Jos. Surf. 'Sdeath, blockhead, I 'm not within—I 'm out
for the day.

Sir Pet. Stay—hold—a thought has struck me :—you shall
be at home.

Jos. Surf. Well, well, let him up.—[*Exit* SERVANT.] He 'll
interrupt Sir Peter, however.   [*Aside.*

Sir Pet. Now, my good friend, oblige me, I entreat you.
Before Charles comes, let me conceal myself somewhere, then

do you tax him on the point we have been talking, and his
answer may satisfy me at once.

Jos. Surf. Oh, fie, Sir Peter! would you have me join in so
mean a trick?—to trepan my brother too?

Sir Pet. Nay, you tell me you are sure he is innocent; if
so, you do him the greatest service by giving him an opportunity to clear himself, and you will set my heart at rest.
Come, you shall not refuse me: [*Going up,*] here, behind
the screen will be—Hey! what the devil! there seems to be
one listener here already—I 'll swear I saw a petticoat!

Jos. Surf. Ha! ha! ha! Well, this is ridiculous enough.
I 'll tell you, Sir Peter, though I hold a man of intrigue to be
a most despicable character, yet, you know, it does not follow
that one is to be an absolute Joseph either! Hark 'ee, 'tis a
little French milliner, a silly rogue that plagues me; and
having some character to lose, on your coming, sir, she ran behind the screen.

Sir Pet. Ah, Joseph! Joseph! Did I ever think that
you——But, egad, she has overheard all I have been saying of
my wife.

Jos. Surf. Oh, 'twill never go any farther, you may depend
upon it!

Sir Pet. No! then, faith, let her hear it out.—Here 's a
closet will do as well.

Jos. Surf. Well, go in there.

Sir Pet. Sly, rogue! sly rogue!   [*Goes into the closet.*

Jos. Surf. A narrow escape, indeed! and a curious situation
I 'm in, to part man and wife in this manner.

Lady Teaz. [*Peeping.*] Couldn't I steal off?

Jos. Surf. Keep close, my angel!

Sir Pet. [*Peeping.*] Joseph, tax him home.

Jos. Surf. Back, my dear friend!

Lady Teaz. [*Peeping.*] Couldn't you lock Sir Peter in?

Jos. Surf. Be still, my life!

Sir Pet. [*Peeping.*] You 're sure the little milliner won't
blab?

Jos. Surf. In, in, my dear Sir Peter!—'Fore Gad, I wish I
had a key to the door.

Enter CHARLES SURFACE.

Chas. Surf. Holla! brother, what has been the matter?
Your fellow would not let me up at first. What! have you
had a Jew or a wench with you?

Jos. Surf. Neither, brother, I assure you.

Chas. Surf. But what has made Sir Peter steal off? I thought he had been with you.

Jos. Surf. He was, brother; but, hearing you were coming, he did not choose to stay.

Chas. Surf. What! was the old gentleman afraid I wanted to borrow money of him?

Jos. Surf. No, sir: but I am sorry to find, Charles, you have lately given that worthy man grounds for great uneasiness.

Chas. Surf Yes, they tell me I do that to a great many worthy men. But how so, pray?

Jos. Surf. To be plain with you, brother, he thinks you are endeavouring to gain Lady Teazle's affections from him.

Chas. Surf. Who, I? O Lud! not I, upon my word.— Ha! ha! ha! ha! so the old fellow has found out that he has got a young wife, has he?—or, what is worse, Lady Teazle has found out she has an old husband?

Jos. Surf. This is no subject to jest on, brother. He who can laugh——

Chas. Surf. True, true, as you were going to say—then, seriously, I never had the least idea of what you charge me with, upon my honour.

Jos. Surf. Well, it will give Sir Peter great satisfaction to hear this.   [*Raising his voice*

Chas. Surf. To be sure, I once thought the lady seemed to have taken a fancy to me; but, upon my soul, I never gave her the least encouragement. Besides, you know my attachment to Maria.

Jos. Surf. But sure, brother, even if Lady Teazle had betrayed the fondest partiality for you——

Chas. Surf. Why, look 'ee, Joseph, I hope I shall never deliberately do a dishonourable action; but if a pretty woman was purposely to throw herself in my way—and that pretty woman married to a man old enough to be her father——

Jos. Surf. Well!

Chas. Surf. Why, I believe I should be obliged to——

Jos. Surf. What?

Chas. Surf. To borrow a little of your morality, that's all. But, brother, do you know now that you surprise me exceedingly, by naming me with Lady Teazle; for, i'faith, I always understood you were her favourite.

Jos. Surf. Oh, for shame, Charles! This retort is foolish.

Chas. Surf. Nay, I swear I have seen you exchange such significant glances——

Jos. Surf. Nay, nay, sir, this is no jest.

Chas. Surf. Egad, I'm serious! Don't you remember one day, when I called here——

Jos. Surf. Nay, pr'ythee, Charles——

Chas. Surf. And found you together——

Jos. Surf. Zounds, sir, I insist——

Chas. Surf. And another time when your servant——

Jos. Surf. Brother, brother, a word with you!—[*Aside.*] Gad, I must stop him.

Chas. Surf. Informed, I say, that——

Jos. Surf. Hush! I beg your pardon, but Sir Peter has overheard all we have been saying. I knew you would clear yourself, or I should not have consented.

Chas Surf. How, Sir Peter! Where is he?

Jos. Surf. Softly, there! [*Points to the closet.*

Chas. Surf. Oh, 'fore Heaven, I'll have him out Sir Peter, come forth!

Jos. Surf. No, no——

Chas. Surf. I say, Sir Peter, come into court.—[*Pulls in* SIR PETER.] What! my old guardian!—What! turn inquisitor, and take evidence incog.? Oh, fie! Oh, fie!

Sir Pet. Give me your hand, Charles—I believe I have suspected you wrongfully; but you mustn't be angry with oseph—'twas my plan!

Chas. Surf. Indeed!

Sir Pet. But I acquit you. I promise you I don't think near so ill of you as I did: what I have heard has given me great satisfaction.

Chas. Surf. Egad, then, 'twas lucky you didn't hear any more. Wasn't it, Joseph?

Sir Pet. Ah! you would have retorted on him

Chas. Surf. Ah, ay, that was a joke.

Sir Pet. Yes, yes, I know his honour too well.

Chas. Surf. But you might as well have suspected him as me in this matter, for all that. Mightn't he, Joseph?

Sir Pet. Well, well, I believe you.

Jos. Surf. Would they were both out of the room! [*Aside*

Sir Pet. And in future, perhaps, we may not be such strangers.

Re enter SERVANT, *and whispers* JOSEPH SURFACE.

Serv. Lady Sneerwell is below, and says she will come up.

Jos. Surf. Lady Sneerwell! Gad's life! she must not come here. [*Exit* SERVANT.] Gentlemen, I beg pardon—I must wait on you down stairs: here is a person come on particular business.

Chas. Surf. Well, you can see him in another room. Sir Peter and I have not met a long time, and I have something to say to him.

Jos. Surf. [*Aside.*] They must not be left together.—[*Aloud.*] I'll send Lady Sneerwell away, and return directly.—[*Aside to* SIR PETER.] Sir Peter, not a word of the French milliner.

Sir Pet. [*Aside to* JOSEPH SURFACE.] I! not for the world! —[*Exit* JOSEPH SURFACE.] Ah, Charles, if you associated more with your brother, one might indeed hope for your reformation. He is a man of sentiment. Well, there is nothing in the world so noble as a man of sentiment.

Chas. Surf. Psha! he is too moral by half; and so apprehensive of his good name, as he calls it, that I suppose he would as soon let a priest into his house as a wench.

Sir Pet. No, no,—come, come,—you wrong him. No, no! Joseph is no rake, but he is no such saint either, in that respect.—[*Aside.*] I have a great mind to tell him—we should have such a laugh at Joseph.

Chas. Surf. Oh, hang him! he's a very anchorite, a young hermit!

Sir Pet. Hark 'ee—you must not abuse him: he may chance to hear of it again, I promise you.

Chas. Surf. Why, you won't tell him?

Sir Pet. No—but—this way.—[*Aside.*] Egad, I'll tell him. —[*Aloud.*] Hark 'ee—have you a mind to have a good laugh at Joseph?

Chas Surf. I should like it of all things.

Sir Pet. Then, i'faith, we will! I'll be quit with him for discovering me. He had a girl with him when I called.

[*Whispers.*

Chas. Surf. What! Joseph? you jest.

Sir Pet. Hush!—a little French milliner—and the best of the jest is—she's in the room now.

Chas. Surf. The devil she is!

Sir Pet. Hush! I tell you. [*Points to the screen*

Chas. Surf. Behind the screen! 'Slife, let's unveil her!

Sir Pet. No, no, he's coming :—you sha'n't, indeed !

Chas. Surf. Oh, egad, we 'll have a peep at the little milliner !

Sir Pet. Not for the world !—Joseph will never forgive me.

Chas. Surf. I 'll stand by you——

Sir Pet Odds, here he is !

        [CHARLES SURFACE *throws down the screen*

    Re-enter JOSEPH SURFACE.

Chas. Surf. Lady Teazle, by all that's wonderful !

Sir Pet. Lady Teazle, by all that's damnable !

Chas. Surf. Sir Peter, this is one of the smartest French milliners I ever saw. Egad, you seem all to have been diverting yourselves here at hide and seek, and I don't see who is out of the secret. Shall I beg your ladyship to inform me ? Not a word !—Brother, will you be pleased to explain this matter ? What ! is Morality dumb too ?—Sir Peter. though I found you in the dark, perhaps you are not so now ! All mute !—Well—though I can make nothing of the affair, I suppose you perfectly understand one another ; so I 'll leave you to yourselves.—[*Going.*] Brother, I 'm sorry to find you have given that worthy man grounds for so much uneasiness. —Sir Peter ! there 's nothing in the world so noble as a man of sentiment !   [*Exit.*

Jos. Surf. Sir Peter—notwithstanding—I confess—that appearances are against me—if you will afford me your patience—I make no doubt—but I shall explain every thing to your satisfaction.

Sir Pet. If you please, sir.

Jos. Surf. The fact is, sir, that Lady Teazle, knowing my pretensions to your ward Maria—I say, sir, Lady Teazle, being apprehensive of the jealousy of your temper—and knowing my friendship to the family—she, sir, I say—called here—in order that—I might explain these pretensions—but on your coming—being apprehensive—as I said—of your jealousy—she withdrew—and this, you may depend on it, is the whole truth of the matter.

Sir Pet. A very clear account, upon my word ; and I dare swear the lady will vouch for every article of it.

Lady Teaz. For not one word of it, Sir Peter !

Sir Pet. How ! don't you think it worth while to agree in the lie ?

Lady Teaz. There is not one syllable of truth in what that gentleman has told you.

Sir Pet. I believe you, upon my soul, ma'am!

Jos. Surf. [*Aside to* LADY TEAZLE.] 'Sdeath, madam, will you betray me?

Lady Teaz. Good Mr. Hypocrite, by your leave, I 'll speak for myself.

Sir Pet. Ay, let her alone, sir; you 'll find she 'll make out a better story than you, without prompting.

Lady Teaz. Hear me, Sir Peter!—I came here on no matter relating to your ward, and even ignorant of this gentleman's pretensions to her. But I came, seduced by his insidious arguments, at least to listen to his pretended passion, if not to sacrifice your honour to his baseness.

Sir Pet. Now. I believe, the truth is coming, indeed!

Jos. Surf. The woman 's mad!

Lady Teaz. No, sir; she has recovered her senses, and your own arts have furnished her with the means.--Sir Peter, I do not expect you to credit me—but the tenderness you expressed for me, when I am sure you could not think I was a witness to it, has so penetrated to my heart, that had I left the place without the shame of this discovery, my future life should have spoken the sincerity of my gratitude. As for that smooth-tongued hypocrite, who would have seduced the wife of his too credulous friend, while he affected honourable addresses to his ward—I behold him now in a light so truly despicable, that I shall never again respect myself for having listened to him. [*Exit.*

Jos. Surf. Notwithstanding all this, Sir Peter, Heaven knows——

Sir Pet. That you are a villain! and so I leave you to your conscience.

Jos. Surf. You are too rash, Sir Peter; you shall hear me The man who shuts out conviction by refusing to——

Sir Pet. Oh, damn your sentiments!

[*Exeunt* SIR PETER *and* JOSEPH SURFACE, *talking*

ACT V.

SCENE I.—*The Library in* JOSEPH SURFACE'S *House*
Enter JOSEPH SURFACE *and* SERVANT.

Jos. Surf. Mr. Stanley! and why should you think I would see him? you must know he comes to ask something.

Ser. Sir, I should not have let him in, but that Mr. Rowley came to the door with him.

Jos. Surf. Psha! blockhead! to suppose that I should now be in a temper to receive visits from poor relations!—Well, why don't you show the fellow up?

Ser. I will, sir.—Why, sir, it was not my fault that Sir Peter discovered my lady——

Jos. Surf. Go, fool!—[*Exit* SERVANT.] Sure Fortune never played a man of my policy such a trick before! My character with Sir Peter, my hopes with Maria, destroyed in a moment! I 'm in a rare humour to listen to other people's distresses! I sha'n't be able to bestow even a benevolent sentiment on Stanley.—So! here he comes, and Rowley with him. I must try to recover myself, and put a little charity into my face, however.   [*Exit*

Enter SIR OLIVER SURFACE *and* ROWLEY.

Sir Oliv. What! does he avoid us? That was he, was it not?

Row. It was, sir. But I doubt you are come a little too abruptly. His nerves are so weak, that the sight of a poor relation may be too much for him. I should have gone first to break it to him.

Sir Oliv. Oh, plague of his nerves! Yet this is he whom Sir Peter extols as a man of the most benevolent way of thinking!

Row. As to his way of thinking, I cannot pretend to decide; for, to do him justice, he appears to have as much speculative benevolence as any private gentleman in the kingdom, though he is seldom so sensual as to indulge himself in the exercise of it.

Sir Oliv. Yet he has a string of charitable sentiments at his fingers' ends.

Row. Or, rather, at his tongue's end, Sir Oliver; for I believe there is no sentiment he has such faith in as that *Charity begins at home.*

Sir Oliv. And his, I presume, is of that domestic sort which never stirs abroad at all.

Row. I doubt you 'll find it so;—but he 's coming. I mustn't seem to interrupt you; and you know, immediately as you leave him, I come in to announce your arrival in your real character.

Sir Oliv. True; and afterwards you 'll meet me at Sir Peter's

Row. Without losing a moment   [*Exit.*

Sir Oliv. I don't like the complaisance of his features.

Re-enter JOSEPH SURFACE.

Jos. Surf. Sir, I beg you ten thousand pardons for keeping you a moment waiting.—Mr. Stanley, I presume.

Sir Oliv. At your service.

Jos. Surf. Sir, I beg you will do me the honour to sit down —I entreat you, sir.

Sir Oliv. Dear sir—there's no occasion.—[*Aside*] Too civil by half!

Jos. Surf. I have not the pleasure of knowing you, Mr. Stanley; but I am extremely happy to see you look so well. You were nearly related to my mother, I think, Mr. Stanley?

Sir Oliv. I was, sir; so nearly that my present poverty, I fear, may do discredit to her wealthy children, else I should not have presumed to trouble you.

Jos. Surf. Dear sir, there needs no apology;—he that is in distress, though a stranger, has a right to claim kindred with the wealthy. I am sure I wish I was one of that class, and had it in my power to offer you even a small relief.

Sir Oliv. If your uncle, Sir Oliver, were here, I should have a friend.

Jos. Surf. I wish he was, sir, with all my heart: you should not want an advocate with him, believe me, sir.

Sir Oliv. I should not need one—my distresses would re-commend me. But I imagined his bounty would enable you to become the agent of his charity.

Jos. Surf. My dear sir, you were strangely misinformed. Sir Oliver is a worthy man, a very worthy man; but avarice, Mr. Stanley, is the vice of age. I will tell you, my good sir, in confidence, what he has done for me has been a mere nothing; though people, I know, have thought otherwise, and, for my part, I never chose to contradict the report.

Sir Oliv. What! has he never transmitted you bullion—rupees—pagodas?

Jos. Surf. Oh, dear sir, nothing of the kind! No, no; a few presents now and then—china, shawls, congou tea, avada-vats, and Indian crackers—little more, believe me.

Sir Oliv. Here's gratitude for twelve thousand pounds!—Avadavats and Indian crackers!   [*Aside.*

Jos. Surf. Then, my dear sir, you have heard, I doubt not, of the extravagance of my brother: there are very few

L

would credit what I have done for that unfortunate young man.

Sir Oliv. Not I, for one!   [*Aside.*

Jos. Surf. The sums I have lent him! Indeed I have been exceedingly to blame; it was an amiable weakness; however, I don't pretend to defend it—and now I feel it doubly culpable, since it has deprived me of the pleasure of serving you, Mr. Stanley, as my heart dictates.

Sir Oliv. [*Aside.*] Dissembler!—[*Aloud.*] Then, sir, you can't assist me?

Jos. Surf. At present, it grieves me to say, I cannot; but, whenever I have the ability, you may depend upon hearing from me

Sir Oliv. I am extremely sorry——

Jos. Surf. Not more than I, believe me; to pity, without the power to relieve, is still more painful than to ask and be denied.

Sir Oliv. Kind sir, your most obedient humble servant.

Jos. Surf. You leave me deeply affected, Mr. Stanley.— William, be ready to open the door.   [*Calls to* SERVANT.

Sir. Oliv. Oh, dear sir, no ceremony.

Jos. Surf. Your very obedient.

Sir Oliv. Your most obsequious.

Jos. Surf. You may depend upon hearing from me, whenever I can be of service.

Sir Oliv. Sweet sir, you are too good!

Jos. Surf. In the meantime I wish you health and spirits.

Sir Oliv. Your ever grateful and perpetual humble servant

Jos. Surf. Sir, yours as sincerely.

Sir Oliv. [*Aside.*] Now I am satisfied.   [*Exit.*

Jos. Surf. This is one bad effect of a good character; it invites application from the unfortunate, and there needs no small degree of address to gain the reputation of benevolence without incurring the expense. The silver ore of pure charity is an expensive article in the catalogue of a man's good qualities; whereas the sentimental French plate I use instead of it makes just as good a show, and pays no tax.

Re-enter ROWLEY.

Row. Mr. Surface, your servant: I was apprehensive of interrupting you, though my business demands immediate attention, as this note will inform you.

Jos. Surf. Always happy to see Mr. Rowley,— a rascal.— [*Aside. Reads the letter.*]   Sir Oliver Surface!—My uncle arrived!

Row. He is, indeed : we have just parted—quite well, after a speedy voyage, and impatient to embrace his worthy nephew.

Jos Surf. I am astonished!—William! stop Mr. Stanley. if he's not gone.   [*Calls to* SERVANT

Row. Oh! he's out of reach, I believe.

Jos. Surf. Why did you not let me know this when you came in together?

Row. I thought you had particular business.   But I must be gone to inform your brother, and appoint him here to meet your uncle.   He will be with you in a quarter of an hour.

Jos. Surf. So he says.   Well, I am strangely overjoyed at his coming.—[*Aside.*]   Never, to be sure, was any thing so damned unlucky!

Row. You will be delighted to see how well he looks.

Jos. Surf. Oh! I'm overjoyed to hear it.—[*Aside.*]   Just at this time!

Row. I'll tell him how impatiently you expect him.

Jos. Surf. Do, do; pray give my best duty and affection.   Indeed, I cannot express the sensations I feel at the thought of seeing him.—[*Exit* ROWLEY.]   Certainly his coming just at this time is the cruellest piece of ill fortune.[*Exit.*

SCENE II.—*A Room in* SIR PETER TEAZLE'S *House.*

Enter MRS. CANDOUR *and* MAID.

Maid. Indeed, ma'am, my lady will see nobody at present.

Mrs. Can. Did you tell her it was her friend Mrs. Candour?

Maid. Yes, ma'am; but she begs you will excuse her.

Mrs. Can. Do go again; I shall be glad to see her, if it be only for a moment, for I am sure she must be in great distress. —[*Exit* MAID.]   Dear heart, how provoking!   I'm not mistress of half the circumstances!   We shall have the whole affair in the newspapers, with the names of the parties at length, before I have dropped the story at a dozen houses.

Enter SIR BENJAMIN BACKBITE.

Oh, dear Sir Benjamin! you have heard, I suppose——

Sir Ben. Of Lady Teazle and Mr. Surface——

Mrs. Can. And Sir Peter's discovery——

Sir Ben. Oh, the strangest piece of business, to be sure!

Mrs. Can. Well, I never was so surprised in my life.   I am so sorry for all parties, indeed.

Sir Ben. Now, I don't pity Sir Peter at all: he was so extravagantly partial to Mr. Surface.

Mrs. Can. Mr. Surface!   Why, 'twas with Charles Lady Teazle was detected.

Sir Ben. No, no, I tell you: Mr. Surface is the gallant.

Mrs. Can. No such thing!   Charles is the man.   'Twas Mr. Surface brought Sir Peter on purpose to discover them.

Sir Ben. I tell you I had it from one——

Mrs. Can. And I have it from one——

Sir Ben. Who had it from one, who had it——

Mrs. Can. From one immediately.   But here comes Lady Sneerwell; perhaps she knows the whole affair.

Enter LADY SNEERWELL.

Lady Sneer. So, my dear Mrs. Candour, here's a sad affair of our friend Lady Teazle!

Mrs. Can. Ay, my dear friend, who would have thought——

Lady Sneer. Well, there is no trusting appearances; though, indeed, she was always too lively for me.

Mrs. Can. To be sure, her manners were a little too free; but then she was so young!

Lady Sneer. And had, indeed, some good qualities.

Mrs. Can. So she had, indeed.   But have you heard the particulars?

Lady Sneer. No; but every body says that Mr. Surface——

Sir Ben. Ay, there; I told you Mr. Surface was the man.

Mrs. Can. No, no: indeed the assignation was with Charles.

Lady Sneer. With Charles!   You alarm me, Mrs. Candour!

Mrs. Can. Yes, yes; he was the lover.   Mr. Surface, to do him justice, was only the informer.

Sir Ben. Well, I'll not dispute with you, Mrs. Candour; but, be it which it may, I hope that Sir Peter's wound will not——

Mrs. Can. Sir Peter's wound!   Oh, mercy!   I didn't hear a word of their fighting.

Lady Sneer. Nor I, a syllable.

Sir Ben. No! what, no mention of the duel?

Mrs. Can. Not a word.

Sir Ben. Oh, yes: they fought before they left the room

Lady Sneer. Pray, let us hear

Mrs. Can. Ay, do oblige us with the duel.

Sir Ben. " *Sir*," says Sir Peter, immediately after the dis-covery, " *you are a most ungrateful fellow.*"

Mrs. Can. Ay, to Charles——

Sir Ben. No, no—to Mr. Surface—*a most ungrateful fel-low; and old as I am, sir*, says he, *I insist on immediate satis-faction.*

Mrs. Can. Ay, that must have been to Charles; for 'tis very unlikely Mr. Surface should fight in his own house.

Sir Ben. Gad's life, ma'am, not at all—*giving me imme-diate satisfaction.*—On this, ma'am, Lady Teazle, seeing Sir Peter in such danger, ran out of the room in strong hysterics, and Charles after her, calling out for hartshorn and water; then, madam, they began to fight with swords——

Enter CRABTREE.

Crab. With pistols, nephew—pistols! I have it from un-doubted authority.

Mrs. Can. Oh, Mr. Crabtree, then it is all true!

Crab. Too true, indeed, madam, and Sir Peter is danger-ously wounded——

Sir Ben. By a thrust in segoon quite through his left side——

Crab. By a bullet lodged in the thorax.

Mrs. Can. Mercy on me! Poor Sir Peter!

Crab. Yes, madam; though Charles would have avoided the matter, if he could.

Mrs. Can. I told you who it was; I knew Charles was the person.

Sir Ben. My uncle, I see, knows nothing of the matter.

Crab. But Sir Peter taxed him with the basest ingra-titude——

Sir Ben. That I told you, you know——

Crab. Do, nephew, let me speak!—and insisted on imme-diate——

Sir Ben. Just as I said——

Crab. Odds life, nephew, allow others to know something too! A pair of pistols lay on the bureau (for Mr. Surface, it seems, had come home the night before late from Salthill, where he had been to see the Montem with a friend, who has a son at Eton), so, unluckily, the pistols were left charged.

Sir Ben. I heard nothing of this.

Crab. Sir Peter forced Charles to take one, and they fired, it seems, pretty nearly together. Charles's shot took effect, as I tell you, and Sir Peter's missed; but, what is very extraordinary, the ball struck against a little bronze Shakspeare that stood over the fire-place, grazed out of the window at a right angle, and wounded the postman, who was just coming to the door with a double letter from Northamptonshire.

Sir Ben. My uncle's account is more circumstantial, I confess; but I believe mine is the true one, for all that.

Lady Sneer. [*Aside.*] I am more interested in this affair than they imagine, and must have better information. [*Exit.*

Sir Ben. Ah! Lady Sneerwell's alarm is very easily accounted for.

Crab. Yes, yes, they certainly do say—but that's neither here nor there.

Mrs. Can. But, pray, where is Sir Peter at present?

Crab. Oh! they brought him home, and he is now in the house, though the servants are ordered to deny him.

Mrs. Can. I believe so, and Lady Teazle, I suppose, attending him.

Crab. Yes, yes; and I saw one of the faculty enter just before me.

Sir Ben. Hey! who comes here?

Crab. Oh, this is he: the physician, depend on 't.

Mrs. Can. Oh, certainly! it must be the physician; and now we shall know.

Enter Sir Oliver Surface.

Crab. Well, doctor, what hopes?

Mrs. Can. Ay, doctor, how's your patient?

Sir Ben. Now, doctor, isn't it a wound with a small-sword?

Crab. A bullet lodged in the thorax, for a hundred!

Sir Oliv. Doctor! a wound with a small-sword! and a bullet in the thorax!—Oons! are you mad, good people?

Sir Ben. Perhaps, sir, you are not a doctor?

Sir Oliv. Truly, I am to thank you for my degree, if I am.

Crab. Only a friend of Sir Peter's, then, I presume. But, sir, you must have heard of his accident?

Sir Oliv. Not a word!

Crab. Not of his being dangerously wounded?

Sir Oliv. The devil he is!

Sir Ben. Run through the body——

Crab. Shot in the breast——

Sir Ben. By one Mr. Surface——

Crab. Ay, the younger.

Sir Oliv. Hey! what the plague! you seem to differ strangely in your accounts : however, you agree that Sir Peter is dangerously wounded.

Sir Ben. Oh, yes, we agree in that.

Crab. Yes, yes, I believe there can be no doubt of that.

Sir Oliv. Then, upon my word, for a person in that situation, he is the most imprudent man alive ; for here he comes, walking as if nothing at all was the matter.

Enter SIR PETER TEAZLE.

Odds heart, Sir Peter! you are come in good time, I promise you; for we had just given you over!

Sir Ben. [*Aside to* CRABTREE.] Egad, uncle, this is the most sudden recovery!

Sir Oliv. Why, man! what do you out of bed with a small-sword through your body, and a bullet lodged in your thorax?

Sir Pet. A small-sword and a bullet!

Sir Oliv. Ay; these gentlemen would have killed you without law or physic, and wanted to dub me a doctor, to make me an accomplice.

Sir Pet. Why, what is all this?

Sir Ben. We rejoice, Sir Peter, that the story of the duel is not true, and are sincerely sorry for your other misfortune.

Sir Pet. So, so; all over the town already!   [*Aside.*

Crab. Though, Sir Peter, you were certainly vastly to blame to marry at your years.

Sir Pet. Sir, what business is that of yours?

Mrs. Can. Though, indeed, as Sir Peter made so good a husband, he 's very much to be pitied.

Sir Pet. Plague on your pity, ma'am! I desire none of it.

Sir Ben. However, Sir Peter, you must not mind the laughing and jests you will meet with on the occasion.

Sir Pet. Sir, sir! I desire to be master in my own house.

Crab. 'Tis no uncommon case, that 's one comfort.

Sir Pet. I insist on being left to myself: without ceremony, I insist on your leaving my house directly!

Mrs. Can. Well, well, we are going; and depend on 't, we 'll make the best report of it we can   [*Exit.*

Sir Pet. Leave my house!

Crab. And tell how hardly you've been treated.   [*Exit.*

Sir Pet. Leave my house!

Sir Ben. And how patiently you bear it.   [*Exit*

Sir Pet. Fiends! vipers! furies! Oh! that their own venom would choke them!

Sir Oliv. They are very provoking indeed, Sir Peter.

Enter ROWLEY.

Row. I heard high words: what has ruffled you, sir?

Sir Pet. Psha! what signifies asking? Do I ever pass a day without my vexations?

Row. Well, I'm not inquisitive

Sir Oliv. Well, Sir Peter, I have seen both my nephews in the manner we proposed.

Sir Pet. A precious couple they are!

Row. Yes, and Sir Oliver is convinced that your judgment was right, Sir Peter.

Sir Oliv. Yes, I find Joseph is indeed the man, after all.

Row. Ay, as Sir Peter says, he is a man of sentiment.

Sir Oliv. And acts up to the sentiments he professes.

Row. It certainly is edification to hear him talk.

Sir Oliv. Oh, he's a model for the young men of the age! —But how's this, Sir Peter? you don't join us in your friend Joseph's praise, as I expected.

Sir Pet. Sir Oliver, we live in a damned wicked world, and the fewer we praise the better.

Row. What! do you say so, Sir Peter, who were never mistaken in your life?

Sir Pet. Psha! plague on you both! I see by your sneering you have heard the whole affair. I shall go mad among you!

Row. Then, to fret you no longer, Sir Peter, we are indeed acquainted with it all. I met Lady Teazle coming from Mr. Surface's so humbled, that she deigned to request me to be her advocate with you.

Sir Pet. And does Sir Oliver know all this?

Sir Oliv. Every circumstance.

Sir Pet. What of the closet and the screen, hey?

Sir Oliv. Yes, yes, and the little French milliner. Oh, I have been vastly diverted with the story! ha! ha! ha!

Sir Pet. 'Twas very pleasant.

Sir Oliv. I never laughed more in my life, I assure you: ah! ah! ah!

Sir Pet. Oh, vastly diverting! ha! ha! ha!

Row. To be sure. Joseph with his sentiments! ha! ha! ha.

Sir Pet. Yes, yes his sentiments! ha! ha! ha! Hypocritical villain!

Sir Oliv. Ay, and tnat rogue Charles to pull Sir Peter out of the closet: ha! ha! ha!

Sir Pet. Ha! ha! 'twas devilish entertaining, to be sure!

Sir Oliv. Ha! ha! ha! Egad, Sir Peter, I should like to have seen your face when the screen was thrown down : ha! ha!

Sir Pet. Yes, yes, my face when the screen was thrown down: ha! ha! ha! Oh, I must never show my head again!

Sir Oliv. But come, come, it isn't fair to laugh at you neither, my old friend; though, upon my soul, I can't help it.

Sir Pet. Oh, pray don't restrain your mirth on my account: it does not hurt me at all! I laugh at the whole affair myself. Yes, yes, I think being a standing jest for all one's acquaintance a very happy situation. Oh, yes. and then of a morning to read the paragraphs about Mr. S——, Lady T——, and Sir P——, will be so entertaining!

Row. Without affectation, Sir Peter, you may despise the ridicule of fools. But I see Lady Teazle going towards the next room: I am sure you must desire a reconciliation as earnestly as she does.

Sir Oliv. Perhaps my being here prevents her coming to you. Well, I'll leave honest Rowley to mediate between you; but he must bring you all presently to Mr. Surface's, where I am now returning, if not to reclaim a libertine, at least to expose hypocrisy.

Sir Pet. Ah, I'll be present at your discovering yourself there with all my heart; though 'tis a vile unlucky place for discoveries.

Row. We'll follow.   [*Exit* SIR OLIVER SURFACE.

Sir Pet. She is not coming here, you see, Rowley.

Row. No, but she has left the door of that room open, you perceive. See, she is in tears.

Sir Pet. Certainly a little mortification appears very becoming in a wife. Don't you think it will do her good to let her pine a little?

Row. Oh, this is ungenerous in you!

Sir Pet. Well, I know not what to think. You remember the letter I found of hers evidently intended for Charles?

Row. A mere forgery, Sir Peter! laid in your way on purpose. This is one of the points which I intend Snake shall give you conviction of.

Sir Pet. I wish I were once satisfied of that. She looks this way. What a remarkably elegant turn of the head she has ; Rowley, I 'll go to her.

Row. Certainly.

Sir Pet. Though, when it is known that we are reconciled, people will laugh at me ten times more.

Row. Let them laugh, and retort their malice only by showing them you are happy in spite of it.

Sir Pet. I' faith, so I will! and, if I 'm not mistaken, we may yet be the happiest couple in the country.

Row. Nay, Sir Peter, he who once lays aside suspicion——

Sir Pet. Hold, Master Rowley! if you have any regard for me, never let me hear you utter any thing like a sentiment: I have had enough of them to serve me the rest of my life.

[*Exeunt.*

Scene III.—*The Library in* Joseph Surface's *House.*

Enter Joseph Surface *and* Lady Sneerwell.

Lady Sneer. Impossible! Will not Sir Peter immediately be reconciled to Charles, and of course no longer oppose his union with Maria? The thought is distraction to me.

Jos. Surf. Can passion furnish a remedy?

Lady Sneer. No, nor cunning either. Oh, I was a fool, an idiot, to league with such a blunderer!

Jos. Surf. Sure, Lady Sneerwell, I am the greatest sufferer; yet you see I bear the accident with calmness.

Lady Sneer. Because the disappointment doesn't reach your heart; your interest only attached you to Maria. Had you felt for her what I have for that ungrateful libertine, neither your temper nor hypocrisy could prevent your showing the sharpness of your vexation.

Jos. Surf. But why should your reproaches fall on me for this disappointment?

Lady Sneer. Are you not the cause of it? Had you not a sufficient field for your roguery in imposing upon Sir Peter, and supplanting your brother, but you must endeavour to seduce his wife? I hate such an avarice of crimes; 'tis an unfair monopoly, and never prospers.

Jos. Surf. Well, I admit I have been to blame. I confess I deviated from the direct road of wrong, but I don't think we're so totally defeated neither.

Lady Sneer. No!

Jos. Surf. You tell me you have made a trial of Snake since we met, and that you still believe him faithful to us?

Lady Sneer. I do believe so.

Jos. Surf. And that he has undertaken, should it be necessary, to swear and prove, that Charles is at this time contracted by vows and honour to your ladyship, which some of his former letters to you will serve to support?

Lady Sneer. This, indeed, might have assisted.

Jos. Surf. Come, come; it is not too late yet.—[*Knocking at the door.*] But hark! this is probably my uncle, Sir Oliver: retire to that room; we'll consult farther when he is gone.

Lady Sneer. Well, but if he should find you out too?

Jos. Surf Oh, I have no fear of that. Sir Peter will hold his tongue for his own credit's sake—and you may depend on it I shall soon discover Sir Oliver's weak side!

Lady Sneer. I have no diffidence of your abilities: only be constant to one roguery at a time

Jos. Surf. I will, I will!—[*Exit* LADY SNEERWELL.] So! 'tis confounded hard, after such bad fortune, to be baited by one's confederate in evil. Well, at all events, my character is so much better than Charles's, that I certainly—hey!—what —this is not Sir Oliver, but old Stanley again. Plague on't that he should return to tease me just now! I shall have Sir Oliver come and find him here—and——

Enter SIR OLIVER SURFACE.

Gad's life, Mr. Stanley, why have you come back to plague me at this time? You must not stay now, upon my word.

Sir Oliv. Sir, I hear your uncle Oliver is expected here, and though he has been so penurious to you, I'll try what he'll do for me.

Jos. Surf. Sir, 'tis impossible for you to stay now, so I must beg——Come any other time, and I promise you, you shall be assisted

Sir Oliv. No: Sir Oliver and I must be acquainted.

Jos. Surf. Zounds, sir! then I insist on your quitting the room directly

Sir Oliv. Nay, sir——

Jos. Surf. Sir, I insist on't!—Here, William! show this gentleman out. Since you compel me, sir, not one moment —this is such insolence.   [*Going to push him out.*

Enter CHARLES SURFACE.

Chas. Surf. Heyday! what's the matter now? What the devil, have you got hold of my little broker here? Zounds, brother, don't hurt little Premium. What's the matter, my little fellow?

Jos. Surf. So! he has been with you too, has he?

Chas. Surf. To be sure, he has. Why, he's as honest a little——But sure, Joseph, you have not been borrowing money too, have you?

Jos. Surf. Borrowing! no! But, brother, you know we expect Sir Oliver here every——

Chas. Surf. O Gad, that's true! Noll mustn't find the little broker here, to be sure.

Jos. Surf. Yet Mr. Stanley insists——

Chas. Surf. Stanley! why his name's Premium.

Jos. Surf. No, sir, Stanley.

Chas. Surf. No, no, Premium.

Jos. Surf. Well, no matter which—but——

Chas. Surf. Ay, ay, Stanley or Premium, 'tis the same thing, as you say; for I suppose he goes by half a hundred names, besides A. B. at the coffee-house.   [*Knocking.*

Jos. Surf. 'Sdeath! here's Sir Oliver at the door.—Now I beg, Mr. Stanley——

Chas. Surf. Ay, ay, and I beg, Mr. Premium——

Sir Oliv. Gentlemen——

Jos. Surf. Sir, by Heaven you shall go '

Chas. Surf. Ay, out with him, certainly!

Sir Oliv. This violence——

Jos. Surf. Sir, 'tis your own fault.

Chas. Surf. Out with him, to be sure.

          [*Both forcing* SIR OLIVER *out*

Enter SIR PETER *and* LADY TEAZLE, MARIA, *and* ROWLEY.

Sir Pet. My old friend, Sir Oliver—hey! What in the name of wonder—here are dutiful nephews—assault their uncle at first visit!

Lady Teaz. Indeed, Sir Oliver, 'twas well we came in to rescue you.

Row. Truly it was; for I perceive, Sir Oliver, the character of old Stanley was no protection to you.

Sir Oliv. Nor of Premium either: the necessities of the former could not extort a shilling from that benevolent gentleman; and with the other I stood a chance of faring worse than my ancestors, and being knocked down without being bid for.

Jos. Surf. Charles!

Chas. Surf. Joseph!

Jos. Surf. 'Tis now complete!

Chas. Surf. Very.

Sir Oliv. Sir Peter, my friend, and Rowley too—look on that elder nephew of mine. You know what he has already received from my bounty; and you also know how gladly I would have regarded half my fortune as held in trust for him: judge then my disappointment in discovering him to be destitute of truth, charity, and gratitude!

Sir Pet. Sir Oliver, I should be more surprised at this declaration, if I had not myself found him to be mean, treacherous, and hypocritical.

Lady Teaz. And if the gentleman pleads not guilty to these, pray let him call me to his character.

Sir Pet. Then, I believe, we need add no more: if he knows himself, he will consider it as the most perfect punishment, that he is known to the world.

Chas. Surf. If they talk this way to Honesty, what will they say to me, by and by?   [*Aside.*

[SIR PETER, LADY TEAZLE, *and* MARIA *retire.*

Sir Oliv. As for that prodigal, his brother, there——

Chas. Surf. Ay, now comes my turn: the damned family pictures will ruin me!   [*Aside.*

Jos. Surf. Sir Oliver—uncle, will you honour me with a hearing?

Chas. Surf. Now, if Joseph would make one of his long speeches, I might recollect myself a little.   [*Aside*

Sir Oliv. I suppose you would undertake to justify yourself?   [*To* JOSEPH SURFACE.

Jos. Surf. I trust I could.

Sir Oliv. [*To* CHARLES SURFACE.] Well, sir!—and you could justify yourself too, I suppose?

Chas. Surf. Not that I know of, Sir Oliver.

Sir Oliv. What!—Little Premium has been let too much into the secret, I suppose?

Chas. Surf True, sir; but they were family secrets, and should not be mentioned again, you know.

Row. Come, Sir Oliver, I know you cannot speak of Charles's follies with anger

Sir Oliv. Odd's heart, no more I can; nor with gravity either. Sir Peter, do you know the rogue bargained with me for all his ancestors; sold me judges and generals by the foot, and maiden aunts as cheap as broken china.

Chas. Surf. To be sure, Sir Oliver, I did make a little free with the family canvas, that's the truth on't. My ancestors may rise in judgment against me, there's no denying it; but believe me sincere when I tell you—and upon my soul I would not say so if I was not—that if I do not appear mortified at the exposure of my follies, it is because I feel at this moment the warmest satisfaction in seeing you, my liberal benefactor.

Sir Oliv. Charles, I believe you. Give me your hand again: the ill-looking little fellow over the settee has made your peace.

Chas. Surf. Then, sir, my gratitude to the original is still increased.

Lady Teaz. [*Advancing.*] Yet, I believe, Sir Oliver, here is one whom Charles is still more anxious to be reconciled to.

[*Pointing to* MARIA.

Sir Oliv. Oh, I have heard of his attachment there; and, with the young lady's pardon, if I construe right—that blush——

Sir Pet. Well, child, speak your sentiments!

Mar. Sir, I have little to say, but that I shall rejoice to hear that he is happy; for me, whatever claim I had to his attention, I willingly resign to one who has a better title.

Chas. Surf. How, Maria!

Sir Pet. Heyday! what's the mystery now? While he appeared an incorrigible rake, you would give your hand to no one else; and now that he is likely to reform I'll warrant you won't have him!

Mar. His own heart and Lady Sneerwell know the cause.

Chas. Surf. Lady Sneerwell!

Jos. Surf. Brother, it is with great concern I am obliged to speak on this point, but my regard to justice compels me, and Lady Sneerwell's injuries can no longer be concealed.

[*Opens the door*

Enter LADY SNEERWELL.

Sir Pet. So! another French milliner! Egad, he has one in every room in the house, I suppose!

Lady Sneer. Ungrateful Charles! Well may you be sur prised, and feel for the indelicate situation your perfidy has forced me into.

Chas. Surf. Pray, uncle, is this another plot of yours? For, as I have life, I don't understand it.

Jos. Surf. I believe, sir, there is but the evidence of one person more necessary to make it extremely clear.

Sir Pet. And that person, I imagine, is Mr. Snake.—Row-ley, you were perfectly right to bring him with us, and pray let him appear.

Row. Walk in, Mr. Snake.

Enter SNAKE.

I thought his testimony might be wanted: however, it happens unluckily, that he comes to confront Lady Sneerwell, not to support her.

Lady Sneer. A villain! Treacherous to me at last! Speak, fellow, have you too conspired against me!

Snake. I beg your ladyship ten thousand pardons: you paid me extremely liberally for the lie in question; but I unfortu nately have been offered double to speak the truth.

Sir Pet. Plot and counter-plot, egad! I wish your lady-ship joy of your negociation.

Lady Sneer. The torments of shame and disappointment on you all!   [*Going*

Lady Teaz. Hold, Lady Sneerwell—before you go, let me thank you for the trouble you and that gentleman have taken, in writing letters from me to Charles, and answering them yourself; and let me also request you to make my respects to the scandalous college, of which you are president, and inform them, that Lady Teazle, licentiate, begs leave to return the diploma they granted her, as she leaves off practice, and kills characters no longer.

Lady Sneer. You too, madam!—provoking—insolent! May your husband live these fifty years!   [*Exit.*

Sir Pet. Oons! what a fury!

Lady Teaz. A malicious creature, indeed!

Sir Pet. What! not for her last wish?

Lady Teaz. Oh, no!

Sir Oliv. Well, sir, and what have you to say now?

Jos. Surf. Sir, I am so confounded, to find that Lady Sneer-well could be guilty of suborning Mr. Snake in this manner, to impose on us all, that I know not what to say: however, lest her revengeful spirit should prompt her to injure my brother, I had certainly better follow her directly. For the man who attempts to——   [*Exit.*

Sir Pet. Moral to the last!

Sir Oliv. Ay, and marry her, Joseph, if you can.   Oil and vinegar!—egad you 'll do very well together.

Row. I believe we have no more occasion for Mr. Snake at present?

Snake. Before I go, I beg pardon once for all, for whatever uneasiness I have been the humble instrument of causing to the parties present.

Sir Pet. Well, well, you have made atonement by a good deed at last.

Snake. But I must request of the company, that it shall never be known.

Sir Pet. Hey! what the plague! are you ashamed of having done a right thing once in your life?

Snake. Ah, sir, consider—I live by the badness of my cha-racter; and, if it were once known that I had been betrayed into an honest action, I should lose every friend I have in the world.

Sir Oliv. Well, well—we 'll not traduce you by saying any thing in your praise, never fear.   [*Exit* SNAKE.

Sir Pet. There 's a precious rogue!

Lady Teaz. See, Sir Oliver, there needs no persuasion now to reconcile your nephew and Maria.

Sir Oliv. Ay, ay, that 's as it should be, and, egad, we 'll have the wedding to-morrow morning.

Chas. Surf. Thank you, dear uncle.

Sir Pet. What, you rogue! don't you ask the girl's consent first?

Chas. Surf. Oh, I have done that a long time—a minute ago—and she has looked yes.

Mar. For shame, Charles!—I protest, Sir Peter, there has not been a word——

Sir Oliv. Well, then, the fewer the better; may your love for each other never know abatement.

Sir Pet. And may you live as happily together as Lady Teazle and I intend to do!

Chas. Surf. Rowley, my old friend, I am sure you congra-
tulate me ; and I suspect that I owe you much.

Sir Oliv. You do, indeed, Charles.

Sir Pet. Ay, honest Rowley always said you would reform

Chas. Surf. Why, as to reforming, Sir Peter, I 'll make no
promises, and that I take to be a proof that I intend to set
about it.   But here shall be my monitor—my gentle guide.—
Ah! can I leave the virtuous path those eyes illumine ?

> Though thou, dear maid, shouldst waive thy beauty's sway,
> Thou still must rule, because I will obey :
> An humble fugitive from Folly view,
> No sanctuary near but Love and you :   [*To the audience.*
> You can, indeed, each anxious fear remove,
> For even Scandal dies, if you approve.   [*Exeunt omnes.*

EPILOGUE.

BY MR. COLMAN.

SPOKEN BY LADY TEAZLE.

I, who was late so volatile and gay,
Like a trade-wind must now blow all one way,
Bend all my cares, my studies, and my vows,
To one dull rusty weathercock—my spouse !
So wills our virtuous bard—the motley Bayes
Of crying epilogues and laughing plays !
Old bachelors, who marry smart young wives,
Learn from our play to regulate your lives :
Each bring his dear to town, all faults upon her—
London will prove the very source of honour.
Plunged fairly in, like a cold bath it serves,
When principles relax, to brace the nerves :
Such is my case ; and yet I must deplore
That the gay dream of dissipation 's o'er.
And say, ye fair ! was ever lively wife,
Born with a genius for the highest life,
Like me untimely blasted in her bloom,
Like me condemn'd to such a dismal doom ?
Save money—when I just knew how to waste it !
Leave London—just as I began to taste it !
    Must I then watch the early crowing cock,
The melancholy ticking of a clock ;
In a lone rustic hall for ever pounded,
With dogs, cats, rats, and squalling brats surrounded

With humble curate can I now retire,
(While good Sir Peter boozes with the squire,)
And at backgammon mortify my soul,
That pants for loo, or flutters at a vole?
Seven's the main!   Dear sound that must expire,
Lost at hot cockles round a Christmas fire;
The transient hour of fashion too soon spent,
Farewell the tranquil mind, farewell content!
Farewell the plumèd head, the cushion'd tête,
That takes the cushion from its proper seat!
That spirit-stirring drum!—card drums I mean,
Spadille—odd trick—pam—basto—king and queen!
And you, ye knockers, that, with brazen throat,
The welcome visitors' approach denote;
Farewell all quality of high renown,
Pride, pomp, and circumstance of glorious town!
Farewell! your revels I partake no more,
And Lady Teazle's occupation's o'er!
All this I told our bard; he smiled, and said 'twas clear,
I ought to play deep tragedy next year.
Meanwhile he drew wise morals from his play,
And in these solemn periods stalk'd away:—
" Bless'd were the fair like you; her faults who stopp'd
And closed her follies when the curtain dropp'd!
No more in vice or error to engage,
Or play the fool at large on life's great stage."

THE CRITIC;

OR,

A TRAGEDY REHEARSED.

A DRAMATIC PIECE IN THREE ACTS.

TO MRS. GREVILLE.

MADAM,—In requesting your permission to address the following pages to you, which, as they aim themselves to be critical, require every protection and allowance that approving taste or friendly prejudice can give them, I yet ventured to mention no other motive than the gratification of private friendship and esteem. Had I suggested a hope that your implied approbation would give a sanction to their defects, your particular reserve, and dislike to the reputation of critical taste, as well as of poetical talent, would have made you refuse the protection of your name to such a purpose. However, I am not so ungrateful as now to attempt to combat this disposition in you. I shall not here presume to argue that the present state of poetry claims and expects every assistance that taste and example can afford it; nor endeavour to prove that a fastidious concealment of the most elegant productions of judgment and fancy is an ill return for the possession of those endowments. Continue to deceive yourself in the idea that you are known only to be eminently admired and regarded for the valuable qualities that attach private friendships, and the graceful talents that adorn conversation. Enough of what you have written has stolen into full public notice to answer my purpose; and you will, perhaps, be the only person, conversant in elegant literature, who shall read this address and not perceive that by publishing your particular approbation of the following drama, I have a more interested object than to boast the true respect and regard with which I have the honour to be, Madam, your very sincere and obedient humble servant,

R. B. SHERIDAN.

DRAMATIS PERSONÆ,

AS ORIGINALLY ACTED AT DRURY LANE THEATRE IN 1779.

SIR FRETFUL PLAGIARY	*Mr. Parsons.*	MR. HOPKINS . . .	*Mr. Hopkins.*
PUFF	*Mr. King.*		
DANGLE	*Mr. Dodd.*	MRS. DANGLE . . .	*Mrs. Hopkins.*
SNEER	*Mr. Palmer.*		
SIGNOR PASTICCIO RITORNELLO . . .	*Mr. Delpini.*	SIGNORE PASTICCIO RITORNELLO . . .	*Miss Field and the Miss Abrams.*
INTERPRETER . . .	*Mr. Baddeley.*		
UNDER PROMPTER	*Mr. Phillimore.*	Scenemen, Musicians, *and* Servants.	

M 2

CHARACTERS OF THE TRAGEDY.

LORD BURLEIGH . .	. *Mr. Moody.*
GOVERNOR OF TILBURY FORT . .	} *Mr. Wrighten.*
EARL OF LEICESTER	} *Mr. Farren.*
SIR WALTER RALEIGH	} *Mr. Burton.*
SIR CHRISTOPHER HATTON . . .	} *Mr. Waldron.*
MASTER OF THE HORSE. . . .	} *Mr. Kenny.*
DON FEROLO WHISKERANDOS. . .	} *Mr. Bannister, jun.*
BEEFEATER	. *Mr. Wright.*

JUSTICE	. *Mr. Packer*
SON	. *Mr. Lamash.*
CONSTABLE	. *Mr. Fawcett.*
THAMES	. *Mr. Gawdry*
TILBURINA	. *Miss Pope.*
CONFIDANT . . .	{ *Mrs. Bradshaw.* }
JUSTICE'S LADY . .	. *Mrs. Johnston.*
FIRST NIECE . . .	. *Miss Collett.*
SECOND NIECE . . .	. *Miss Kirby.*

Knights, Guards, Constables, Sentinels, Servants, Chorus, Rivers, Attendants, &c., &c.

SCENE,—LONDON: *in* DANGLE'S *House during the First Act, and throughout the rest of the Play in* DRURY LANE THEATRE.

PROLOGUE,

BY THE HONOURABLE RICHARD FITZPATRICK.

THE sister muses, whom these realms obey,
Who o'er the drama hold divided sway,
Sometimes, by evil counsellors, 'tis said,
Like earth-born potentates have been misled.
In those gay days of wickedness and wit,
When Villiers criticised what Dryden writ,
The tragic queen, to please a tasteless crowd,
Had learn'd to bellow, rant, and roar so loud,
That frighten'd Nature, her best friend before,
The blustering beldam's company forswore;
Her comic sister, who had wit 'tis true,
With all her merits, had her failings too;
And would sometimes in mirthful moments use
A style too flippant for a well-bred muse;
Then female modesty abash'd began
To seek the friendly refuge of the fan,
Awhile behind that slight intrenchment stood,
Till driven from thence, she left the stage for good.
In our more pious, and far chaster times,
These sure no longer are the Muse's crimes!
But some complain that, former faults to shun,
The reformation to extremes has run.
The frantic hero's wild delirium past,
Now insipidity succeeds bombast;
So slow Melpomene's cold numbers creep,
Here dulness seems her drowsy court to keep,
And we are scarce awake, whilst you are fast asleep.

Thalia, once so ill-behaved and rude,
Reform'd, is now become an arrant prude;
Retailing nightly to the yawning pit
The purest morals, undefiled by wit!
Our author offers, in these motley scenes,
A slight remonstrance to the drama's queens:
Nor let the goddesses be over nice;
Free-spoken subjects give the best advice.
Although not quite a novice in his trade.
His cause to-night requires no common aid.
To this, a friendly, just, and powerful court,
I come ambassador to beg support.
Can he undaunted brave the critic's rage?
In civil broils with brother bards engage?
Hold forth their errors to the public eye,
Nay more, e'en newspapers themselves defy?
Say, must his single arm encounter all?
By numbers vanquish'd, e'en the brave may fall;
And though no leader should success distrust,
Whose troops are willing, and whose cause is just;
To bid such hosts of angry foes defiance,
His chief dependence must be, your alliance.

ACT I.

Scene I.—*A Room in* DANGLE'S *House.*

MR. *and* MRS. DANGLE *discovered at breakfast, and reading newspapers.*

Dang. [Reading.] *Brutus to Lord North.—Letter the second on the State of the Army*—Psha! *To the first L dash D of the A dash Y.—Genuine extract of a Letter from St. Kitt's.— Coxheath Intelligence.—It is now confidently asserted that Sir Charles Hardy*—Psha! nothing but about the fleet and the nation!—and I hate all politics but theatrical politics.— Where's the Morning Chronicle?

Mrs. Dang. Yes, that's your Gazette

Dang. So, here we have it.—[Reads.] *Theatrical intelligence extraordinary.—We hear there is a new tragedy in rehearsal at Drury Lane Theatre, called the Spanish Armada, said to be written by Mr. Puff, a gentleman well known in the theatrical world. If we may allow ourselves to give credit to the report of the performers, who, truth to say, are in general but indifferent judges, this piece abounds with the most striking and received beauties of modern composition.*—So! I am very glad my friend Puff's tragedy is in such forwardness.—Mrs Dangle, my dear, you will be very glad to hear that Puff's tragedy——

Mrs. Dang. Lord, Mr. Dangle, why will you plague me about such nonsense?—Now the plays are begun I shall have no peace.—Isn't it sufficient to make yourself ridiculous by your passion for the theatre, without continually teasing me to join you? Why can't you ride your hobby-horse without desiring to place me on a pillion behind you, Mr. Dangle?

Dang. Nay, my dear, I was only going to read——

Mrs. Dang. No, no; you will never read anything that's worth listening to. You hate to hear about your country; there are letters every day with Roman signatures, demonstrating the certainty of an invasion, and proving that the nation is utterly undone. But you never will read any thing to entertain one.

Dang. What has a woman to do with politics, Mrs. Dangle?

Mrs. Dang. And what have you to do with the theatre, Mr. Dangle? Why should you affect the character of a critic? I have no patience with you!—haven't you made yourself the jest of all your acquaintance by your interference in matters where you have no business? Are you not called a theatrical Quidnunc, and a mock Mæcenas to second-hand authors?

Dang. True; my power with the managers is pretty notorious. But is it no credit to have applications from all quarters for my interest—from lords to recommend fiddlers, from ladies to get boxes, from authors to get answers, and from actors to get engagements?

Mrs. Dang. Yes, truly; you have contrived to get a share in all the plague and trouble of theatrical property, without the profit, or even the credit of the abuse that attends it.

Dang. I am sure, Mrs. Dangle, you are no loser by it, however; you have all the advantages of it. Mightn't you, last winter, have had the reading of the new pantomime a fortnight previous to its performance? And doesn't Mr. Fosbrook let you take places for a play before it is advertised, and set you down for a box for every new piece through the season? And didn't my friend, Mr. Smatter, dedicate his last farce to you at my particular request, Mrs. Dangle?

Mrs. Dang. Yes; but wasn't the farce damned, Mr. Dangle? And to be sure it is extremely pleasant to have one's house made the motley rendezvous of all the lackeys of literature:

the very high 'Change of trading authors and jobbing critics?
—Yes, my drawing-room is an absolute register office for can-
didate actors, and poets without character.—Then to be continually alarmed with misses and ma'ams piping hysteric
changes on Juliets and Dorindas, Pollys, and Ophelias; and
the very furniture trembling at the probationary starts and
unprovoked rants of would-be Richards and Hamlets!—And
what is worse than all, now that the manager has monopolized
the Opera House, haven't we the signors and signoras calling
here, sliding their smooth semibreves, and gargling glib divi-
sions in their outlandish throats—with foreign emissaries and
French spies, for aught I know, disguised like fiddlers and
figure-dancers?

Dang. Mercy! Mrs. Dangle!

Mrs. Dang. And to employ yourself so idly at such an
alarming crisis as this too—when, if you had the least spirit,
you would have been at the head of one of the Westminster
associations—or trailing a volunteer pike in the Artillery
Ground! But you—o' my conscience, I believe, if the French
were landed to-morrow, your first inquiry would be, whether
they had brought a theatrical troop with them.

Dang. Mrs. Dangle, it does not signify—I say the stage is
the Mirror of Nature, and the actors are *the Abstract and brief
Chronicles of the Time:* and pray what can a man of sense
study better?—Besides, you will not easily persuade me that
there is no credit or importance in being at the head of a band
of critics, who take upon them to decide for the whole town,
whose opinion and patronage all writers solicit, and whose recommendation no manager dares refuse.

Mrs. Dang. Ridiculous!—Both managers and authors of
the least merit laugh at your pretensions.—The public is their
critic—without whose fair approbation they know no play can
rest on the stage, and with whose applause they welcome such
attacks as yours, and laugh at the malice of them, where they
can't at the wit.

Dang. Very well, madam—very well!

Enter SERVANT.

Ser. Mr. Sneer, sir, to wait on you.

Dang. Oh, show Mr. Sneer up.—[*Exit* SERVANT.] Plague
on 't, now we must appear loving and affectionate, or Sneer
will hitch us into a story.

Mrs. Dang. With all my heart; you can t be more ridiculous than you are.

Dang. You are enough to provoke——

Ha! my dear Sneer, I am vastly glad to see you.—My dear, here's Mr. Sneer.

Mrs. Dang. Good morning to you, sir.

Dang. Mrs. Dangle and I have been diverting ourselves with the papers. Pray, Sneer, won't you go to Drury Lane Theatre the first night of Puff's tragedy?

Sneer. Yes; but I suppose one shan't be able to get in, for on the first night of a new piece they always fill the house with orders to support it. But here, Dangle, I have brought you two pieces, one of which you must exert yourself to make the managers accept, I can tell you that; for 'tis written by a person of consequence.

Dang. So! now my plagues are beginning.

Sneer. Ay, I am glad of it, for now you'll be happy. Why, my dear Dangle, it is a pleasure to see how you enjoy your volunteer fatigue, and your solicited solicitations.

Dang. It's a great trouble—yet, egad, it's pleasant too.— Why, sometimes of a morning I have a dozen people call on me at breakfast-time, whose faces I never saw before, nor ever desire to see again.

Sneer. That must be very pleasant indeed!

Dang. And not a week but I receive fifty letters, and not a line in them about any business of my own.

Sneer. An amusing correspondence!

Dang. [Reading.] *Bursts into tears, and exit.*—What, is this a tragedy?

Sneer. No, that's a genteel comedy, not a translation—only taken from the French: it is written in a style which they have lately tried to run down; the true sentimental, and nothing ridiculous in it from the beginning to the end.

Mrs. Dang. Well, if they had kept to that, I should not have been such an enemy to the stage; there was some edification to be got from those pieces, Mr. Sneer!

Sneer. I am quite of your opinion, Mrs. Dangle: the theatre, in proper hands, might certainly be made the school of morality; but now, I am sorry to say it, people seem to go there principally for their entertainment!

Mrs. Dang. It would have been more to the credit of tho managers to have kept it in the other line.

Sneer. Undoubtedly, madam; and hereafter perhaps to have had it recorded, that in the midst of a luxurious and dissipated age, they preserved two houses in the capital, where the conversation was always moral at least, if not entertaining!

Dang. Now, egad, I think the worst alteration is in the nicety of the audience!—No *double-entendre*, no smart innuendo admitted; even Vanbrugh and Congreve obliged to undergo a bungling reformation!

Sneer. Yes, and our prudery in this respect is just on a par with the artificial bashfulness of a courtesan, who increases the blush upon her cheek in an exact proportion to the diminution of her modesty.

Dang. Sneer can't even give the public a good word! But what have we here?—This seems a very odd——

Sneer. Oh, that's a comedy, on a very new plan; replete with wit and mirth, yet of a most serious moral! You see it is called *The Reformed House-breaker;* where, by the mere force of humour, house-breaking is put into so ridiculous a light, that if the piece has its proper run, I have no doubt but that bolts and bars will be entirely useless by the end of the season.

Dang. Egad, this is new indeed!

Sneer. Yes; it is written by a particular friend of mine, who has discovered that the follies and foibles of society are subjects unworthy the notice of the comic muse, who should be taught to stoop only at the greater vices and blacker crimes of humanity—gibbeting capital offences in five acts, and pillorying petty larcenies in two.—In short, his idea is to dramatise the penal laws, and make the stage a court of ease to the Old Bailey.

Dang. It is truly moral.

Re-enter SERVANT.

Ser. Sir Fretful Plagiary, sir.

Dang. Beg him to walk up.—[*Exit* SERVANT.] Now, Mrs. Dangle, Sir Fretful Plagiary is an author to your own taste.

Mrs. Dang. I confess he is a favourite of mine, because everybody else abuses him.

Sneer. Very much to the credit of your charity, madam, if not of your judgment

Dang. But, egad, he allows no merit to any author but himself, that 's the truth on 't—though he 's my friend.

Sneer. Never.—He is as envious as an old maid verging on the desperation of six-and-thirty; and then the insidious humility with which he seduces you to give a free opinion on any of his works, can be exceeded only by the petulant arroganco with which he is sure to reject your observations.

Dang. Very true, egad—though he 's my friend.

Sneer. Then his affected contempt of all newspaper strictures; though, at the same time, he is the sorest man alive, and shrinks like scorched parchment from the fiery ordeal of true criticism : yet is he so covetous of popularity, that he had rather be abused than not mentioned at all.

Dang. There 's no denying it—though he is my friend.

Sneer. You have read the tragedy he has just finished, haven't you ?

Dang. O yes ; he sent it to me yesterday.

Sneer. Well, and you think it execrable, don't you?

Dang. Why, between ourselves, egad, I must own—though he is my friend—that it is one of the most——He 's here— [*Aside*]—finished and most admirable perform——

Sir Fret. [*Without.*] Mr. Sneer with him, did you say?

Enter SIR FRETFUL PLAGIARY.

Dang Ah, my dear friend !—Egad, we were just speaking of your tragedy.—Admirable, Sir Fretful, admirable!

Sneer You never did any thing beyond it, Sir Fretful—never in your life.

Sir Fret. You make me extremely happy : for without a compliment, my dear Sneer, there isn't a man in the world whose judgment I value as I do yours and Mr. Dangle's.

Mrs. Dang. They are only laughing at you, Sir Fretful ; for it was but just now that——

Dang. Mrs. Dangle !—Ah, Sir Fretful, you know Mrs. Dangle.—My friend Sneer was rallying just now :—he knows how she admires you, and——

Sir Fret. O Lord, I am sure Mr. Sneer has more taste and sincerity than to——[*Aside*] A damned double-faced fellow!

Dang. Yes, yes—Sneer will jest—but a better humoured——

Sir Fret. Oh, I know——

Dang. He has a ready turn for ridicule—his wit costs him nothing.

Sir Fret. No, egad—or I should wonder how he came by it.   [*Aside.*

Mrs. Dang Because his jest is always at the expense of his friend.   [*Aside*

Dang. But, Sir Fretful, have you sent your play to the managers yet?—or can I be of any service to you?

Sir Fret. No, no, I thank you: I believe the piece had sufficient recommendation with it.—I thank you though.—I sent it to the manager of Covent Garden Theatre this morning.

Sneer. I should have thought now, that it might have been cast (as the actors call it) better at Drury Lane.

Sir Fret. O lud! no—never send a play there while I live—hark'ee!   [*Whispers* SNEER.

Sneer. Writes himself!—I know he does.

Sir Fret. I say nothing—I take away from no man's merit —am hurt at no man's good fortune—I say nothing.—But this I will say—through all my knowledge of life, I have observed —that there is not a passion so strongly rooted in the human heart as envy

Sneer. I believe you have reason for what you say, indeed.

Sir Fret. Besides—I can tell you it is not always so safe to leave a play in the hands of those who write themselves.

Sneer. What, they may steal from them, hey, my dear Plagiary?

Sir Fret. Steal!—to be sure they may; and, egad, serve your best thoughts as gypsies do stolen children, disfigure them to make 'em pass for their own.

Sneer. But your present work is a sacrifice to Melpomene, and he, you know, never——

Sir Fret. That's no security: a dexterous plagiarist may do any thing. Why, sir, for aught I know, he might take out some of the best things in my tragedy, and put them into his own comedy.

Sneer. That might be done, I dare be sworn.

Sir Fret. And then, if such a person gives you the least hint or assistance, he is devilish apt to take the merit of the whole——

Dang. If it succeeds.

Sir Fret. Ay, but with regard to this piece, I think I can hit that gentleman, for I can safely swear he never read it.

Sneer. I'll tell you how you may hurt him more.

Sir Fret. How?

Sneer. Swear he wrote it.

Sir Fret. Plague on 't now, Sneer. I shall take it ill !—I believe you want to take away my character as an author.

Sneer. Then I am sure you ought to be very much obliged to me.

Sir Fret. Hey !—sir !——

Dang. Oh, you know, he never means what he says.

Sir Fret. Sincerely then—you do like the piece?

Sneer. Wonderfully !

Sir Fret. But come now, there must be something that you think might be mended, hey ?—Mr Dangle, has nothing struck you?

Dang. Why, faith, it is but an ungracious thing, for the most part, to——

Sir Fret. With most authors it is just so indeed ; they are in general strangely tenacious !   But, for my part, I am never so well pleased as when a judicious critic points out any defect to me ; for what is the purpose of showing a work to a friend, if you don't mean to profit by his opinion?

Sneer. Very true.—Why then, though I seriously admire the piece upon the whole, yet there is one small objection ; which, if you 'll give me leave, I 'll mention.

Sir Fret. Sir, you can't oblige me more.

Sneer. I think it wants incident.

Sir Fret. Good God ! you surprise me !—wants incident !

Sneer. Yes ; I own I think the incidents are too few.

Sir Fret. Good God ! Believe me, Mr. Sneer, there is no person for whose judgment I have a more implicit deference. But I protest to you, Mr. Sneer, I am only apprehensive that the incidents are too crowded.—My dear Dangle, how does it strike you?

Dang. Really I can't agree with my friend Sneer.   I think the plot quite sufficient ; and the four first acts by many degrees the best I ever read or saw in my life.   If I might venture to suggest any thing, it is that the interest rather falls off in the fifth.

Sir Fret. Rises, I believe you mean, sir

Dang. No, I don't, upon my word.

Sir Fret. Yes, yes, you do, upon my soul !—it certainly don't fall off, I assure you.—No, no ; it don't fall off.

Dang. Now, Mrs. Dangle, didn't you say it struck you in the same light?

Mrs. Dang. No, indeed, I did not—I did not see a fault in any part of the play, from the beginning to the end.

Sir Fret. Upon my soul, the women are the best judges after all!

Mrs. Dang. Or, if I made any objection, I am sure it was to nothing in the piece; but that I was afraid it was, on the whole, a little too long.

Sir Fret. Pray, madam, do you speak as to duration of time; or do you mean that the story is tediously spun out?

Mrs. Dang. O lud! no.—I speak only with reference to the usual length of acting plays.

Sir Fret. Then I am very happy—very happy indeed—because the play is a short play, a remarkably short play. I should not venture to differ with a lady on a point of taste; but, on these occasions, the watch, you know, is the critic.

Mrs. Dang. Then, I suppose, it must have been Mr Dangle's drawling manner of reading it to me.

Sir Fret. Oh, if Mr. Dangle read it, that's quite another affair!—But I assure you, Mrs. Dangle, the first evening you can spare me three hours and a half, I'll undertake to read you the whole from beginning to end, with the prologue and epilogue, and allow time for the music between the acts.

Mrs. Dang. I hope to see it on the stage next.

Dang. Well, Sir Fretful, I wish you may be able to get rid as easily of the newspaper criticisms as you do of ours.

Sir Fret. The newspapers! Sir, they are the most villanous — licentious — abominable — infernal — Not that I ever read them—no—I make it a rule never to look into a news paper.

Dang. You are quite right; for it certainly must hurt an author of delicate feelings to see the liberties they take.

Sir Fret. No, quite the contrary! their abuse is, in fact, the best panegyric—I like it of all things. An author's reputation is only in danger from their support.

Sneer. Why that's true—and that attack, now, on you the other day——

Sir Fret. What? where?

Dang. Ay, you mean in a paper of Thursday: it was completely ill-natured, to be sure.

Sir Fret. Oh, so much the better.—Ha! ha! ha! I wouldn't have it otherwise.

Dang. Certainly it is only to be laughed at; for——

Sir Fret. You don't happen to recollect what the fellow said, do you?

Sneer. Pray, Dangle—Sir Fretful seems a little an-xious——

Sir Fret. O lud, no!—anxious!—not I,—not the least.—I—but one may as well hear, you know.

Dang. Sneer, do you recollect?—[*Aside to* SNEER.] Make out something.

Sneer. [*Aside to* DANGLE.] I will.—[*Aloud.*] Yes, yes, I remember perfectly.

Sir Fret. Well, and pray now—not that it signifies—what might the gentleman say?

Sneer. Why, he roundly asserts that you have not the slightest invention or original genius whatever; though you are the greatest traducer of all other authors living.

Sir Fret. Ha! ha! ha!—very good!

Sneer. That as to comedy, you have not one idea of your own, he believes, even in your common-place-book—where stray jokes and pilfered witticisms are kept with as much method as the ledger of the lost and stolen office.

Sir Fret. Ha! ha! ha!—very pleasant!

Sneer. Nay, that you are so unlucky as not to have the skill even to steal with taste:—but that you glean from the refuse of obscure volumes, where more judicious plagiarists have been before you; so that the body of your work is a composition of dregs and sediments—like a bad tavern's worst wine.

Sir Fret. Ha! ha!

Sneer. In your more serious efforts, he says, your bombast would be less intolerable, if the thoughts were ever suited to the expression; but the homeliness of the sentiment stares through the fantastic encumbrance of its fine language, like a clown in one of the new uniforms!

Sir Fret. Ha! ha!

Sneer. That your occasional tropes and flowers suit the general coarseness of your style, as tambour sprigs would a ground of linsey-woolsey; while your imitations of Shakspeare resemble the mimicry of Falstaff's page, and are about as near the standard of the original.

Sir Fret. Ha!

Sneer. In short, that even the finest passages you steal are of no service to you; for the poverty of your own language prevents their assimilating; so that they lie on the surface

like lumps of marl on a barren moor, encumbering what it is
not in their power to fertilise!

Sir Fret. [*After great agitation.*] Now, another person
would be vexed at this.

Sneer. Oh! but I wouldn't have told you—only to divert
you.

Sir Fret. I know it—I am diverted.—Ha! ha! ha!—not
the least invention!—Ha! ha! ha!—very good!—very good!

Sneer. Yes—no genius! ha! ha! ha!

Dang. A severe rogue! ha! ha! ha! But you are quite
right, Sir Fretful, never to read such nonsense.

Sir Fret. To be sure—for if there is any thing to one's
praise, it is a foolish vanity to be gratified at it; and, if it is
abuse,—why one is always sure to hear of it from one damned
good-natured friend or another!

Enter SERVANT

Ser. Sir, there is an Italian gentleman, with a French interpreter, and three young ladies, and a dozen musicians, who
say they are sent by Lady Rondeau and Mrs. Fugue.

Dang. Gadso! they come by appointment!—Dear Mrs
Dangle, do let them know I'll see them directly.

Mrs. Dang. You know, Mr. Dangle, I shan't understand a
word they say.

Dang. But you hear there's an interpreter.

Mrs. Dang. Well, I'll try to endure their complaisance till
you come. [*Exit*

Ser. And Mr. Puff, sir, has sent word that the last rehearsal
is to be this morning, and that he'll call on you presently.

Dang. That's true—I shall certainly be at home.—[*Exit*
SERVANT.] Now, Sir Fretful, if you have a mind to have justice
done you in the way of answer, egad, Mr. Puff's your man.

Sir Fret. Psha! Sir, why should I wish to have it answered,
when I tell you I am pleased at it?

Dang True, I had forgot that. But I hope you are not
fretted at what Mr. Sneer——

Sir Fret. Zounds! no, Mr. Dangle; don't I tell you these
things never fret me in the least?

Dang. Nay, I only thought——

Sir Fret. And let me tell you, Mr. Dangle, 'tis damned
affronting in you to suppose that I am hurt when I tell you I
am not

Sneer. But why so warm, Sir Fretful ?

Sir Fret. Gad's life !   Mr. Sneer, you are as absurd as Dangle : how often must I repeat it to you, that nothing can vex me but your supposing it possible for me to mind the damned nonsense you have been repeating to me !— and, let me tell you, if you continue to believe this, you must mean to insult me, gentlemen—and, then, your disrespect will affect me no more than the newspaper criticisms--and I shall treat it with exactly the same calm indifference and philosophic contempt—and so your servant.   [*Exit.*

Sneer. Ha! ha! ha! poor Sir Fretful! Now will he go and vent his philosophy in anonymous abuse of all modern critics and authors.—But, Dangle, you must get your friend Puff to take me to the rehearsal of his tragedy.

Dang. I 'll answer for 't, he 'll thank you for desiring it. But come and help me to judge of this musical family : they are recommended by people of consequence, I assure you.

Sneer. I am at your disposal the whole morning ;—but I thought you had been a decided critic in music as well as in literature.

Dang So I am—but I have a bad ear. I'faith, Sneer, though, I am afraid we were a little too severe on Sir Fretful —though he is my friend.

Sneer. Why, 'tis certain, that unnecessarily to mortify the vanity of any writer is a cruelty which mere dulness never can deserve ; but where a base and personal malignity usurps the place of literary emulation, the aggressor deserves neither quarter nor pity.

Dang. That 's true, egad !—though he 's my friend !

SCENE II.—*A Drawing-room in* DANGLE's *House.*

MRS. DANGLE, SIGNOR PASTICCIO RITORNELLO, SIGNORE PAS-
TICCIO RITORNELLO, INTERPRETER, *and* MUSICIANS, *discovered.*

Interp. Je dis, madame, j'ai l'honneur to introduce et de vous demander votre protection pour le signor Pasticcio Ritor-nello et pour sa charmante famille.

Signor Past. Ah ! vosignoria, noi vi preghiamo di favoritevi colla vostra protezione.

1 *Signora Past.* Vosignoria fatevi questi grazie.

2 *Signora Past.* Si, signora.

Interp. Madame—me interpret.—C'est à dire—in English —qu'ils vous prient de leur faire l'honneur——

Mrs. Dang. I say again, gentleman, I don't understand a word you say.

Signor Past. Questo signore spiegherò——

Interp. Oui—me interpret.—Nous avons les lettres de recommendation pour monsieur Dangle de——

Mrs. Dang. Upon my word, sir, I don't understand you.

Signor Past. La contessa Rondeau è nostra padrona.

3 *Signora Past.* Si, padre, et miladi Fugue.

Interp. O!—me interpret.—Madame, ils disent—in English—Qu'ils ont l'honneur d'être protégés de ces dames.—You understand?

Mrs. Dang No, sir,—no understand!

Enter DANGLE and SNEER.

Interp. Ah, voici monsieur Dangle!

All Italians. Ah! signor Dangle!

Mrs. Dang. Mr. Dangle, here are two very civil gentlemen trying to make themselves understood, and I don't know which is the interpreter.

Dang. Eh, bien!

[*The* INTERPRETER *and* SIGNOR PASTICCIO *here speak at the same time.*

Interp. Monsieur Dangle, le grand bruit de vos talens pour la critique, et de votre intérêt avec messieurs les directeurs à tous les théâtres——

Signor Past. Vosignoria siete si famoso par la vostra conoscenza, e vostra interessa colla le direttore da——

Dang. Egad, I think the interpreter is the hardest to be understood of the two!

Sneer. Why, I thought, Dangle, you had been an admirable linguist!

Dang. So I am, if they would not talk so damned fast.

Sneer. Well, I'll explain that—the less time we lose in hearing them the better—for that, I suppose, is what they are brought here for.

[*Speaks to* SIGNOR PASTICCIO—*they sing trios, &c.,* DANGLE *beating out of time*

Enter SERVANT and whispers DANGLE.

Dang. Show him up.—[*Exit* SERVANT.] Bravo! admirable

N

bravissimo! admirablissimo!—Ah! Sneer! where will you find voices such as these in England?

Sneer. Not easily.

Dang. But Puff is coming.—Signor and little signoras obligatissimo!—Sposa signora Danglena—Mrs. Dangle, shall I beg you to offer them some refreshments, and take their address in the next room.

[*Exit* Mrs. DANGLE *with* SIGNOR PASTICCIO, SIGNORE PASTICCIO, MUSICIANS, *and* INTERPRETER, *ceremoniously.*

Re-enter SERVANT.

Ser. Mr Puff, sir.   [*Exit.*

Enter PUFF.

Dang. My dear Puff!

Puff. My dear Dangle, how is it with you?

Dang. Mr. Sneer, give me leave to introduce Mr. Puff to you.

Puff. Mr. Sneer is this?—Sir, he is a gentleman whom I have long panted for the honour of knowing—a gentleman whose critical talents and transcendent judgment——

Sneer. Dear Sir——

Dang. Nay, don't be modest, Sneer; my friend Puff only talks to you in the style of his profession.

Sneer. His profession!

Puff Yes, sir; I make no secret of the trade I follow: among friends and brother authors, Dangle knows I love to be frank on the subject, and to advertise myself *vivâ voce.*—I am, sir, a practitioner in panegyric, or, to speak more plainly, a professor of the art of puffing, at your service—or anybody else's.

Sneer. Sir, you are very obliging!—I believe, Mr. Puff, I have often admired your talents in the daily prints.

Puff. Yes, sir, I flatter myself I do as much business in that way as any six of the fraternity in town.—Devilish hard work all the summer, friend Dangle,—never worked harder! But, hark'ee,—the winter managers were a little sore, I believe.

Dang. No; I believe they took it all in good part.

Puff. Ay! then that must have been affectation in them; for, egad, there were some of the attacks which there was no laughing at!

Sneer. Ay, the humorous ones.—But I should think, Mr

Puff, that authors would in general be able to do this sort of work for themselves.

Puff. Why, yes—but in a clumsy way. Besides, we look on that as an encroachment, and so take the opposite side. I dare say, now, you conceive half the very civil paragraphs and advertisements you see to be written by the parties concerned, or their friends? No such thing: nine out of ten manufac-tured by me in the way of business.

Sneer. Indeed!

Puff. Even the auctioneers now—the auctioneers, I say—though the rogues have lately got some credit for their lan-guage—not an article of the merit theirs: take them out of their pulpits, and they are as dull as catalogues!—No, sir; 'twas I first enriched their style—'twas I first taught them to crowd their advertisements with panegyrical superlatives, each epithet rising above the other, like the bidders in their own auction-rooms! From me they learned to inlay their phrase-ology with variegated chips of exotic metaphor: by me too their inventive faculties were called forth:—yes, sir, by me they were instructed to clothe ideal walls with gratuitous fruits —to insinuate obsequious rivulets into visionary groves—to teach courteous shrubs to nod their approbation of the grate-ful soil; or on emergencies to raise upstart oaks, where there never had been an acorn; to create a delightful vicinage with out the assistance of a neighbour; or fix the temple of Hygeia in the fens of Lincolnshire!

Dang. I am sure you have done them infinite service; for now, when a gentleman is ruined, he parts with his house with some credit.

Sneer. Service! if they had any gratitude, they would erect a statue to him; they would figure him as a presiding Mer-cury, the god of traffic and fiction, with a hammer in his hand instead of a caduceus.—But pray, Mr. Puff, what first put you on exercising your talents in this way?

Puff. Egad, sir, sheer necessity!—the proper parent of an art so nearly allied to invention. You must know, Mr. Sneer, that from the first time I tried my hand at an advertisement, my success was such, that for some time after I led a most extraordinary life indeed!

Sneer. How, pray.

Puff. Sir, I supported myself two years entirely by my mis-fortunes

Sneer. By your misfortunes!

Puff. Yes, sir, assisted by long sickness, and other occasional disorders; and a very comfortable living I had of it.

Sneer. From sickness and misfortunes! You practised as a doctor and an attorney at once?

Puff. No, egad; both maladies and miseries were my own.

Sneer. Hey! what the plague!

Dang. 'Tis true, i'faith.

Puff. Hark'ee!—By advertisements—*To the charitable and humane!* and *To those whom Providence hath blessed with affluence!*

Sneer. Oh, I understand you.

Puff. And, in truth, I deserved what I got; for I suppose never man went through such a series of calamities in the same space of time. Sir, I was five times made a bankrupt, and reduced from a state of affluence, by a train of unavoidable misfortunes: then, sir, though a very industrious tradesman, I was twice burned out, and lost my little all both times: I lived upon those fires a month. I soon after was confined by a most excruciating disorder, and lost the use of my limbs: that told very well; for I had the case strongly attested, and went about to collect the subscriptions myself.

Dang. Egad, I believe that was when you first called on me.

Puff. In November last?—O no; I was at that time a close prisoner in the Marshalsea, for a debt benevolently contracted to serve a friend. I was afterwards twice tapped for a dropsy, which declined into a very profitable consumption. I was then reduced to—O no—then, I became a widow with six helpless children, after having had eleven husbands pressed, and being left every time eight months gone with child, and without money to get me into an hospital!

Sneer. And you bore all with patience, I make no doubt?

Puff. Why, yes; though I made some occasional attempts at *felo de se;* but as I did not find those rash actions answer, I left off killing myself very soon. Well, sir, at last, what with bankruptcies, fires, gouts, dropsies, imprisonments, and other valuable calamities, having got together a pretty handsome sum, I determined to quit a business which had always gone rather against my conscience, and in a more liberal way still to indulge my talents for fiction and embellishments,

through my favourite channels of diurnal communication—
and so, sir, you have my history.

Sneer. Most obligingly communicative indeed! and your confession, if published, might certainly serve the cause of true
charity, by rescuing the most useful channels of appeal to
benevolence from the cant of imposition. But surely, Mr.
Puff, there is no great mystery in your present profession?

Puff. Mystery, sir! I will take upon me to say the matter
was never scientifically treated nor reduced to rule before.

Sneer. Reduced to rule!

Puff. O lud, sir, you are very ignorant, I am afraid!—Yes,
sir, puffing is of various sorts; the principal are, the puff
direct, the puff preliminary, the puff collateral, the puff collusive, and the puff oblique, or puff by implication. These all
assume, as circumstances require, the various forms of Letter to
the Editor, Occasional Anecdote, Impartial Critique, Observation from Correspondent, or Advertisement from the Party

Sneer. The puff direct, I can conceive——

Puff. O yes, that's simple enough! For instance,—a new
comedy or farce is to be produced at one of the theatres
(though by-the-by they don't bring out half what they ought
to do)—the author, suppose Mr. Smatter, or Mr. Dapper, or
any particular friend of mine—very well; the day before it is
to be performed, I write an account of the manner in which it
was received; I have the plot from the author, and only add
—" characters strongly drawn—highly coloured—hand of a
master—fund of genuine humour—mine of invention—neat
dialogue—Attic salt." Then for the performance—" Mr. Dodd
was astonishingly great in the character of Sir Harry   That
universal and judicious actor, Mr. Palmer, perhaps never appeared to more advantage than in the colonel;—but it is not
in the power of language to do justice to Mr. King: indeed
he more than merited those repeated bursts of applause which
he drew from a most brilliant and judicious audience. As to
the scenery—the miraculous powers of Mr. De Loutherbourg's
pencil are universally acknowledged. In short, we are at a
loss which to admire most, the unrivalled genius of the author,
the great attention and liberality of the managers, the wonderful abilities of the painter, or the incredible exertions of all
the performers."

Sneer. That's pretty well indeed, sir.

Puff. Oh, cool!—quite cool!—to what I sometimes do.

Sneer. And do you think there are any who are influenced by this?

Puff. O lud, yes, sir! the number of those who undergo the fatigue of judging for themselves is very small indeed.

Sneer. Well, sir, the puff preliminary?

Puff. O, that, sir, does well in the form of a caution. In a matter of gallantry now—Sir Flimsy Gossamer wishes to be well with Lady Fanny Fete—he applies to me—I open trenches for him with a paragraph in the Morning Post.— " It is recommended to the beautiful and accomplished Lady F four stars F dash E to be on her guard against that dangerous character, Sir F dash G; who, however pleasing and insinuating his manners may be, is certainly not remarkable for the *constancy of his attachments!*"—in italics.   Here, you see, Sir Flimsy Gossamer is introduced to the particular notice of Lady Fanny, who perhaps never thought of him before—she finds herself publicly cautioned to avoid him, which naturally makes her desirous of seeing him : the observation of their acquaintance causes a pretty kind of mutual embarrassment; this produces a sort of sympathy of interest, which if Sir Flimsy is unable to improve effectually, he at least gains the credit of having their names mentioned together, by a particular set, and in a particular way—which nine times out of ten is the full accomplishment of modern gallantry.

Dang. Egad, Sneer, you will be quite an adept in the business!

Puff. Now, sir, the puff collateral is much used as an appendage to advertisements, and may take the form of anecdote.—" Yesterday, as the celebrated George Bonmot was sauntering down St. James's Street, he met the lively Lady Mary Myrtle coming out of the park:—' Good God, Lady Mary, I 'm surprised to meet you in a white jacket,—for I expected never to have seen you, but in a full-trimmed uniform and a light horseman's cap!'—' Heavens, George, where could you have learned that?'—' Why,' replied the wit, ' I just saw a print of you, in a new publication called the Camp Magazine; which, by the by, is a devilish clever thing, and is sold at No. 3, on the right hand of the way, two doors from the printing-office, the corner of Ivy Lane, Paternoster Row, price only one shilling.'"

Sneer. Very ingenious indeed!

Puff. But the puff collusive is the newest of any; for it
acts in the disguise of determined hostility. It is much used
by bold booksellers and enterprising poets.—" An indignant
correspondent observes, that the new poem called *Beelzebub's
Cotillon*, or *Proserpine's Fête Champêtre*, is one of the most
unjustifiable performances he ever read. The severity with
which certain characters are handled is quite shocking: and
as there are many descriptions in it too warmly coloured for
female delicacy, the shameful avidity with which this piece is
bought by all people of fashion is a reproach on the taste of
the times, and a disgrace to the delicacy of the age." Here
you see the two strongest inducements are held forth;
first, that nobody ought to read it; and secondly, that everybody buys it: on the strength of which the publisher boldly
prints the tenth edition, before he had sold ten of the first;
and then establishes it by threatening himself with the pillory,
or absolutely indicting himself for *scan. mag.*

Dang. Ha! ha! ha;—'gad, I know it is so.

Puff. As to the puff oblique, or puff by implication, it is
too various and extensive to be illustrated by an instance: it
attracts in titles and presumes in patents; it lurks in the li-
mitation of a subscription, and invites in the assurance of
crowd and incommodation at public places; it delights to draw
forth concealed merit, with a most disinterested assiduity;
and sometimes wears a countenance of smiling censure and
tender reproach. It has a wonderful memory for parliament-
ary debates, and will often give the whole speech of a favoured
member with the most flattering accuracy. But, above all, it
is a great dealer in reports and suppositions. It has the
earliest intelligence of intended preferments that will reflect
honour on the patrons; and embryo promotions of modest gentlemen, who know nothing of the matter themselves. It can
hint a ribbon for implied services in the air of a common report; and with the carelessness of a casual paragraph, suggest officers into commands, to which they have no pretension
but their wishes. This, sir, is the last principal class of the
art of puffing—an art which I hope you will now agree with
me is of the highest dignity, yielding a tablature of benevolence and public spirit; befriending equally trade, gallantry,
criticism, and politics: the applause of genius—the register
of charity—the triumph of heroism—the self-defence of con
tractors--the fame of orators—and the gazette of ministers

Sneer. Sir, I am completely a convert both to the importance and ingenuity of your profession ; and now, sir, there is
but one thing which can possibly increase my respect for you,
and that is, your permitting me to be present this morning at
the rehearsal of your new trage——

Puff. Hush, for heaven's sake !—*My* tragedy !—Egad,
Dangle, I take this very ill : you know how apprehensive I
am of being known to be the author.

Dang. I' faith I would not have told—but it 's in the papers,
and your name at length in the Morning Chronicle.

Puff. Ah ! those damned editors never can keep a secret
—Well, Mr. Sneer, no doubt you will do me great honour—
I shall be infinitely happy—highly flattered——

Dang. I believe it must be near the time—shall we go together ?

Puff. No ; it will not be yet this hour, for they are always
late at that theatre : besides, I must meet you there, for I
have some little matters here to send to the papers, and a few
paragraphs to scribble before I go.—[*Looking at memorandums.*] Here is *A conscientious Baker, on the subject of the
Army Bread ;* and *A Detester of visible Brickwork, in favour
of the new-invented Stucco ;* both in the style of Junius, and
promised for to-morrow. The Thames navigation too is at
a stand. Misomud or Anti shoal must go to work again directly.—Here too are some political memorandums—I see ;
ay—*To take Paul Jones, and get the Indiamen out of the
Shannon—reinforce Byron—compel the Dutch to—*so !—I
must do that in the evening papers, or reserve it for the
Morning Herald ; for I know that I have undertaken to morrow, besides, to establish the unanimity of the fleet in the Public Advertiser, and to shoot Charles Fox in the Morning
Post.—So, egad, I ha'n't a moment to lose !

Dang. Well, we 'll meet in the Green Room.

[*Exeunt severally.*

ACT II.

Scene 1.—*The Theatre, before the Curtain.*

Enter Dangle, Puff, *and* Sneer.

Puff. No, no, sir ; what Shakspeare says of actors may be
better applied to the purpose of plays ; they ought to be *the*

abstract and brief chronicles of the time. Therefore when history, and particularly the history of our own country, furnishes any thing like a case in point, to the time in which an author writes, if he knows his own interest, he will take advantage of it; so, sir, I call my tragedy *The Spanish Armada;* and have laid the scene before Tilbury Fort

Sneer. A most happy thought, certainly!

Dang. Egad it was—I told you so. But pray now, I don't understand how you have contrived to introduce any love into it.

Puff. Love! oh, nothing so easy! for it is a received point among poets, that where history gives you a good heroic outline for a play, you may fill up with a little love at your own discretion: in doing which, nine times out of ten, you only make up a deficiency in the private history of the times. Now I rather think I have done this with some success.

Sneer. No scandal about Queen Elizabeth, I hope?

Puff. O lud! no, no;—I only suppose the governor of Tilbury Fort's daughter to be in love with the son of the Spanish admiral.

Sneer. Oh, is that all!

Dang. Excellent, i' faith! I see at once. But won't this appear rather improbable?

Puff. To be sure it will—but what the plague! a play is not to show occurrences that happen every day, but things just so strange, that though they never did, they might happen.

Sneer. Certainly nothing is unnatural, that is not physically impossible.

Puff. Very true—and for that matter Don Ferolo Whisker-andos, for that's the lover's name, might have been over here in the train of the Spanish Ambassador; or Tilburina, for that is the lady's name, might have been in love with him, from having heard his character, or seen his picture; or from knowing that he was the last man in the world she ought to be in love with—or for any other good female reason.—However, sir, the fact is, that though she is but a knight's daughter, egad! she is in love like any princess!

Dang. Poor young lady! I feel for her already! for I can conceive how great the conflict must be between her passion and her duty; her love for her country, and her love for Don Ferolo Whiskerandos!

Puff. Oh, amazing!—her poor susceptible heart is swayed to and fro by contending passions like——

Enter UNDER PROMPTER.

Und. Promp. Sir, the scene is set, and every thing is ready to begin, if you please.

Puff. Egad, then we 'll lose no time.

Und Promp. Though, I believe, sir, you will find it very short, for all the performers have profited by the kind permission you granted them.

Puff. Hey! what?

Und. Promp. You know, sir, you gave them leave to cut out or omit whatever they found heavy or unnecessary to the plot, and I must own they have taken very liberal advantage of your indulgence.

Puff. Well, well.—They are in general very good judges, and I know I am luxuriant.—Now, Mr. Hopkins, as soon as you please.

Und. Promp. [*To the* Orchestra.] Gentlemen, will you play a few bars of something, just to——

Puff. Ay, that's right; for as we have the scenes and dresses, egad, we 'll go to 't, as if it was the first night's performance ;—but you need not mind stopping between the acts —[*Exit* UNDER PROMPTER.—Orchestra *play—then the bell rings.*] So! stand clear, gentlemen. Now you know there will be a cry of Down! down!—Hats off!—Silence!—Then up curtain, and let us see what our painters have done for us.

[*Curtain rises.*

SCENE II.—*Tilbury Fort.*

" *Two* SENTINELS *discovered asleep.*"

Dang. Tilbury Fort!—very fine indeed!

Puff. Now, what do you think I open with?

Sneer. Faith, I can't guess——

Puff. A clock.—Hark!—[*Clock strikes.*] I open with a clock striking, to beget an awful attention in the audience : it also marks the time, which is four o'clock in the morning, and saves a description of the rising sun, and a great deal about gilding the eastern hemisphere.

Dang. But pray, are the sentinels to be asleep?

Puff. Fast as watchmen.

Sneer. Isn't that odd though at such an alarming crisis?

Puff. To be sure it is,—but smaller things must give way to a striking scene at the opening ; that's a rule. And the case is, that two great men are coming to this very spot to be-

gin the piece : now, it is not to be supposed they would open
their lips, if these fellows were watching them ; so, egad, I
must either have sent them off their posts, or set them asleep.

Sneer. Oh, that accounts for it.—But tell us, who are these
coming?

Puff. These are they—Sir Walter Raleigh, and Sir Christopher Hatton. You 'll know Sir Christopher by his turning
out his toes—famous, you know, for his dancing. I like to
preserve all the little traits of character.—Now attend.

"*Enter* SIR WALTER RALEIGH *and* SIR CHRISTOPHER HATTON.
Sir Christ. True, gallant Raleigh !"—

Dang. What, they had been talking before?

Puff. O yes; all the way as they came along.—[*To the*
Actors.] I beg pardon, gentlemen, but these are particular
friends of mine, whose remarks may be of great service to us
—[*To* SNEER *and* DANGLE.] Don't mind interrupting them
whenever any thing strikes you.

"*Sir Christ.* True, gallant Raleigh !
        But oh, thou champion of thy country's fame,
        There is a question which I yet must ask :
        A question which I never ask'd before.—
        What mean these mighty armaments ?
        This general muster ? and this throng of chiefs ?"

Sneer. Pray, Mr. Puff, how came Sir Christopher Hatton
never to ask that question before?

Puff. What, before the play began ?—how the plague could
he ?

Dang. That 's true, i' faith !

Puff. But you will hear what he thinks of the matter

"*Sir Christ.* Alas! my noble friend, when I behold
        Yon tented plains in martial symmetry
        Array'd ; when I count o'er yon glittering lines
        Of crested warriors, where the proud steeds neigh
        And valour-breathing trumpet's shrill appeal,
        Responsive vibrate on my listening ear ;
        When virgin majesty herself I view,
        Like her protecting Pallas, veil'd in steel,
        With graceful confidence exhort to arms !
        When, briefly, all I hear or see bears stamp
        Of martial vigilance and stern defence,
        I cannot but surmise—forgive, my friend,
        If the conjecture's rash—I cannot but
        Surmise the state some danger apprehends !

Sneer. A very cautious conjecture that.

Puff. Yes, that's his character; not to give an opinion but on secure grounds.—Now then.

"*Sir Walt.* O most accomplish'd Christopher!"——

Puff. He calls him by his christian name, to show that they are on the most familiar terms

" *Sir Walt.* O most accomplish'd Christopher! I find
        Thy staunch sagacity still tracks the future,
        In the fresh print of the o'ertaken past."

   Puff. Figurative!

" *Sir Walt.* Thy fears are just.
Sir Christ. But where? whence? when? and what
        The danger is,—methinks I fain would learn.
Sir Walt. You know, my friend, scarce two revolving suns,
        And three revolving moons, have closed their course,
        Since haughty Philip, in despite of peace,
        With hostile hand hath struck at England's trade.
Sir Christ. I know it well.
Sir Walt. Philip, you know, is proud Iberia's king!
Sir Christ. He is.
Sir Walt.   His subjects in base bigotry
        And Catholic oppression held;—while we,
        You know, the Protestant persuasion hold.
Sir Christ. We do.
Sir Walt. You know, beside, his boasted armament,
        The famed Armada, by the Pope baptized,
        With purpose to invade these realms——
Sir Christ.   Is sail'd,
        Our last advices so report.
Sir Walt. While the Iberian admiral's chief hope,
        His darling son——
Sir Christ.   Ferolo Whiskerandos hight——
Sir Walt. The same—by chance a prisoner hath been ta'en,
        And in this fort of Tilbury——
Sir Christ.   Is now
        Confined—'tis true, and oft from yon tall turret's top
        I've mark'd the youthful Spaniard's haughty mien—
        Unconquer'd, though in chains.
Sir Walt.   You also know"——

Dang Mr. Puff, as he knows all this, why does Sir Walter go on telling him?

Puff. But the audience are not supposed to know any thing of the matter, are they?

Sneer. True; but I think you manage ill: for there certainly appears no reason why Sir Walter should be so communicative.

Puff. 'Fore Gad, now, that is one of the most ungrateful observations I ever heard!—for the less inducement he has to tell all this, the more, I think, you ought to be obliged to him; for I am sure you'd know nothing of the matter without it.

Dang. That's very true, upon my word.

Puff. But you will find he was not going on

"*Sir Christ.* Enough, enough—'tis plain—and I no more
          Am in amazement lost!"——

Puff. Here, now you see, Sir Christopher did not in fact ask any one question for his own information.

Sneer No, indeed: his has been a most disinterested curiosity!

Dang. Really, I find, we are very much obliged to them both.

Puff. To be sure you are. Now then for the commander-in-chief, the Earl of Leicester, who, you know, was no favourite but of the queen's.—We left off—*in amazement lost!*

"*Sir Christ.*   Am in amazement lost.
          But, see where noble Leicester comes! supreme
          In honours and command.
Sir Walt. .   And yet, methinks,
          At such a time, so perilous, so fear'd,
          That staff might well become an abler grasp.
Sir Christ. . And so, by Heaven! think I; but soft, he's here!"

Puff. Ay, they envy him!

Sneer. But who are these with him?

Puff. Oh! very valiant knights: one is the governor of the fort, the other the master of the horse. And now, I think, you shall hear some better language: I was obliged to be plain and intelligible in the first scene, because there was so much matter of fact in it; but now, i'faith, you have trope, figure, and metaphor, as plenty as noun-substantives.

"*Enter* EARL OF LEICESTER, GOVERNOR, MASTER OF THE HORSE,
                              KNIGHTS, &c.

Leic. . . . How's this, my friends! is't thus your new-fledged zeal
          And plumèd valour moulds in roosted sloth?
          Why dimly glimmers that heroic flame,
          Whose reddening blaze, by patriot spirit fed,
          Should be the beacon of a kindling realm?
          Can the quick current of a patriot heart
          Thus stagnate in a cold and weedy converse,
          Or freeze in tideless inactivity?
          No! rather let the fountain of your valour
          Spring through each stream of enterprise,
          Each petty channel of conducive daring,
          Till the full torrent of your foaming wrath
          O'erwhelm the flats of sunk hostility!'"

Puff. There it is—followed up!

"*Sir Walt.* No more!—the freshening breath of thy rebuke
            Hath fill'd the swelling canvas of our souls!
            And thus, though fate should cut the cable of
                                      [*All take hands.*
            Our topmost hopes, in friendship's closing line
            We'll grapple with despair, and if we fall,
            We'll fall in glory's wake!
Leic. . . . There spoke old England's genius!
            Then, are we all resolved?
All. . . . . We are—all resolved.
Leic. . . . To conquer—or be free?
All. . . . . To conquer, or be free.
Leic. . . . All?
All. . . . . All."

Dang. Nem. con. egad!

Puff. O yes!—where they do agree on the stage, their
unanimity is wonderful!

"*Leic.* . . Then let's embrace—and now——   [*Kneels.*"

Sneer. What the plague, is he going to pray?

Puff. Yes; hush!—in great emergencies, there is nothing
like a prayer.

"*Leic.* . . . O mighty Mars!"

Dang. But why should he pray to Mars?

Puff. Hush!

"*Leic.* . . .   If in thy homage bred,
            Each point of discipline I've still observed;
            Nor but by due promotion, and the right
            Of service, to the rank of major-general
            Have risen; assist thy votary now!
Gov. . . . Yet do not rise—hear me!   [*Kneels.*
Mast. . . . And me!   [*Kneels.*
Knight. . . And me!   [*Kneels.*
Sir Walt. . And me!   [*Kneels.*
Sir Christ. And me!   [*Kneels.*"

Puff. Now pray altogether.

"*All.* . . . Behold thy votaries submissive beg,
            That thou wilt deign to grant them all they ask;
            Assist them to accomplish all their ends,
            And sanctify whatever means they use
            To gain them!"

Sneer. A very orthodox quintetto!

Puff. Vastly well, gentlemen!—Is that well managed or
not? Have you such a prayer as that on the stage?

Sneer. Not exactly.

Leic. [*To* PUFF.] But, sir, you haven't settled how we are to get off here.

Puff. You could not go off kneeling, could you?

Sir Walt. [*To* PUFF.] O no, sir; impossible!

Puff. It would have a good effect, i' faith, if you could exeunt praying!—Yes, and would vary the established mode of springing off with a glance at the pit.

Sneer. Oh, never mind, so as you get them off!—I 'll answer for it, the audience won't care how.

Puff. Well, then, repeat the last line standing, and go off the old way.

" *All.* . . . And sanctify whatever means we use
　　　　　To gain them.　　　　　　　[*Exeunt.*"

Dang. Bravo! a fine exit.

Sneer. Well, really, Mr Puff——

Puff. Stay a moment!

　　　　　　" *The* SENTINELS *get up.*

1 *Sent.* . . All this shall to Lord Burleigh's ear.

2 *Sent.* . . 'Tis meet it should.　　　[*Exeunt.*"

Dang. Hey!—why, I thought those fellows had been asleep?

Puff. Only a pretence; there 's the art of it: they were spies of Lord Burleigh's.

Sneer. But isn't it odd they never were taken notice of, not even by the commander-in-chief?

Puff. O lud, sir! if people, who want to listen or over hear, were not always connived at in a tragedy, there would be no carrying on any plot in the world.

Dang. That 's certain!

Puff. But take care, my dear Dangle! the morning-gun is going to fire.　　　　　　　　　[*Cannon fires*

Dang. Well, that will have a fine effect!

Puff. I think so, and helps to realise the scene.—[*Cannon twice.*] What the plague! three morning guns! there never is but one!—Ay, this is always the way at the theatre: give those fellows a good thing, and they never know when to have done with it.—You have no more cannon to fire?

Und. Promp. [*Within.*] No, sir.

Puff. Now, then, for soft music.

Sneer. Pray what 's that for?

Puff. It shows that Tilburina is coming;—nothing intro-duces you a heroine like soft music. Here she comes!

Dang. And her confidant, I suppose?

Puff. To be sure! Here they are—inconsolable to the minuet in Ariadne!   [*Soft music.*

"*Enter* TILBURINA *and* CONFIDANT.

Tilb. . . Now has the whispering breath of gentle morn
          Bid Nature's voice and Nature's beauty rise;
          While orient Phœbus, with unborrow'd hues,
          Clothes the waked loveliness which all night slept
          In heavenly drapery !   Darkness is fled.
          Now flowers unfold their beauties to the sun,
          And, blushing, kiss the beam he sends to wake them—
          The striped carnation, and the guarded rose,
          The vulgar wallflower, and smart gillyflower,
          The polyanthus mean—the dapper daisy,
          Sweet-william, and sweet marjoram—and all
          The tribe of single and of double pinks !
          Now, too, the feather'd warblers tune their notes
          Around, and charm the listening grove.   The lark !
          The linnet ! chaffinch ! bullfinch ! goldfinch ! greenfinch !
          But O, to me no joy can they afford !
          Nor rose, nor wallflower, nor smart gillyflower,
          Nor polyanthus mean, nor dapper daisy,
          Nor William sweet, nor marjoram—nor lark,
          Linnet, nor all the finches of the grove !"

Puff. Your white handkerchief, madam !——

Tilb. I thought, sir, I wasn't to use that till *heart-rending* woe.

Puff O yes, madam, at *the finches of the grove*, if you please

" *Tilb.* . . . .   Nor lark,
          Linnet, nor all the finches of the grove !   [*Weeps.*"

Puff. Vastly well, madam !

Dang. Vastly well, indeed !

" *Tilb.* . . For, O, too sure, heart-rending woe is now
          The lot of wretched Tilburina !"

Dang. Oh !—'tis too much !

Sneer Oh !—it is indeed !

" *Con.* . . Be comforted, sweet lady ; for who knows,
          But Heaven has yet some milk-white day in store ?

Tilb. . . . Alas ! my gentle Nora,
          Thy tender youth as yet hath never mourn'd
          Love's fatal dart.   Else wouldst thou know, that when
          The soul is sunk in comfortless despair,
          It cannot taste of merriment."

Dang. That's certain !

" *Con.* . . . But see where your stern father comes :
          It is not meet that he should find you thus."

Puff. Hey, what the plague!—what a cut is here! Why, what is become of the description of her first meeting with Don Whiskerandos—his gallant behaviour in the sea fight—and the simile of the canary-bird?

Tilb. Indeed, sir, you 'll find they will not be missed.

Puff. Very well, very well!

Tilb. [*To* Confidant.] The cue, ma'am. if you please·

" *Con.* . . It is not meet that he should find you thus.

Tilb. . . . Thou counsel'st right; but 'tis no easy task
  For barefaced grief to wear a mask of joy.

Enter Governor.

Gov. . . . How 's this!—in tears?—O Tilburina, shame!
  Is this a time for maudling tenderness,
  And Cupid's baby woes?—Hast thou not heard
  That haughty Spain's pope-consecrated fleet
  Advances to our shores, while England's fate,
  Like a clipp'd guinea, trembles in the scale?

Tilb. . . . Then is the crisis of my fate at hand!
  I see the fleets approach—I see——"

Puff. Now, pray, gentlemen, mind. This is one of the most useful figures we tragedy writers have, by which a hero or heroine, in consideration of their being often obliged to overlook things that are on the stage, is allowed to hear and see a number of things that are not.

Sneer. Yes; a kind of poetical second-sight!

Puff. Yes.—Now then, madam.

" *Tilb.* . . .   I see their decks
  Are clear'd!—I see the signal made!
  The line is form'd!—a cable's length asunder!—
  I see the frigates station'd in the rear;
  And now, I hear the thunder of the guns!
  I hear the victor's shouts!—I also hear
  The vanquish'd groan!—and now 'tis smoke—and now
  I see the loose sails shiver in the wind!
  I see—I see—what soon you 'll see——

Gov. . . . Hold, daughter! peace! this love hath turn'd thy brain:
  The Spanish fleet thou canst not see—because
  —It is not yet in sight!"

Dang. Egad, though, the governor seems to make no allowance for this poetical figure you talk of

Puff. No, a plain matter-of-fact man;—that 's his character

" *Tilb.* . . But will you then refuse his offer?

Gov. . . . I must—I will—I can—I ought—I do.

Tilb. . . . Think what a noble price.

Gov. . . . No more—you urge in vain.

Tilb. . . . His liberty is all he asks."

O

Sneer. All who asks, Mr. Puff? Who is——

Puff. Egad, sir, I can't tell! Here has been such cutting and slashing, I don't know where they have got to myself.

Tilb. Indeed, sir, you will find it will connect very well.

" —And your reward secure."

Puff. Oh, if they hadn't been so devilish free with their cutting here, you would have found that Don Whiskerandos has been tampering for his liberty, and has persuaded Tilburina to make this proposal to her father. And now, pray observe the conciseness with which the argument is conducted. Egad, the *pro* and *con* goes as smart as hits in a fencing-match. It is indeed a sort of small-sword logic, which we have borrowed from the French.

```
" Tilb. . . A retreat in Spain !
Gov.  . . . Outlawry here !
Tilb. . . . Your daughter's prayer ?
Gov.  . . . Your father's oath.
Tilb. . . . My lover !
Gov.  . . . My country !
Tilb. . . . Tilburina !
Gov.. . . . England !
Tilb. . . . A title !
Gov.  . . . Honour !
Tilb.. . . . A pension !
Gov.. . . . Conscience !
Tilb.. . . . A thousand pounds !
Gov.. . . . Ha ! thou hast touch'd me nearly !"
```

Puff. There you see—she threw in *Tilburina*, Quick, parry quarte with *England!*—Ha! thrust in tierce *a title!*—parried by *honour*. Ha! *a pension* over the arm!—put by by *conscience*. Then flankonade with *a thousand pounds*—and a palpable hit, egad!

```
" Tilb. . . Canst thou—
          Reject the suppliant, and the daughter too
Gov.. . . . No more ; I would not hear thee plead in vain :
          The father softens—but the governor
          Is fix'd !                          [Exit.
```

Dang. Ay, that antithesis of persons is a most established figure.

```
" Tilb. . . 'Tis well,—hence then, fond hopes,—fond passion, hence ;
          Duty, behold I am all over thine——
Whisk. . . [Without.] Where is my love—my——
Tilb. . . . Ha !
```

Enter Don Ferolo Whiskerandos.

```
Whisk. . . My beauteous enemy !——"
```

Puff O dear, ma'am, you must start a great deal more than that! Consider, you had just determined in favour of duty—when, in a moment, the sound of his voice revives your passion—overthrows your resolution—destroys your obedience. If you don't express all that in your start, you do nothing at all

Tilb. Well, we'll try again!

Dang. Speaking from within has always a fine effect

Sneer. Very

" *Whisk.* . My conquering Tilburina! How! is 't thus
We meet? why are thy looks averse? what means
That falling tear—that frown of boding woe?
Ha! now indeed I am a prisoner!
Yes, now I feel the galling weight of these
Disgraceful chains—which, cruel Tilburina!
Thy doating captive gloried in before.—
But thou art false, and Whiskerandos is undone!

Tilb. . . . O no! how little dost thou know thy Tilburina!

Whisk. . . Art thou then true?—Begone cares, doubts, and fears,
I make you all a present to the winds;
And if the winds reject you—try the waves."

Puff. The wind, you know, is the established receiver of all stolen sighs, and cast-off griefs and apprehensions.

" *Tilb.* . . . Yet must we part!—stern duty seals our doom:
Though here I call yon conscious clouds to witness,
Could I pursue the bias of my soul,
All friends, all right of parents, I'd disclaim,
And thou, my Whiskerandos, shouldst be father
And mother, brother, cousin, uncle, aunt,
And friend to me!

Whisk. . . Oh, matchless excellence! and must we part?
Well, if—we must—we must—and in that case
The less is said the better."

Puff. Heyday! here's a cut!—What, are all the mutual protestations out?

Tilb. Now, pray, sir, don't interrupt us just here: you ruin our feelings.

Puff. Your feelings!—but zounds, my feelings, ma'am!

Sneer No; pray don't interrupt them.

" *Whisk.* . One last embrace.
Tilb. . . . Now,—farewell, for ever.
Whisk. . . For ever!
Tilb. . . . Ay, for ever!   [*Going.*"

Puff. 'Sdeath and fury!—Gad's life!—sir! madam! if you go out without the parting look, you might as well dance out. Here, here!

Con. But pray, sir, how am I to get off here?

Puff. You! pshaw! what the devil signifies how you get off! edge away at the top, or where you will—[*Pushes the* CON-FIDANT *off.*] Now, ma'am, you see——

Tilb. We understand you, sir

" Ay, for ever.

Both. . . Oh! [*Turning back, and exeunt.—Scene closes."*

Dang. Oh, charming!

Puff. Hey!—'tis pretty well, I believe: you see I don't attempt to strike out any thing new—but I take it I improve on the established modes,

Sneer. You do, indeed! But pray is not Queen Elizabeth to appear?

Puff. No, not once—but she is to be talked of for ever; so that, egad, you'll think a hundred times that she is on the point of coming in.

Sneer. Hang it, I think it's a pity to keep her in the green room all the night.

Puff. O no, that always has a fine effect—it keeps up expectation.

Dang. But are we not to have a battle?

Puff. Yes, yes, you will have a battle at last; but, egad, it's not to be by land, but by sea—and that is the only quite new thing in the piece.

Dang. What, Drake at the Armada, hey?

Puff. Yes, i'faith—fire-ships and all; then we shall end with the procession. Hey, that will do, I think?

Sneer. No, doubt on 't.

Puff. Come, we must not lose time; so now for the under plot.

Sneer. What the plague, have you another plot?

Puff. O Lord, yes; ever while you live have two plots to your tragedy. The grand point in managing them is only to let your under-plot have as little connection with your main-plot as possible.—I flatter myself nothing can be more distinct than mine; for as in my chief plot the characters are all great people, I have laid my under-plot in low life; and as the former is to end in deep distress, I make the other end as happy as a farce.—Now, Mr. Hopkins, as soon as you please.

Enter UNDER PROMPTER

Und. Promp. Sir, the carpenter says it is impossible you can go to the park scene yet.

Puff. The park scene! no! I mean the description sceno here, in the wood.

Und. Promp. Sir, the performers have cut it out.

Puff Cut it out!

Under Promp. Yes, sir.

Puff. What! the whole account of Queen Elizabeth?

Under Promp. Yes, sir.

Puff. And the description of her horse and side-saddle?

Under Promp. Yes, sir.

Puff. So, so; this is very fine indeed!—Mr Hopkins, how the plague could you suffer this?

Mr. Hop. [*Within.*] Sir, indeed the pruning-knife——

Puff. The pruning-knife—zounds!—the axe! Why, here has been such lopping and topping, I shan't have the bare trunk of my play left presently!—Very well, sir—the performers must do as they please; but, upon my soul, I'll print it every word.

Sneer. That I would, indeed.

Puff. Very well, sir; then we must go on.—Zounds! I would not have parted with the description of the horse!—Well, sir, go on.—Sir, it was one of the finest and most laboured things.—Very well, sir; let them go on.—There you had him and his accoutrements, from the bit to the crupper. —Very well, sir; we must go to the park scene.

Under Promp. Sir, there is the point: the carpenters say, that unless there is some business put in here before the drop, they shan't have time to clear away the fort, or sink Gravesend and the river.

Puff. So! this is a pretty dilemma, truly!—Gentlemen, you must excuse me—these fellows will never be ready, unless I go and look after them myself.

Sneer. O dear, sir, these little things will happen.

Puff To cut out this scene!—but I'll print it—egad, I'll print it every word!   [*Exeunt.*

ACT III

SCENE I.—*The Theatre, before the Curtain*

Enter PUFF, SNEER, *and* DANGLE.

Puff Well, we are ready; now then for the justices.

[*Curtain rises*

" JUSTICES, CONSTABLES, &c., *discovered.*"

Sneer. This, I suppose, is a sort of senate scene.

Puff. To be sure; there has not been one yet

Dang. It is the under-plot, isn't it?

Puff. Yes.—What, gentlemen, do you mean to go at once to the discovery scene?

Just. If you please, sir.

Puff. Oh, very well!—Hark'ee, I don't choose to say any thing more; but, i' faith, they have mangled my play in a most shocking manner.

Dang. It's a great pity!

Puff. Now, then, Mr. Justice, if you please.

" *Just.* . . . Are all the volunteers without?

Const. . . .   They are.
　　　　　Some ten in fetters, and some twenty drunk.

Just. . . . Attends the youth, whose most opprobrious fame
　　　　　And clear convicted crimes have stamp'd him soldier?

Const. . . . He waits your pleasure; eager to repay
　　　　　The blest reprieve that sends him to the fields
　　　　　Of glory, there to raise his branded hand
　　　　　In honour's cause.

Just. . . . . .   'Tis well—'tis justice arms him!
　　　　　Oh! may he now defend his country's laws
　　　　　With half the spirit he has broke them all!
　　　　　If 'tis your worship's pleasure, bid him enter.

Const. . . . I fly, the herald of your will.   [*Exit.*"

Puff. Quick, sir.

Sneer. But, Mr. Puff, I think not only the Justice, but the clown seems to talk in as high a style as the first hero among them.

Puff. Heaven forbid they should not in a free country!— Sir, I am not for making slavish distinctions, and giving all the fine language to the upper sort of people.

Dang. That's very noble in you, indeed.

　　　　　" *Enter* JUSTICE'S LADY."

Puff. Now, pray mark this scene.

" *Lady.* . . Forgive this interruption, good my love;
　　　　　But as I just now pass'd a prisoner youth,
　　　　　Whom rude hands hither lead, strange bodings seized
　　　　　My fluttering heart, and to myself I said,
　　　　　An if our Tom had lived, he'd surely been
　　　　　This stripling's height!

Just. . . . Ha! sure some powerful sympathy directs
　　　　　Us both——
　　　　　　　Re-enter CONSTABLE *with* SON.
　　　　　　　What is thy name?

Son. . . My name is Tom Jenkins—*alias* have I none——
　　　　　'Though orphan'd, and without a friend!

Just. . . .   Thy parents!
Son. . . . My father dwelt in Rochester—and was,
            As I have heard—a fishmonger—no more."

Puff. What, sir, do you leave out the account of your birth,
parentage and education?
    Son. They have settled it so, sir, here.
    Puff. Oh! oh!

" *Lady.* . . How loudly nature whispers to my heart!
            Had he no other name?
Son. . . .   I 've seen a bill
            Of his sign'd Tomkins, creditor.
Just.. . . . This does indeed confirm each circumstance
            The gipsy told!—Prepare!
Son. . . . .   I do.
Just. . . . . No orphan, nor without a friend art thou—
            I am thy father; here 's thy mother; there
            Thy uncle—this thy first cousin, and those
            Are all your near relations!
Lady. . . . O ecstacy of bliss!
Son. . . . . O most unlook'd for happiness!
Just. . . . . O wonderful event! [*They faint alternately in each other's arms.*"

Puff. There, you see relationship, like murder, will out.

" *Just.* . . Now let 's revive—else were this joy too much!
            But come—and we 'll unfold the rest within;
            And thou, my boy, must needs want rest and food.
            Hence may each orphan hope, as chance directs,
            To find a father—where he least expects!"   [*Exeunt.*"

Puff. What do you think of that?
Dang. One of the finest discovery-scenes I ever saw!—
Why, this under-plot would have made a tragedy itself.
Sneer. Ay, or a comedy either
Puff. And keeps quite clear you see of the other.

Enter SCENEMEN, *taking away the seats.*

Puff. The scene remains, does it?
Sceneman. Yes, sir.
Puff. You are to leave one chair, you know.—But it is always awkward in a tragedy, to have you fellows coming in in
your playhouse liveries to remove things.—I wish that could
be managed better.—So now for my mysterious yeoman

" *Enter* BEEFEATER.

Beef. . . . Perdition catch my soul, but I do love thee."

Sneer Haven't I heard that line before?
Puff. No, I fancy not.—Where, pray?

Dang. Yes, I think there is something like it in Othello.

Puff. Gad! now you put me in mind on 't, I believe there is—but that 's of no consequence; all that can be said is, that two people happened to hit on the same thought—and Shakspeare made use of it first, that 's all.

Sneer. Very true

Puff. Now, sir, your soliloquy—but speak more to the pit, if you please—the soliloquy always to the pit, that 's a rule

" *Beef.* . . Though hopeless love finds comfort in despair,
It never can endure a rival's bliss !
But soft—I am observed.   [*Exit.*"

Dang. That 's a very short soliloquy

Puff. Yes—but it would have been a great deal longer if he had not been observed.

Sneer. A most sentimental Beefeater that, Mr. Puff!

Puff. Hark'ee—I would not have you be too sure that he is a Beefeater.

Sneer. What, a hero in disguise?

Puff. No matter—I only give you a hint.   But now for my principal character.   Here he comes—Lord Burleigh in person !   Pray, gentlemen step this way—softly—I only hope the Lord High Treasurer is perfect—if he is but perfect!

" *Enter* LORD BURLEIGH, *goes slowly to a chair, and sits.*"

Sneer. Mr. Puff!

Puff. Hush!—Vastly well, sir ! vastly well ! a most interesting gravity !

Dang. What isn't he to speak at all ?

Puff. Egad, I thought you 'd ask me that !—Yes, it is a very likely thing—that a minister in his situation, with the whole affairs of the nation on his head, should have time to talk !— But hush ! or you 'll put him out.

Sneer. Put him out ! how the plague can that be, if he 's not going to say any thing !

Puff. There 's the reason ! why, his part is to think; and how the plague do you imagine he can think if you keep talking ?

Dang. That 's very true, upon my word !

" LORD BURLEIGH *comes forward, shakes his head, and exit.*"

Sneer. He is very perfect indeed ! Now, pray what did he mean by that ?

Puff. You don't take it ?

Sneer. No, I don't, upon my soul.

Puff. Why, by that shake of the head, he gave you to understand that even though they had more justice in their cause, and wisdom in their measures—yet, if there was not a greater spirit shown on the part of the people, the country would at last fall a sacrifice to the hostile ambition of the Spanish monarchy.

Sneer. The devil! did he mean all that by shaking his head?

Puff. Every word of it—if he shook his head as I taught him.

Dang. Ah! there certainly is a vast deal to be done on the stage by dumb show and expression of face; and a judicious author knows how much he may trust to it.

Sneer. Oh, here are some of our old acquaintance.

" *Enter* SIR CHRISTOPHER HATTON *and* SIR WALTER RALEIGH.

Sir Christ. My niece and your niece too!
     By Heaven! there's witchcraft in 't.—He could not else
     Have gain'd their hearts.—But see where they approach:
     Some horrid purpose lowering on their brows!
Sir Walt. Let us withdraw and mark them.   [*They withdraw.*"

Sneer. What is all this?

Puff. Ah! here has been more pruning!—but the fact is, these two young ladies are also in love with Don Whiskerandos.—Now, gentlemen, this scene goes entirely for what we call situation and stage effect, by which the greatest applause may be obtained, without the assistance of language, sentiment, or character: pray mark!

" *Enter the two* NIECES.

1*st Niece.* . Ellena here!
     She is his scorn as much as I—that is
     Some comfort still!"

Puff. O dear, madam, you are not to say that to her face!—aside, ma'am, aside.—The whole scene is to be aside.

"1*st Niece.* She is his scorn as much as I—that is
     Some comfort still.   [*Aside.*
2*nd Niece.* I know he prizes not Pollina's love;
     But Tilburina lords it o'er his heart.   [*Aside.*
1*st Niece.* . But see the proud destroyer of my peace.
     Revenge is all the good I've left.   [*Aside.*
2*nd Niece.* He comes, the false disturber of my quiet.
     Now, vengeance do thy worst.   [*Aside.*

Enter DON FEROLO WHISKERANDOS.

Whisk. . . O hateful liberty—if thus in vain
     I seek my Tilburina!

Both Nieces. . . And ever shalt!

    Sir Christopher Hatton *and* Sir Walter Raleigh *come forward.*

Sir Christ. and Sir Walt. Hold! we will ¿venge you.

Whisk. . . Hold you—or see your nieces bleed!

> *[The two* Nieces *draw their two daggers to strike* Whisker-
> andos: *the two* Uncles *at the instant, with their two
> swords drawn, catch their two* Nieces' *arms, and turn
> the points of their swords to* Whiskerandos, *who imme-
> diately draws two daggers, and holds them to the two*
> Nieces' *bosoms."*

Puff. There's situation for you! there's an heroic group!
—You see the ladies can't stab Whiskerandos—he durst not
strike them, for fear of their uncles—the uncles durst not kill
him, because of their nieces—I have them all at a dead lock!
—for every one of them is afraid to let go first.

Sneer. Why, then they must stand there for ever!

Puff. So, they would, if I hadn't a very fine contrivance
for 't.—Now mind——

    " *Enter* Beefeater, *with his halberd.*

Beef. . . . In the queen's name I charge you all to drop
    Your swords and daggers!

> *[They drop their swords and daggers."*

Sneer. That is a contrivance indeed!

Puff. Ay—in the queen's name.

" *Sir Christ.* Come, niece!

Sir Walter. Come, niece!   [*Exeunt with the two* Nieces.

Whisk. . . What's he, who bids us thus renounce our guard?

Beef. . . . Thou must do more—renounce thy love!

Whisk. . . Thou liest—base Beefeater!

Beef. . . . .   Ha! hell! the lie!
    By Heaven thou'st roused the lion in my heart!
    Off, yeoman's habit!—base disguise! off! off!

> *[Discovers himself, by throwing off his upper dress, and ap-
> pearing in a very fine waistcoat.*

    Am I a Beefeater now?
    Or beams my crest as terrible as when
    In Biscay's Bay I took thy captive sloop?"

Puff. There, egad! he comes out to be the very captain of
the privateer who had taken Whiskerandos prisoner—and was
himself an old lover of Tilburina's.

Dang. Admirably managed, indeed!

Puff. Now, stand out of their way.

Whisk. . . I thank thee, Fortune, that hast thus bestowed
    A weapon to chastise this insolent. [*Takes up one of the swords*

Beef. . . . I take thy challenge, Spaniard, and I thank thee,
Fortune, too !   [*Takes up the other sword.*"

Dang. That's excellently contrived !—It seems as if the two uncles had left their swords on purpose for them.

Puff. No, egad, they could not help leaving them.

" *Whisk.* . Vengeance and Tilburina !

Beef.   Exactly so——
[*They fight—and after the usual number of rounds given,* WHISKERANDOS *falls.*

Whisk. . . O cursèd parry !—that last thrust in tierce
Was fatal.—Captain, thou hast fenced well !
And Whiskerandos quits this bustling scene
For all eter——

Beef. . . .   ——nity—he would have added, but stern death
Cut short his being, and the noun at once ! "

Puff. Oh, my dear sir, you are too slow : now mind me.
—Sir, shall I trouble you to die again ?

" *Whisk.* . And Whiskerandos quits this bustling scene
For all eter——

Beef . . . .   ——nity—he would have added,——"

Puff. No, sir—that's not it—once more, if you please

Whisk. I wish, sir, you would practise this without me—I can't stay dying here all night.

Puff. Very well ; we'll go over it by-and-by.—[*Exit* WHIS-KERANDOS.] I must humour these gentlemen !

" *Beef.* . . Farewell, brave Spaniard ! and when next "——

Puff. Dear sir, you needn't speak that speech, as the body has walked off.

Beef. That's true, sir—then I'll join the fleet.

Puff. If you please.—[*Exit* BEEFEATER.] Now, who comes on ?

" *Enter* GOVERNOR, *with his hair properly disordered.*

Gov. . . . . . A hemisphere of evil planets reign !
And every planet sheds contagious frenzy !
My Spanish prisoner is slain ! my daughter,
Meeting the dead corse borne along, has gone
Distract !   [*A loud flourish of trumpets.*
But hark ! I am summon'd to the fort :
Perhaps the fleets have met ! amazing crisis !
O Tilburina ! from thy aged father's beard
Thou'st pluck'd the few brown hairs which time had left !
[*Exit.*"

Sneer Poor gentleman !

Puff. Yes—and no one to blame but his daughter!

Dang. And the planets——

Puff. True.—Now enter Tilburina!

Sneer. Egad, the business comes on quick here.

Puff. Yes, sir—now she comes in stark mad in white satin

Sneer. Why in white satin?

Puff. O Lord, sir—when a heroine goes mad, she always goes into white satin.—Don't she, Dangle?

Dang. Always—it 's a rule.

Puff. Yes—here it is—[*Looking at the book.*] "Enter Tilburina stark mad in white satin, and her confidant stark mad in white linen."

"*Enter* TILBURINA *and* CONFIDANT, *mad, according to custom.*"

Sneer. But, what the deuce, is the confidant to be mad too?

Puff. To be sure she is: the confidant is always to do whatever her mistress does; weep when she weeps, smile when she smiles, go mad when she goes mad.—Now, madam confidant—but keep your madness in the back-ground, if you please.

" *Tilb.* . . The wind whistles—the moon rises—see,
They have kill'd my squirrel in his cage :
Is this a grasshopper?—Ha! no; it is my
Whiskerandos—you shall not keep him—
I know you have him in your pocket—
An oyster may be cross'd in love!—Who says
A whale 's a bird?—Ha! did you call, my love?—
He 's here! he 's there!—He 's everywhere!
Ah me! he 's nowhere!   [*Exit.*"

Puff. There, do you ever desire to see any body madder than that?

Sneer. Never, while I live!

Puff. You observed how she mangled the metre?

Dang Yes—egad, it was the first thing made me suspect she was out of her senses!

Sneer. And pray what becomes of her?

Puff. She is gone to throw herself into the sea, to be sure—and that brings us at once to the scene of action, and so to my catastrophe—my sea-fight, I mean.

Sneer. What, you bring that in at last?

Puff. Yes, yes—you know my play is called *The Spanish Armada;* otherwise, egad, I have no occasion for the battle at

all.—Now then for my magnificence!—my battle!—my noise!
—and my procession!—You are all ready?

Und. Promp. [*Within.*] Yes, sir

Puff Is the Thames dressed?

" *Enter* THAMES *with two* ATTENDANTS."

Thames. Here I am, sir.

Puff. Very well, indeed!—See, gentlemen, there 's a river
for you!—This is blending a little of the masque with my
tragedy—a new fancy, you know—and very useful in my
case; for as there must be a procession, I suppose Thames,
and all his tributary rivers, to compliment Britannia with
a fête in honour of the victory.

Sneer. But pray, who are these gentlemen in green with
him?

Puff. Those?—those are his banks.

Sneer. His banks?

Puff. Yes, one crowned with alders, and the other with
a villa!—you take the allusions?—But hey! what the plague!
you have got both your banks on one side.—Here, sir, come
round.—Ever while you live, Thames, go between your
banks.—[*Bell rings.*] There, so! now for 't!—Stand aside
my dear friends!—Away, Thames!

[*Exit* THAMES *between his banks.*

[*Flourish of drums, trumpets, cannon, &c. &c. Scene
changes to the sea—the fleets engage—the music plays
" Britons strike home."—Spanish fleet destroyed by
fire-ships, &c.—English fleet advances—music plays
" Rule Britannia."—The procession of all the English
rivers, and their tributaries, with their emblems, &c.,
begins with Handel's water music, ends with a chorus,
to the march in Judas Maccabæus.—During this scene,*
PUFF *directs and applauds every thing—then*

Puff. Well, pretty well—but not quite perfect.—So, ladies
and gentlemen, if you please, we 'll rehearse this piece again
to-morrow.   [*Curtain drops*

www.ingramcontent.com/pod-product-compliance
Lightning Source LLC
Chambersburg PA
CBHW030825270326
41928CB00007B/902